Rationality, Justice and the Social Contract

Rationality, Justice and the Social Contract

Themes from *Morals by Agreement*

Edited by
David Gauthier and Robert Sugden

Ann Arbor
The University of Michigan Press

Published in the United States of America by
The University of Michigan Press
1996 1995 1994 1993 4 3 2 1

Library of Congress Cataloging-in-Publication Data applied for.
ISBN 0-472-10394-6

Contents

The contributors vii

Preface ix

1 **The contractarian enterprise** 1
Robert Sugden

2 **Between Hobbes and Rawls** 24
David Gauthier

3 **The agriculture of the mind** 40
Martin Hollis

4 **Practical reason, collective rationality and contractarianism** 53
Julian Nida-Rümelin

5 **Justice, social union and the separateness of persons** 75
Albert Weale

6 **Right constraints?** 95
Percy B. Lehning

7 **Equal rationality and initial endowments** 116
Robert E. Goodin

8 **Bargaining and morality** 131
Ken Binmore

9 Rationality and impartiality: Is the contractarian enterprise possible? 157
Robert Sugden

10 Uniting separate persons 176
David Gauthier

References 193

Index 199

Contributors

Ken Binmore is Professor of Economics at University College, London and at the University of Michigan.

David Gauthier is Professor of Philosophy at the University of Pittsburgh.

Robert Goodin is Professorial Fellow in Philosophy at the Australian National University.

Martin Hollis is Professor of Philosophy at the University of East Anglia, Norwich.

Percy Lehning is Professor of Government at Erasmus University, Rotterdam.

Julian Nida-Rümelin is Professor at the Centre for Ethics in the Sciences and Humanities, University of Tübingen.

Robert Sugden is Professor of Economics at the University of East Anglia, Norwich.

Albert Weale is Professor of Government at the University of Essex.

Preface

In the last twenty years, following the publication of John Rawls's *A Theory of Justice* in 1971, moral philosophers, political theorists and economists have given a good deal of attention to the contractarian idea of justice – the idea that principles of justice are those that everyone, in some suitably defined initial position, would agree to accept as binding. In 1986, David Gauthier published his contribution to this debate, *Morals by Agreement.* The controversy that it aroused led Robert Sugden to select it as the basis of a conference which he organized at the Centre for Public Choice Studies at the University of East Anglia, at which a group of philosophers, political theorists and economists discussed Gauthier's work.

The book grew out of that conference, and takes *Morals by Agreement* as the starting point for an evaluation of the contractarian enterprise. The papers given at that conference by Gauthier, Sugden, Martin Hollis, Julian Nida-Rümelin, Albert Weale and Percy Lehning form the basis of six of its chapters. The other four chapters include papers by Robert Goodin and Ken Binmore, who were unable to attend the conference, an introduction in which Sugden sets the scene, and a conclusion in which Gauthier is allowed a final word.

We are grateful to the editors of *Ethics* and to the University of Chicago Press for permission to publish Chapter 9, which previously appeared as an article in that journal. Sugden's work in editing this volume was carried out as part of a project, 'The Foundations of Rational Choice Theory', which is financed by the Economic and Social Research Council of the UK. Throughout the volume, references to *Morals by Agreement* are given simply by page numbers, such as '(p. 23)'.

David Gauthier

Robert Sugden

Preface

1

The contractarian enterprise

Robert Sugden

A just society, according to John Rawls, should be capable of being viewed as a 'voluntary scheme' (1971, p. 13); it should be grounded on principles of 'reciprocity', of 'cooperation among equals for mutual advantage' (p. 14). This ideal provides the starting point for a body of social, political and economic thought which is often called *contractarianism.* In his monumental *A Theory of Justice*, Rawls presents a contractarian theory of justice which has been enormously influential in setting the agenda for debate about social justice. Among the many subsequent contributions to the contractarian enterprise, David Gauthier's *Morals by Agreement* is probably the most significant and almost certainly the most controversial. The present volume evaluates the contractarian enterprise in the light of Gauthier's work.

1 *Morals by Agreement*

The contractarian enterprise is simultaneously an enterprise in moral philosophy, in political theory, and in economics. It seeks answers to questions about the moral obligations we owe to one another, about the legitimate functions of government and the nature of our obligations to it, and about justice in the distribution of income and wealth. Its mode of enquiry is to consider how rational individuals, each concerned with his or her own interests, might agree to cooperate for mutual benefit; thus the theory of rational choice – the core of economic theory – is brought to bear on philosophical and political questions. In *Morals by Agreement,* Gauthier challenges many cherished ideas about how these questions should be answered and about the content of the theory of rational choice. These challenges provide the themes of this volume.

Gauthier is perhaps most radical of all in his approach to moral philosophy. He rejects the common idea that there is a distinction between prudential reasoning and moral reasoning, between asking 'What is it in my interest to do?' and asking 'What ought I to do?'. The idea that there is a distinct mode of moral reasoning, drawing on our 'moral sense' or 'moral intuitions', is, he suggests, a hangover from religious thinking. Asserting that he is writing 'moral theory for adults' (1988b, p. 385), he claims to derive moral principles from a theory of rational choice in which each individual pursues his or her own interests. He is determined to avoid injecting moral premisses into his conception of rationality, as writers in the Kantian tradition might be said to do, and as Rawls does when he requires that principles of justice are to be agreed by 'contracting parties' who do not know their own identities or interests. Thus, the link between rationality and morality is much closer for Gauthier than for most contractarian writers. Whether rationality and morality can be linked so closely is one of the central questions that this volume addresses.

Gauthier, like Rawls, sees a just society as one that is based on cooperation among equals for mutual advantage. He provides a sketch of the kind of society that could count as just, given this contractarian conception of justice and given his own account of rational (and moral) cooperation. Gauthier's picture of a just society is significantly different from Rawls's. Rawls draws egalitarian conclusions from contractarian premisses. Rawls's well-known *difference principle* states that 'the higher expectations of those better situated are just if and only if they work as part of a scheme which improves the expectations of the least advantaged members of society' (1971, p. 75). The distribution of income generated by a market economy is unlikely to satisfy the difference principle; that principle typically requires redistribution from rich to poor. Gauthier, in contrast, sees the perfectly competitive market of economic theory as a paradigm of rational cooperation – and hence of justice. A world of perfectly competitive markets, he argues, would be a 'morally free zone, a zone within which the constraints of morality would have no place' (p. 84). In such a world, there would be no call for morality, and there would be no argument of social justice for redistributing income. The theoretical debate between Rawls's and Gauthier's brands of contractarianism parallels the political debate between those who see the redistribution of income as a proper activity of government and those who deny this. This debate forms a second central theme in this volume.

Much of the argument of *Morals by Agreement* is conducted within the framework of the theory of rational choice, as this is conventionally understood by economists and decision theorists. But at two crucial points, Gauthier argues that the conventional theory is mistaken, and substitutes a theory of his own. At these points, *Morals by Agreement* is a contribution to economic theory, and not merely an application of economic theory to philosophical and political issues. Gauthier's arguments raise fundamental questions about the theory of rational choice and about the nature of rationality: this provides a third theme for this volume.

One of these points of divergence concerns the theory of bargaining. Social cooperation generates benefits that would not exist otherwise: in the language of economics, there are 'gains from trade', or in Gauthier's phrase, there is a *cooperative surplus.* Gauthier argues that rational individuals, bargaining over the division of this surplus, would settle on a particular division which, since uniquely rational, is uniquely just. Here he appeals to his own theory of bargaining, which he defends against its better-known rivals.

The second point of divergence concerns the rationality of complying with an agreement, once made. Granted that an agreement to cooperate would benefit everyone, were everyone to comply with it, is it rational for each individual to comply? What if (as Hobbes seems to have thought) the problem of securing social cooperation is a many-player Prisoner's Dilemma, in which each individual does better by not complying, irrespective of whether others comply or not? The standard answer of rational choice theory is that, in such a case, rational individuals would not comply with their agreements. In the absence of some external mechanism for enforcing agreements, agreement would be pointless and cooperation would be impossible to achieve. Gauthier disagrees, arguing that it is rational to be disposed to keep the agreements that one has rationally entered into. In making this argument, Gauthier is challenging ideas which are at the core of the conventional theory of rational choice.

2 The appeal of contractarianism

The attention which Rawls's and Gauthier's work has received is a testimony, not merely to the quality and depth of their arguments, but also to the appeal that contractarian ways of thinking have to present-day readers. In their different ways, Rawls and Gauthier present an approach to political and moral theory that many people (including myself) find attractive: we want the contractarian enterprise to succeed. What are the sources of this appeal?

One significant feature of the contractarian approach is that it does not presuppose any particular conception of a good life or of a good society. As Buchanan (1975, p. 1) puts it, contractarian theorists do not presume to 'play God' by setting themselves up as judges of ultimate goodness. In this respect, the alternative to contractarianism is to found a theory of justice or morality on arguments about the proper ends of human life. Much philosophical effort, over thousands of years, has been spent on inconclusive debate about the true nature of a good life or a good society. The contractarian approach offers a method of bypassing this debate altogether. By thinking of society as a scheme of cooperation, we avoid having to ask what really is good in an absolute sense. Even if we cannot agree on common ends, we can cooperate for mutual benefit. Society, on this view, is merely a mechanism that we use in common to achieve our separate ends.

Utilitarian theories have had a rather similar kind of appeal to those who are sceptical about absolute notions of goodness. In principle, of course, traditional utilitarianism does rest on a particular theory of the good – the theory that goodness consists in pleasure or happiness. But pleasure is located in individuals, and it is natural to suppose that each person is the best judge of what gives him or her pleasure. Utilitarianism has gradually evolved into 'welfarism'–the view that the welfare of society is an aggregate of the welfares of its members, and that the welfare of any individual is to be judged by appeal to his or her own preferences. The besetting problem of welfarism, however, is that it requires us to aggregate the preferences of individuals: the history of welfare economics is the history of unsuccessful attempts to aggregate preferences. This is another problem that the contractarian approach may be able to bypass: we may be able to identify the terms on which rational individuals would agree to cooperate without making any interpersonal comparisons of welfare.

Another attractive feature of contractarian theories is that they are designed to be endorsed by every member of society. Rawls speaks of a 'public conception of justice' and of 'public acceptance' of principles of justice (1971, pp. 5, 13). A contractarian theory does more than identify the characteristics of a just society: it justifies that society *to its members*, in terms which each of them can accept. In contrast, a theory based on a particular view about the nature of the good life or the good society can be accepted only by those who endorse that view. Such a theory, of course, claims to offer justifications which everyone *ought* to accept. (If some conception of the nature of goodness is, as the theory claims, the true one, then it is true for everyone, whether they recognize this or not.) But such a theory cannot generate a *public* conception of justice unless everyone agrees about what is good: and it is hard to believe that this will ever be the case.

Utilitarian theories sometimes fail to satisfy this condition of publicness by containing what might be called 'secret clauses' – arguments whose validity depends on their *not* being generally accepted. For example, a utilitarian theory can recommend the propagation of such non-utilitarian beliefs as that it is always wrong to lie, steal, or kill. On balance, the argument goes, welfare is maximized if people accept such constraints as morally absolute, even though this absolute status cannot really be justified (Smart, 1973, pp. 50–1). This may provide a justification for propagating a traditional moral code, but the justification cannot be a *public* one. As Williams (1973, p. 138) puts it, utilitarians who appeal to such secret clauses are reasoning like benevolent colonial administrators, trying to do good by stealth. In insisting on public justifications, contractarianism appeals to democratic sensibilities.

A further feature of the contractarian approach is that it limits the demands that society can make on the individual, or that individuals can make on each other. The contractarian idea of reciprocity implies that the members of society are entitled to demand of one another that each contributes his or her share of the costs of projects which provide benefits to all: there is no licence for free riding. But if society is a scheme of cooperation for mutual advantage, then there must be some level at which each individual benefits from society. The imposition of a harm on one person can never be justified solely in terms of the benefits that others enjoy as a consequence of that harm. Instead, it must be justified as part of some larger scheme of which the person being harmed, like everyone else, is a beneficiary. Thus, as Rawls (1971, pp. 3–4) puts it, 'Each person possesses an inviolability founded on justice that even the welfare of society as a whole cannot override. ... [Justice] does not allow that the sacrifices imposed on a few are outweighed by the larger sum of advantages enjoyed by many.' Gauthier is making a similar point when he writes of 'the moral priority of the individual to society and its institutions' (p. 222).

This view of the relationship between individual and society has some implications about which even the most committed contractarians are uneasy. If justice is wholly a matter of reciprocity, do we have any obligation to support people who are so severely handicapped that they can offer us nothing in return? (A similar question might be asked about our obligations to animals.) Gauthier has to concede that the handicapped lie 'beyond the pale of a morality tied to mutuality' (p. 268); if we have moral duties in these cases, his theory cannot account for them. (Each of us may feel *sympathy* for the handicapped, and if so, the welfare of the handicapped will be among the ends we pursue; but this is a matter of preference, not moral obligation.) There is also a problem in fixing a reference point from which to measure benefit and harm. If we are to say that social cooperation must benefit everyone, we have to specify some pre-social or non-social state of affairs with which to make comparisons: this is the *baseline* (or, in older versions of contract theory, the 'state of nature'). How the baseline should be specified is a crucial and problem-ridden issue in contractarian theory, about which I shall say more later. But, despite these real problems, there surely is something attractive about the idea that the individual has moral priority over society and that society's claims on the individual must be grounded in reciprocity.

All these features of contractarian thinking may be brought together by saying that, for contractarians, a just society is one that rests on the consent of its members. Opponents sometimes argue that this notion of consent is a sham, covering up the forces of power and command which hold real societies together. Jasay (1989, pp. 17–19, 80–5) puts this point forcefully when he suggests that contractarianism began – in the work of writers like Hobbes – as a 'special plea' for strong states that in reality were established and maintained by force. On this view, contractarianism is an ideology which, by using the concept of consent to camouflage the reality of command, serves to reconcile us to the power relations that govern our lives. We might understand the attractions of such an ideology while recognizing it to be false.

In Chapter 2 of this volume, in which he relates *Morals by Agreement* to the contractarian tradition as a whole, Gauthier faces up to this criticism. He recognizes that, in much of this tradition, it is only in a weak sense of the word that society can be said to rest on 'consent'. In Hobbes's *Leviathan* (1651), the powers of the sovereign are created by a contract to which everyone is a party, and so there is *prior* consent; but once the agreement has been struck, there is no more scope for autonomous choice in the political realm. The sovereign is appointed to enforce a contract of peace between individuals; each person keeps the terms of the contract because of the fear of punishment. In a further and in some ways more disturbing way, Hobbes limits the autonomy of the sovereign's subjects. As part of the contract, each subject subordinates his natural reason – his own sense of right and wrong – to the reason of the sovereign. He agrees that the sovereign's laws will dictate to him 'what is really good' (Hobbes, 1841, p. 194). A similar idea can be found in Rousseau's (1762) account of the social contract, in which the act of contract brings about a moral transformation in the individuals who are parties to it: they come to identify with the 'general will'.

Like many liberals, Gauthier is reluctant to accept that social cooperation can be maintained only by the police powers of the state, or that it has to be bought at the cost of moral autonomy. But how else are we to explain why individuals comply with an agreement to cooperate? Rawls (1971, pp. 561–3) answers this question by presupposing that his contracting parties regard moral personality as the fundamental aspect of the self, and that to have a moral personality is to have a capacity for a 'sense of justice'. But, for Gauthier, this amounts to presupposing what a contractarian theory is supposed to show: that it is rational to act according to principles of justice. Gauthier sees his own theory, and in particular, his theory of compliance, as showing that social cooperation can rest on the genuine consent of rational and morally autonomous individuals.

3 Rationality and morality

Rawls and Gauthier are agreed that the object of the contractarian enterprise is to construct a coherent theory from which principles of justice or morality can be derived, and that these principles ought to correspond, to some degree at least, with our prior convictions about what is just or moral. (Who are the 'we' who hold the prior convictions? Rawls and Gauthier both presuppose that they and their readers belong to a society with a reasonable degree of consensus on moral matters.) Rawls (1971, pp. 17–22) says that the object is a state of 'reflective equilibrium' in which our theoretically derived principles match our 'considered convictions' about the cases to which they apply. In order to reach this state, we may have to tailor our theory to match our prior convictions, or we may have to reconsider our prior convictions if they turn out to be inconsistent with our theory. Probably we shall have to do a bit of both.

It may seem to matter less to Gauthier than to Rawls that the conclusions of his theory should match our prior convictions. He recognizes (and is not unduly concerned by the observation) that there may be significant differences between his conclusions and those of 'conventional morality' (p. 6). But he devotes much of the final third of *Morals by Agreement* to an attempt to persuade the reader that his conclusions can be endorsed as principles of morality. There is a good reason for his doing this. *Morals by Agreement* is presented as a theory of *morals*. If it is to be a theory of morals, its conclusions must be recognizably moral principles.

Here Rawls and Gauthier part company. Rawls takes it as given that a theory of justice must be impartial, and tries to construct a theory which can be accepted by anyone *who is prepared to take an impartial viewpoint*. He imagines an 'original position' in which individuals have to choose the principles of justice which are to govern their society, but lowers a 'veil of ignorance' so that no one knows anything about his or her personal identity. This device is presented as a way of modelling, or making vivid, 'commonly shared presumptions' about the nature of the impartiality that should characterize a theory of justice (Rawls, 1971, pp. 11–22, 136–42). But all this leaves open the question of why anyone should allow his choices to be constrained by considerations of justice. Rawls simply *assumes* that individuals are 'capable of a sense of justice', so that (within certain limits) they can rely on one another to respect the constraints which justice imposes on them (p. 145).

Gauthier's aim is much more ambitious. He sets out to construct a theory of morality whose prescriptions will be accepted, and acted on, by any fully rational person. He is, he says, 'committed to showing why an individual, reasoning from non-moral premisses, would accept the constraints of morality on his choices (p. 5). He assumes only that individuals are rational in the sense of having consistent preferences. Nothing is assumed about the content of those preferences. In particular, there is no assumption that individuals take an interest in one another's interests, or that they feel affection or sympathy for one another, or that they have any prior sense of justice or morality. Gauthier's project is to work out the implications of assuming rationality (in this narrow sense) and nothing more. He tries to show that rational individuals would choose to accept certain constraints on their pursuit of their own ends, in return for others accepting similar constraints. These constraints constitute a morality.

Gauthier sees his project as an attempt to give morality a firm grounding that it would otherwise lack. He is conscious of the possibility that what we take to be our sense of morality might turn out to be no more than a relic of religious and superstitious modes of thinking. The strategy of *Morals by Agreement*, he says:

> offers us the only plausible way of defending morality against what I take to be the fate of religion. Religious practice and religious language are, or until recently have been, ubiquitous in human life. But if we take religion at face value, and ask ourselves what must be the case if the claims of religion, literally construed so that they possess ordinary truth-value, are some of them to be true, then we find ourselves driven to an account of the world that is prodigal in admitting into its ontology entities that play no role in our best explanations and justifications. ... The only theory of religion that, to my mind, has the least credibility, is an error theory. [I am not easy about this, but] I should be even more uneasy were I to suppose that morality would share the fate of religion, so that our moral claims, literally construed, would, to be true, require us to accept a prodigal and ultimately incredible ontology. (1988a, p. 175)

Or, as he says in another paper:

> Morals by agreement is an attempt to challenge Nietzsche's prescient remark, 'As the will to truth ... gains self consciousness ... morality will gradually perish'. It is an attempt to write moral theory for adults, for persons who live consciously in a post-anthropomorphic, post-theocentric, post-technocratic world. It is an attempt to allay the fear, or suspicion, or hope, that without a foundation in objective value or objective reason, in sympathy or in sociality, the moral enterprise must fail. (1988b, p. 385)

At the core of all this is the thought that traditional moral theory relies on the supposed existence of entities, such as God or goodness, which are external to human life yet somehow matter. A defensible morality should dispense with such mysterious entities, and accept that life has no meaning outside itself. There is also the more particular suggestion that the standard theory of rational choice has the same firm grounding as, say, the biological theory of evolution or the theory of gravitation. The concepts used in expected utility theory and game theory have, it is implied, the same sort of credibility as, say, the concept of a gene, or the concept of mass. Thus the theory of rational choice is the obvious place in which to ground morality. If Gauthier is right, then the failure of his project would be one more nail in the coffin of morality.

We might, however, look at things the other way round. Is the standard theory of rational choice really so well grounded? Suppose Gauthier's project fails, and we find that moral choices cannot be accommodated within the theory. Must we then conclude that it is morality that is at fault? Perhaps the fault lies in the standard theory of rational choice. Perhaps moral choices *are* rational, by virtue of some form of valid reasoning which the standard theory of choice is too restrictive to take account of. This possibility is explored by Martin Hollis in Chapter 3 of this volume, and by Julian Nida-Rümelin in Chapter 4.

Hollis characterizes the standard theory of rational choice as *instrumental*: a choice is rational if it is the best means of achieving given ends. He argues that human beings are not, and could never be, instrumentally rational in all their dealings with one another. Further, the theory of rational choice would not work at all if its agents were *always* instrumentally rational. Gauthier himself seems to be conscious of this problem in the latter part of *Morals by Agreement*, where he distinguishes between 'real human beings' and 'economic men and women', and suggests that it is because we are the former that we can act on moral constraints (pp. 315–17). To understand some kinds of choices, Hollis argues, we need a theory of *expressive* rationality, in which a person's action is rational by virtue of the kind of person he is. Hollis suggests that expressive rationality might provide the key to the problem of reconciling morality and rationality.

An alternative way of explaining moral choices is offered by the Kantian approach, in which rationality requires each individual to act in such a way that he can will the maxim of his action to be a universal law. For Kant, the moral requirement of impartiality is built into the notion of rationality at the outset. Nida-Rümelin argues that the Kantian approach offers the most convincing way of understanding how it is that people sometimes behave cooperatively in situations that take the form of the Prisoner's Dilemma. He considers a number of ways in which such cooperative behaviour might be brought within the scope of the standard theory of rational choice, and argues that these are all unsatisfactory. If Nida-Rümelin is right, then 'our best explanations and justifications' of human action do, after all, depend on entities which lie outside the standard theory, or require at least a major modification of the rational choice paradigm.

4 Social justice and the problem of the baseline

Gauthier's theory of social justice is not egalitarian. It treats the distribution of income that would be generated by a perfectly competitive market, however unequal, as just: the market is a 'morally free zone'. Given the strategy of his argument, Gauthier has to justify this claim in two distinct ways. Clearly, he has to show that his conclusions are implied by the logic of rational choice. I shall say more about this aspect of Gauthier's argument in Sections 5 and 6 of this chapter. But, in addition, he has to show that his theory is a theory of *justice*, and not merely of rational self-interest. To achieve this, he seeks to persuade us that his theory expresses the contractarian ideal of society as a scheme of cooperation among equals for mutual advantage. How far he succeeds in this task is discussed by Albert Weale in Chapter 5, by Percy Lehning in Chapter 6 and by Robert Goodin in Chapter 7.

In a contractarian theory, the ideas of cooperation and mutual advantage have to be defined relative to some baseline: we need to know what each person brings to the bargaining process, as chips to bargain with. Clearly, those who have most to bargain with are likely to be able to settle on the most favourable terms. So if the outcome of the process is to be defended as just, the baseline must itself have some properties of fairness or justice.

Gauthier's baseline is a state of affairs in which there is no coercion. Coercion is defined in terms of one person's 'taking advantage' of another. One person takes advantage of another if he betters his own situation through an interaction which worsens the other's situation. 'Bettering' and 'worsening' are interpreted relative to the outcome that each person could have expected *in the absence of the other* (pp. 200–5). Suppose that Esau lives the life of a hunter–gatherer in a land of virgin forest. If Jacob takes the fruit that Esau has collected, he takes advantage of him. (By making indirect use of Esau's labour, Jacob makes himself better off than he would have been in Esau's absence). But if Jacob burns down the forest and sets up as a cattle rancher, ignoring Esau altogether, he does not take advantage of him. (Esau's situation is worsened, but Jacob is no better off than he would have been, had there been no Esau.) Gauthier sees the rule that one person should not take advantage of another as a kind of natural law, which 'introduces a rudimentary structure of rights into natural interaction' (p. 208). He presents his analysis of natural law as a development of that given by Locke in his *Two Treatises of Government* (1690), although there are some significant differences. (In the case of Jacob and Esau, for example, Locke's natural law would allow Jacob to clear some of the forest, but only if there was 'enough, and as good left' for Esau to make use of (Locke, 1690, Book 2, Chapter 5).) Gauthier claims that his baseline is 'both rational and impartial' (p. 209). If he can show that the baseline is impartial, Gauthier can argue that the agreements made by his bargainers are not merely rational, but also just.

Gauthier defends his baseline by comparing it with the apparently very different baseline in Rawls's *A Theory of Justice.* In one well-known passage, Rawls (1971, pp. 101–2) interprets his difference principle as 'an agreement to regard the distribution of natural talents as a common asset and to share in the benefits of this distribution whatever it turns out to be'. Those who have greater natural abilities do not deserve them; they have merely been lucky. The difference principle is a 'fair way of meeting the arbitrariness of fortune'. Gauthier agrees with Rawls that differences in natural abilities are undeserved, but rejects the idea that justice requires us to compensate for these differences, claiming that such a view of justice fails to 'take seriously the individuality of persons' (p. 254). For Gauthier, human individuality cannot be separated from the natural contingencies which give rise to differences in natural abilities. A just scheme of cooperation is one that can be justified to each person *as she is*, and not to each person as she would be, were the arbitrariness of fortune to be corrected.

It is tempting to see Rawls's and Gauthier's conclusions about distributive justice as arising out of fundamentally opposed positions on the moral significance of inequalities in natural abilities. Gauthier, we might say, treats each person as the owner of his or her natural abilities, while Rawls treats everyone's natural abilities as a common pool, to which all members of society have equal rights. But this would be too simple. Weale and Lehning both argue that, despite Rawls's reference to the distribution of natural talents as a 'common asset', he does not treat these talents as common property, to be used as society chooses. In Rawls's just society, each person remains the owner of her own abilities, and these may not be used without her consent. If society is to make use of a person's talents, it must offer her sufficient reward to induce her to supply them.

On one reading of Rawls, his theory of justice, just as much as Gauthier's, is concerned with the division of a cooperative surplus. The difference principle applies to income and wealth, and not to natural abilities themselves. Income and wealth are almost wholly created by social cooperation. It is sobering to consider what standard of living any one of us could hope to secure, were there no cooperation among human beings. As Adam Smith (1776, pp. 23–4) recognized in his famous comparison between the standards of living of the Scottish day-labourer and the African king – 'the absolute master of the lives and liberties of ten thousand naked savages' – even the most successful predation is no substitute for the division of labour. And the people whose abilities earn the greatest rewards in a market economy – best-selling novelists, film stars, top business executives – are not necessarily those who would be most successful in a state of nature. Rawls may be saying no more than that, since everyone is (almost) equally dependent on social cooperation, no one is entitled to a greater share of the cooperative surplus than anyone else. This seems to be the force of one of Rawls's explanations of the difference principle:

> The intuitive idea is that since everyone's well-being depends upon a scheme of cooperation without which no one could have a satisfactory life, the division of advantages should be such as to draw forth the willing cooperation of everyone taking part in it, including those least well situated. (1971, p. 15)

Gauthier, presumably, would reply that the difference principle is neither a rational nor a fair way to divide the cooperative surplus. Even if everyone is equally dependent on social cooperation, some people *contribute* more than others to the surplus, and the division of the surplus should reflect this. Justice, according to Gauthier, requires that each person's share of the surplus should be proportioned to his contribution (p. 254). In Gauthier's theory of bargaining, each person's initial claim on the cooperative surplus is equal to the value of his marginal contribution to it. That is, the amount a person claims is the amount by which the cooperative surplus would be reduced, were he not to participate. As Gauthier puts it:

> Each person's claim is bounded by the extent of his participation in cooperative interaction. For if someone were to press a claim to what would be brought about by the co-operative interaction of others, then those others would prefer to exclude him from agreement. (p. 134)

Thus Jane the lawyer can make a larger claim than Joe the shop assistant, even though their situations would be equally desperate in the absence of cooperation. Gauthier argues that rational bargainers will divide the cooperative surplus so that each person's share of the surplus is proportionate to his claim. So Jane will get a larger share of the surplus.

As Weale points out, however, Gauthier sometimes seems to be attracted by a much more Rawlsian position. Gauthier considers the case of Wayne Gretzky, the hockey player who can command an enormous income because of his unique talents. Gretzky, we are asked to suppose, would be willing to play hockey for a much more modest salary. The amount he receives in excess of the salary that would just induce him to play is, in the language of economics, *factor rent*. Gauthier accepts that Gretzky has 'the right to his unique hockey skills' and that 'he may use them as he pleases', but he denies that he has a right to the rent that they command (p. 273). In a passage that could almost have been written by Rawls, Gauthier says:

> Society may be considered as a single co-operative enterprise. The benefit represented by factor rent is part of the surplus afforded by that enterprise, for it arises only in social interaction. ... Each person, as a contributor to social interaction, shares in the production of the benefit represented by factor rent. ... In so far as this surplus takes the form of a single, transferable good, each member of society is entitled to an equal portion of it. (p. 274)

Gauthier uses this argument to justify the taxation of factor rent.

Weale argues that Gauthier's position on factor rent is inconsistent. If we accept Gauthier's account of the baseline and his theory of bargaining, we must say that each person will rationally claim the value of his marginal contribution to the social product. If the sum of these claims is greater than the cooperative surplus, each claim must be scaled down (in the same proportion). But there is no question of anyone receiving *more* than his marginal contribution. Simplifying Gauthier's example a little, we might say that value is created by the interaction of Gretzky and a large number of spectators: the value attaches to the spectators' enjoyment of watching Gretzky play. Collectively, the spectators are essential for the creation of this value, just as Gretzky is. But Gretzky's marginal contribution is equal to the whole of the cooperative surplus, since in his absence, there would be no surplus. In contrast, each individual spectator's marginal contribution is tiny, since in the absence of any one spectator, Gretzky could still entertain the others. Thus if the surplus is divided in proportion to marginal contributions, Gretzky will get the lion's share. It seems that Gretzky *does* have a right to the rent that his skills command in the market.

This example illustrates a much more general point. Given Gauthier's theory of bargaining, no one will be paid more than the value of his marginal product. So if the cooperative surplus is just large enough to allow everyone to be paid the value of his marginal product, then the rational (and just) outcome must be for each person to be paid this value. In a competitive market, each person *is* paid the value of his marginal product. Thus each individual is entitled (in Gauthier's terms) to the price that his labour commands in a competitive market. And this implies an entitlement to factor rent.

However, it is only under conditions of constant returns to scale that each person can be paid the value of his marginal product. (This well-known condition for the 'exhaustion of the product' follows from the mathematics of Euler's Theorem.) If there are increasing returns to scale, then a competitive equilibrium is not possible. In this case, the total product is insufficient to allow every factor to be paid its marginal product; in Gauthier's terms, the total of individuals' claims exceeds the cooperative surplus. Taking up a thought of Arrow's (1984, p. 188), Weale suggests that real market economies are characterized by increasing returns, and that this allows a contractarian case to be made for the redistribution of income.

Goodin takes issue with a different aspect of Gauthier's conception of the baseline, pointing to the way in which inequalities in initial endowments affect bargaining power. Bargaining is a risky enterprise: a person who fails to make concessions runs the risk that there will be no agreement at all. Thus those people who can view the breakdown of negotiations with the greatest composure can afford to take the largest risks: they have the most bargaining power, and need to make the smallest concessions. And the people who have least to fear from a breakdown of negotiations are those whose initial endowments are greatest. In this sense, larger endowments imply greater bargaining power. This may make sense as a description of real bargaining between rational individuals, but can it be treated as a property of a *fair* procedure? Goodin argues not.

5 Rational bargaining

A contractarian theory is designed to generate conclusions that are acceptable to everyone, even though individuals may remain committed to different and sometimes conflicting ends. The usual approach, and the one taken by Gauthier, is to show that the conclusions of the theory represent an acceptable solution to a bargaining problem. For each individual, the most preferred outcome would be for his own ends to be accepted by everyone else. But since others think similarly about their own ends, no one can realistically expect to get his own way completely; compromise is necessary. If the compromise is to be acceptable, each party to the bargain must be satisfied that he has settled on the best terms he could achieve, given that he was dealing with other people, as rational as himself, each of whom was trying to get the best possible terms for himself.

If we are to take this approach, we need a theory of rational bargaining. Gauthier offers such a theory, which may roughly be summarized as follows. Suppose there are n individuals, who can generate a cooperative surplus if they all agree to participate in some joint project. Their problem is to agree on how to divide this surplus between them. If they fail to agree, and so no cooperative surplus is generated, they remain in the *initial bargaining position*, in which each person i achieves the utility level u_i^*. Each person begins by making a *claim* u_i' (that is, he proposes that everyone agrees to a solution in which i achieves the utility level u_i'). At this stage, i acts as if he were making an absolutely final proposal, which the others must either accept in full or reject. Thus he claims the largest possible share of the cooperative surplus, subject to the constraint that if the others were to accept his proposal, they would be no worse off than if they chose not to deal with him at all. The intuitive idea is that this is the largest claim for which i can credibly threaten to hold out.

Each person then makes a *concession* in order to reach agreement. If the agreement gives person i a utility level of u_i, then i's *relative concession* is defined as $(u_i' - u_i)/(u_i' - u_i^*)$. Gauthier argues that if the bargainers are equally rational, 'no one can expect any other rational person to be willing to make a concession if he would not be willing to make a similar concession' (p. 145). Interpreting 'similar' in terms of the magnitude of relative concessions, this leads to the conclusion that agreement will be reached at the point which minimizes the value of the largest relative concession. Gauthier calls this the principle of *minimax relative concession.* In most cases, this principle implies that everyone makes the same relative concession as everyone else, or in other words, that the cooperative surplus is divided in proportion to individuals' claims.

This theory belongs to the class of *axiomatic* bargaining theories. Axiomatic theories use a stripped-down model of a bargaining problem, in which the game is fully described by a set of possible outcomes (defined in terms of the players' utility levels) and by a 'threat point' or 'initial bargaining position'. Any other information about the bargaining problem is taken to be irrelevant to the calculations of rational players. Given any bargaining problem, described in this way, the object of axiomatic bargaining theory is to find a unique solution – an outcome that fully rational players would accept as the best that each could achieve, given the rationality of the others. Such theories work by postulating necessary properties of a rational solution, and then by showing that, for any given bargaining problem, there is one and only one outcome which satisfies all those properties. Gauthier's theory of bargaining is a variant of an axiomatic bargaining theory put forward by Kalai and Smorodinsky (1975), and which has never gained wide acceptance. Most economists and game theorists prefer to use the *Nash bargaining solution* (Nash, 1950 and 1953). Using Gauthier's notation, and assuming a game between two players i and j, the Nash bargaining solution is the outcome (u_i, u_j) which maximizes the *Nash product* $(u_i - u_i^*)(u_j - u_j^*)$.

In Chapter 8 of this volume, Ken Binmore explains the logic of the Nash bargaining solution and gives a game-theorist's view of Gauthier's principle of minimax relative concession. Binmore argues that a satisfactory theory of bargaining should start from assumptions about the nature of the negotiation process. (For example: Do players make proposals in turn, or simultaneously? What are the costs of delay in reaching agreement? Is there any deadline at which the game ends, and if so, who is able to make the final proposal?) If the negotiation process is fully described, it can be modelled as a 'non-cooperative' game, which can then be analyzed using the standard tools of game theory. Gauthier's and Nash's theories of bargaining are both attempts to short-circuit the problem of specifying the negotiation process. Such theories, in Binmore's view, can be defended only to the extent that the solutions they generate would also be generated by the non-cooperative approach, given plausible assumptions about the negotiation process. Binmore argues that the Nash bargaining solution can be defended on these grounds, but Gauthier's principle of minimax relative concession cannot. In the final chapter of this volume, Gauthier tells us that he would no longer wish to defend the principle of minimax relative concession. Having been persuaded by Rubinstein's (1982) theory of non-cooperative bargaining, he has come to accept that what he said about bargaining in *Morals by Agreement* 'is simply undercut by the non-cooperative approach'; rational bargaining would yield the Nash solution.

While defending his own theory against Nash's in *Morals by Agreement*, Gauthier remarked that the differences between the two theories were matters of 'infighting among bargaining theorists' which need not concern his more philosophical readers (p. 146). He seems to have thought that the broad conclusions of *Morals by Agreement* would have been much the same had he used Nash's theory instead. Barry (1989a) explores the implications of Nash's bargaining theory for contractarian theories of justice and the results are, indeed, similar to Gauthier's. (Barry argues that the Nash bargaining solution is rational but not just. His grounds for calling it unjust are very similar to those used by Goodin against Gauthier's solution.) Gauthier's particular theory of bargaining, then, is not essential for the main thrust of *Morals by Agreement*.

What is essential is that *some* theory of bargaining, of the same general type as Gauthier's or Nash's, can be defended by an appeal to principles of rationality. Gauthier's project is to derive *moral* principles from an analysis of rational choice. He wants to be able to argue that the outcomes of rational bargaining satisfy certain standards of fairness or impartiality, by virtue of which the principles of rational bargaining are also principles of morality. His strategy is to exploit the idea that fully rational bargainers are *equally* rational. Thus, according to Gauthier, a rational bargainer will make only those concessions that *any* rational bargainer would have made in the same situation. In this sense, any principle which determines what concessions rational bargainers will make is necessarily impersonal.

Gauthier's argument for minimax relative concession is closely related to an argument first presented by Zeuthen (1930) and later refined by Harsanyi (1977). Zeuthen and Harsanyi also start from the claim that no rational bargainer will make a concession that another rational bargainer, in the same situation, would not make. However, Zeuthen and Harsanyi offer a different way of measuring concessions. Using this measure, they argue that fully rational bargainers would agree on the Nash bargaining solution. In relation to this measure, the Nash bargaining solution may be said to be impersonal.

Impersonality is not quite the same thing as impartiality, and we might still want to argue (as Goodin and Barry do) that particular principles for solving bargaining problems, though impersonal, are unjust. Nevertheless, there is a close association between the two concepts, and Gauthier's line of argument depends on this association. In Chapter 9, I argue that this whole approach – the approach of Gauthier, Zeuthen and Harsanyi – rests on the ungrounded assumption that bargaining games have unique solutions, which fully rational players, by virtue of their rationality, will accept. In another paper, I have argued that Rubinstein's non-cooperative theory – the theory now endorsed by Gauthier – depends on a similar assumption (Sugden, 1991b). *If* we know that there is a principle which uniquely determines the concessions that rational bargainers will make, then we may be able to deduce that the principle will be impartial in the Gauthier–Zeuthen–Nash sense of treating like cases alike. But how do we know that any such principle exists? If no such principle exists, the link between rationality and impartiality is broken.

6 Compliance

Conventional theories of bargaining (such as Nash's) assume that individuals come to the bargaining table endowed with clearly defined rights, which they seek to exchange. And they assume that if a bargain is struck, it will be honoured. These are reasonable simplifying assumptions for many of the cases studied by economists, in which bargaining takes place against the background of a law of contract, enforceable through the courts. But contractarian theories typically start with a state of nature, in which there are no institutions for defining and enforcing rights. Such theories have to explain how individuals come to have endowments, and why they comply with the bargains they have made.

The oldest and most robust answer is that given by Hobbes, which is discussed by Gauthier in Chapter 2 of this volume. In Hobbes's state of nature, 'every man has a right to every thing' (1651, Chapter 14). Everyone is free to do whatever he judges most conducive to his own preservation, irrespective of the consequences for other people. Each person's endowment, then, consists of the strength and cunning which he can use to defend himself and to prey on others. The war of all against all can be brought to an end, to everyone's benefit, if each person accepts constraints on how he will use this endowment. But, for Hobbes, mutual recognition of this fact is not enough to bring about peace. A peace agreement would be worthless unless it was in each person's interest to comply with that agreement: 'covenants, without the sword, are but words, and of no strength to secure a man at all' (Chapter 17). Thus Hobbes's contracting parties agree to establish an absolute government with sufficient power to enforce compliance.

Buchanan's *The Limits of Liberty* (1975) offers a modern-dress version of Hobbes's contractarianism. Buchanan starts from a state of nature very much like Hobbes's. The individuals in Buchanan's state of nature have endowments of goods as well as of physical strength and cunning, but a person's endowment consists simply of those goods that he is able to acquire by whatever means – by productive labour or by predation – and to maintain in his control in the face of predation by others. This *natural distribution* of goods may be thought of as an equilibrium state of the war of all against all. For Buchanan, it also represents the initial bargaining position for any social contract. If there are inequalities in the natural distribution, some people being better predators than others, then these inequalities will tend to be carried forward into the post-contract society. Although he allows a limited role for 'ethical constraints' (pp. 74–7), Buchanan generally follows Hobbes in assuming that individuals will comply with their agreements only if it is in their interests to do so. Compliance, for Buchanan, is secured mainly by the threat of punishment.

On one view, *The Limits of Liberty* is a clear-sighted analysis of society as a scheme of cooperation for mutual advantage. This, it might be said, is where the logic of the contractarian enterprise leads us, if we refuse to be diverted by sentimentality and wishful thinking, and if we make no Rawlsian appeal to a sense of justice. But few people (and certainly not Buchanan himself) would claim that *The Limits of Liberty* offers us a theory of justice or of morality.

Gauthier avoids reaching Hobbes's and Buchanan's conclusions by presenting a different theory of compliance. Suppose that Alice and Bruce would both benefit from an arrangement whereby Alice (at some cost to herself) performs some service for Bruce on Monday and then Bruce (at some cost to himself) performs a service for Alice on Tuesday. Suppose that this is the only interaction that there will ever be between these two people, and that no one else will know what they do. On a standard game-theoretic analysis, neither service will be performed. On Tuesday, Bruce has no reason to incur a cost, merely to benefit Alice, even if she benefited him on Monday. As a rational person, Bruce will not perform the service. But Alice knows this on Monday, and so can predict that Bruce will not perform, even if she performs on Monday. So she has no reason to perform either. This is a classic problem of compliance: both individuals stand to benefit by an agreement to cooperate, but they cannot rely on each other to honour the agreement.

Gauthier uses the term *straightforward maximization* for the kind of forward-looking rationality that standard game theory attributes to Bruce: Bruce is taken to be a straightforward maximizer, or SM. Gauthier then describes a different kind of reasoning, which he calls *constrained maximization.* If Bruce is a constrained maximizer, or CM, he will promise to perform on Tuesday, conditional on Alice's performing on Monday. On Tuesday, and if Alice has performed, Bruce will reason something like this: 'Alice performed because she believed (rightly) that I was disposed to keep my promises. People's dispositions are not opaque to one another; if I had not really been disposed to keep my promises, she would probably not have formed that belief. Thus it is to my overall advantage that I have this disposition and act on it, rather than being an SM. So I shall act on it.'

Gauthier argues that, because people are often able to detect one another's dispositions, CMs will tend to do better than SMs. (CMs will be trusted when SMs are not.) The SM always chooses the action that maximizes her expected utility, as viewed from the time each choice is made; but she does not achieve as much utility as she would have done, had she not been disposed to choose in this way. Thus it is rational to acquire the disposition of a CM rather than that of an SM.

As Gauthier shows in Chapter 2 of this volume, Hobbes uses a somewhat similar argument in his famous answer to the Foole. Hobbes considers a case like that of Bruce's promise to Alice, which he calls a 'covenant of mutual trust'. He argues that if the covenant is made in a state of nature, Alice has no adequate assurance that Bruce will perform his part of the bargain: 'he which performeth first, does but betray himself to his enemy'. Thus Alice may declare the covenant void 'upon any reasonable suspicion' (1651, Chapter 14). But what if Alice *does* perform? Hobbes considers the case 'where one of the parties has performed already'. (On Hobbes's analysis, of course, this is a case that will not often arise in a state of nature.) Then 'there is the question whether it be against reason, that is against the benefit of the other to perform, or not. And I say it is not against reason' (1651, Chapter 15). Hobbes's argument in support of this claim takes the form of an answer to the Foole who denies it.

The concept of constrained maximization and the idea of attributing rationality to dispositions rather than to actions are central to Gauthier's claim to show that it is rational to be moral. In voluntarily imposing constraints on herself – in being willing to reject the action that maximizes her expected utility – the CM is acting in a recognizably moral way. But the disposition to act in this way is utility-maximizing and thus rational.

Most commentators have been unconvinced by this argument, although it has found some support. The most notable supporter is McClennen (1988, 1990), whose own theory of 'resolute' choice is in many ways similar to Gauthier's theory of constrained maximization. I have argued in another paper (Sugden, 1991a) that some common objections to Gauthier's and McClennen's positions are unfounded. In this volume, however, the critics are to the fore.

In Chapter 8, Binmore challenges Gauthier's argument from the perspective of mainstream game theory. Binmore regards straightforward maximization as the only possible conception of rationality for game theory. Appealing to a 'revealed preference' interpretation of preference and utility, he argues that it is tautologically true that players maximize utility at every point in a game. If the concept of constrained maximization is to make sense, it must be re-interpreted as a property of the game being played, rather than of the players' reasoning. Thus, for example, Bruce would be able to make a credible commitment to keep his promise if he could set up some mechanism which, in the event of his not keeping the promise, would hurt him in a sufficiently unpleasant way. But such a mechanism, if it exists, should be modelled as part of the game.

In Chapters 3 and 4 of this volume, Hollis and Nida-Rümelin raise more philosophical doubts about the moral psychology of constrained maximization. Hollis is prepared to accept that a person's having made a promise might be a sufficient reason for him to keep it, but he is not convinced that this position is compatible with Gauthier's instrumental view of rationality. Nida-Rümelin argues for the stronger conclusion that rationality requires each person to act cooperatively in situations of the Prisoner's Dilemma kind; but he questions whether this form of rationality is consistent with any kind of maximization.

Gauthier's theory of compliance is linked to his theory of rights. Recall that Gauthier's analysis of rational bargaining requires an 'initial bargaining position', which forms a baseline for defining the cooperative surplus. If the outcomes of bargaining are to have the properties of impartiality that Gauthier hopes to find – and which he must find if he is to derive morality from rationality – then the initial bargaining position must satisfy some property of fairness. Gauthier achieves this by requiring a baseline in which there is no coercion. But the nature of Gauthier's project prevents him from introducing moral premises. He needs to show that individuals, each rationally pursuing his or her own interests and with no desire to be fair, would accept a fair baseline for bargaining.

The problem is illustrated by Gauthier's Parable of the Slaves (pp. 190–1). We are asked to imagine a stable society of masters and slaves, maintained by the power of the masters. Slavery is an inefficient system of economic organization, and so both masters and slaves would gain if slavery were abolished: there is scope for bargaining. On the face of it, the initial bargaining position is the *status quo*, in which the masters are much better off than the slaves. If we define the cooperative surplus in relation to this baseline, then (according to Gauthier's theory) the outcome of rational bargaining will be a non-slave society in which the former masters remain better off than the former slaves. To use Buchanan's language, an inequality in the natural distribution, reflecting the masters' success as predators, has been carried over to the post-contract society.

Gauthier considers this analysis but rejects it, on the grounds that compliance with such a bargain would be irrational on the part of the former slaves. It is rational to dispose oneself to comply with the bargains one has made, but only for the case of bargains which have been made from a non-coercive initial position: 'Someone disposed to comply with agreements that left untouched the fruits of predation would simply invite others to engage in predatory and coercive activities as a prelude to bargaining' (pp. 192, 195).

There is an interesting contrast here with Hobbes. Recall that Hobbes argues, against the Foole, that it is rational to comply with the covenants one has made, provided the other party has performed first. Hobbes makes no exception for cases in which the initial bargaining position was coercive:

> Covenants entered into by fear, in the condition of mere nature, are obligatory. For example, if I covenant to pay a ransom, or service of my life, to an enemy; I am bound by it: for it is a contract, wherein one receiveth the benefit of life; the other is to receive money, or service for it; and consequently, where no other law, as in the condition of mere nature, forbiddeth the performance, the covenant is valid. (1651, Chapter 15)

In this case, Gauthier sides with the Foole; but we may wonder if he is being consistent. It is in the nature of war that prisoners are captured, and that the most convenient way of dealing with prisoners of war is to kill them. In some cases, however, there is scope for a mutually beneficial arrangement, whereby the captor provides the prisoner with a safe passage home in return for a sufficiently large ransom. In Hobbes's case, the captor must perform first, releasing the prisoner in return for a promise of payment. This looks like a classic case in which it would pay to be a CM. A rational captor will release those prisoners who can be trusted to keep their promises; the others (including the Gauthiers who object to the coercive nature of the initial bargaining position) will be killed.

Gauthier may reply that someone who could be trusted to keep all his promises would make himself a target for kidnappers, motivated only by the prospect of a ransom. This is true, but notice that in Hobbes's example (at least, as I have interpreted it) the captor has adequate reason for taking prisoners, even if he cannot ransom them. Similarly in the Parable of the Slaves: the masters have adequate reason for holding slaves, even if there is no prospect of bargaining with them. Following Gauthier's advice will not prevent you from being enslaved, if there are would-be masters with the power to enslave you. It will merely prevent you from negotiating your release. If we can choose our dispositions, it seems rational to choose one which can discriminate between the kidnapping case and the others. But to draw this conclusion would be to undermine Gauthier's strategy for removing coercion from the initial bargaining position.

Gauthier distinguishes between the disposition to be *broadly compliant* and the disposition to be *narrowly compliant.* Someone who is broadly compliant is disposed to comply with any agreement he or she makes; someone who is narrowly compliant is disposed to comply with agreement, but only if the initial bargaining position was non-coercive. Gauthier argues that it is rational to acquire the second disposition but not the first (pp. 177–84, 225–7). His argument here has a similar structure to his argument for the principle of minimax relative concession. The idea is that, since individuals are assumed to be equally rational, it cannot be rational for one person to make a greater sacrifice than anyone else in order to achieve cooperation. Thus:

> It is rational for each person to be sufficiently compliant that society is possible if others are equally compliant; it is not rational to be so compliant that society is possible if others are less compliant; therefore it is rational for each person to be narrowly compliant. (p. 227)

As in his theory of bargaining, Gauthier uses the assumption of equal rationality to show that rationality requires us to accept constraints which apply impartially to all of us.

This argument seems to presuppose that there is a unique degree of compliance which is rationally prescribed. Facing the problem 'How compliant should I be?', Gauthier's individuals use the premiss that this problem has a unique solution to help them find what that solution is. But, as I argue in Chapter 9, we may not be entitled to assume that problems involving the interaction of rational agents have unique solutions. If I am right, then we may not be able to show that equally rational agents will abide by impartial constraints.

7 Success or failure?

Morals by Agreement can be read as a single piece of argument, leading to a breathtaking conclusion: that morality can be derived from rationality. Seen in this way, almost every part of the argument is necessary; if Gauthier is wrong at almost any point, the conclusion cannot be sustained. Like a piece of precision engineering, Gauthier's construction has no redundant components. Since many of these components are novel, it is hardly surprising that most of the contributors to this volume – like most other commentators on *Morals by Agreement* – have been unconvinced by at least one component, and thus have been unable to accept the argument as a whole. Gauthier, however, remains undaunted, as the final chapter of this volume shows.

But even if *Morals by Agreement* is ultimately judged to fail to achieve its highest ambitions, it makes many important contributions to the contractarian enterprise. Perhaps most fundamentally, Gauthier shows how a theory of justice can be based on the idea of bargaining between rational individuals who know their own identities and interests. Any such theory requires a baseline: Gauthier shows how we might construct a baseline by developing Locke's theory of natural rights. Even if this baseline cannot be shown to be an implication of a theory of rational choice, it might still be defended on moral grounds: Gauthier gives us such a defence. We might, then, find Gauthier's moral theory persuasive while rejecting some parts of his account of rationality. Conversely, we might recognize the importance of Gauthier's contributions to the theory of rational choice – particularly his account of constrained maximization – without seeing any connection between rationality and morality. This volume is a tribute to the richness and fertility of *Morals by Agreement*.

2

Between Hobbes and Rawls

David Gauthier

In *A Theory of Justice* John Rawls tells us:

> My aim is to present a conception of justice which generalizes and carries to a higher level of abstraction the familiar theory of the social contract as found, say, in Locke, Rousseau, and Kant ... the guiding idea is that the principles of justice for the basic structure of society are the object of the original agreement. They are the principles that free and rational persons concerned to further their own interests would accept in an initial position of equality as defining the fundamental terms of their association. (1971, p. 11)

To this passage he appends a note, part of which reads 'For all of its greatness, Hobbes's *Leviathan* raises special problems'. What these problems are, we are never told.

Putting his reference to Hobbes temporarily to one side, I want to recall a very natural interpretation of Rawls's enterprise. It is an interpretation that in the light of Rawls's subsequent work, and indeed, even in the light of the full development of *A Theory of Justice*, cannot be sustained, but that does not affect its interest. It is the interpretation first advanced, to the best of my knowledge, by Robert Paul Wolff.

Wolff supposes that Rawls began his thought 'with as narrow and morally neutral a conception of rational agency as can plausibly be drawn ... that men seek happiness'. And Rawls then reflected, 'Clearly, the bare notion of rational agency is insufficient for a rationally defended morality, but is there anything that can be added to these elements, short of the mere positing of substantive moral claims, that will yield a rational argument for a moral principle ...?' This principle is to satisfy certain desiderata of which the two most relevant to my present enquiry are that it 'not deviate wildly from ... our strongest moral convictions' and that it take 'the inviolability and dignity of moral personality as fundamental' (Wolff, 1977, p. 13).

Now, Wolff (pp. 13, 15) continues, Rawls turned to 'the tradition of the social contract ... in its Rousseauean form'. For Rousseau, the social contract effects 'a moral transformation', giving each individual 'the opportunity for the first time to have or exercise a general will' (p. 14). But what can this mean?

> At this point, Rawls had an idea. It was ... one of the loveliest ideas in the history of social and political theory. ... Rawls proposed to construct a formal model of a society of rationally self-interested individuals, whom he would imagine to be engaged in what the modern theory of rational choice calls a *bargaining game*. His intuition was that if ... he posited a group of individuals whose nature and motives were those usually assumed in contract theory – then with a single additional quasi-formal, substantively empty constraint, he could prove, as a formal theorem in the theory of rational choice, that *the* solution to the bargaining game was a moral principle having the [desired] characteristics (p. 16).

The constraint is simply that once the principle is chosen 'on the basis of a calculation of self-interest', then the bargainers – who are now the members of society – 'will abide by ... [it] in all future cases, including those in which ... it is not in their self-interest so to abide'. In agreeing to and abiding by the principle individuals are morally transformed (p. 17).

When I first read Wolff's account, I realized how well he had captured my own initial understanding of Rawls's aim, and how presciently he had characterized what had become my own project in moral theory. Of course in ascribing to Rawls the introduction of a bargaining game, one would have to face his claim 'that the parties have no basis for bargaining in the usual sense' (Rawls, 1971, p. 139), but I shall leave this aside for the moment. And not quite all of the needed elements were in place. In particular, in Wolff's initial account, both the rationale for engaging in the bargaining game and the constraint of commitment to the principles chosen through bargaining are left unmotivated. But we may approach these omissions best by considering first Rawls's own characterization of a society as 'a cooperative venture for mutual advantage', and his insistence that 'A set of principles is required for choosing among the various social arrangements which determine' the division of this advantage among the members (1971, p. 4).

We may think of the idea of mutual advantage as motivating the bargaining game. It might at first seem that Rawls's formal model would enable us to show what rational persons, taking no interest in one another's interests, would agree to *if* they were to bargain together about principles governing their future or prospective interaction, but would leave us asking why it would be rational for such persons to come to the bargaining table in the first place. The answer, implicit in the idea of society as 'a cooperative venture for mutual advantage', is that such bargaining is in each person's interest. Without principles governing their interaction, individuals would find themselves in a state of nature – a state with the internal structure of a generalized prisoner's dilemma. We need not accept Hobbes's peculiarly gloomy representation of our natural condition to see it in this way; Locke, Hume, and Rousseau all give accounts that, while substantively different, are formally similar. Thus persons come to the bargaining table because they want to escape the costs of natural unconstrained interaction, and share in the benefits of social cooperation. The principles to which they agree are those adherence to which best enables them to achieve these aims. And note that these aims are formal. The idea is simply that each person has the general *formal* aim of maximizing the overall fulfilment of her material or substantive aims; the desire to escape the costs of the state of nature and share in the benefits of society may then be derived from this formal aim. We need say nothing about the content of the particular concerns or interests that persons have, in order to recognize that each stands to benefit from cooperation with her fellows. Or at least, we need impose only the very minimal requirement that each person's interests be such that overall they can be more effectively fulfilled through cooperation.

The idea that an initial social bargain would result in a moral principle invites a number of questions. One is why we should take the bargaining outcome to be a *moral* principle. What invests the bargaining of persons, each seeking to advance her own concerns, with *moral* significance? A second is what would result from an initial bargain among persons seeking a principle or principles to govern their social interaction. A third is whether our own moral principles and practices are potential or possible outcomes of such an initial social bargain. I want to pursue the first of these matters, putting the others to one side. In particular – to bring my own enquiries explicitly in to the present argument – I am not concerned here with the adequacy of the account that I have offered in *Morals by Agreement* and elsewhere of the principle that would result from an initial social bargain – of minimax relative concession. I want to focus simply on the idea of investing the bargaining outcome, whatever it may be, with moral significance. This is the core idea of contractarian *ethics.*

To pursue it I shall raise a seemingly different issue. On Wolff's interpretation of Rawls, morality is derived from (i) a morally neutral idea of the rational agent, (ii) the idea of a social contract as a rational bargain among such agents, whose motivation is assumed to be non-tuistic, and (iii) the constraint of commitment to the outcome of the bargain. I have shown how Rawls's conception of society motivates non-tuistic rational agents to make a social contract. In viewing society as a cooperative venture for mutual advantage, each person recognizes the rationality of agreeing to principles that make such a society possible, provided both that others also agree, and that they are then committed to adhere to the agreed principles. Thus the rationale for engaging in the bargaining game is in place. This part of the argument needs no moral premisses. But what of the constraint of commitment to the principles chosen through baragaining? Is it also rational, or is it still unmotivated? I have not yet considered this question. We do not yet know what premisses this part of the argument requires. I propose to bring Hobbes back into our discussion and look to him for an answer.

Hobbes's argument begins from his characterization of the natural condition of mankind. He recognizes that it has the structure of a generalized prisoner's dilemma, and he insists that it is a moral vacuum, a condition from which all moral constraints and requirements are absent. 'The notions of Right and Wrong, Justice and Injustice have there no place' (1651, Chapter 13). In the state of nature 'private Appetite is the measure of Good, and Evill', and 'Reason ... dictateth to every man his own good' (1651, Chapter 15). Although Hobbes speaks of a person exercising the right of nature in using 'his own power ... for the preservation of his own Nature' (1651, Chapter 14), yet right has here no moral significance, since 'Neither by the word *right* is anything else signified, than that liberty which every man hath to make use of his natural faculties according to right reason' (Hobbes, 1978, p. 115). The state of nature is neither an evaluative nor a normative vacuum, but the good of appetite and the right of reason are *morally* empty.

Hobbes says that the right of nature is 'a Right to every thing' (1651, Chapter 14), but his thought is not perspicuously expressed. Properly speaking, natural right is coextensive with natural reason; whatever a person's reason determines as a means to his good, that he does with right. Whatever one would do to achieve one's ends, one may do. To think of natural right in this way is to treat it as unconstrained, existing in a moral vacuum. For Hobbes, it is also to treat it as giving rise to a generalized prisoner's dilemma. Indeed, 'as long as this naturall Right of every man to every thing endureth, there can be no security to any man ... of living out the time, which Nature ordinarily alloweth men to live' (1651, Chapter 14). The unconstrained right of nature is manifest in the war of every man against every man.

'And Reason suggesteth convenient Articles of Peace, upon which men may be drawn to agreement. These Articles, are they, which otherwise are called the Lawes of Nature' (1651, Chapter 13). The laws of nature are rational precepts or rules, 'dictates of Reason' (1651, Chapter 15), that constrain right – 'RIGHT, consisteth in liberty to do, or to forbeare;

Whereas LAW, determineth, and bindeth to one of them'. The first law commands persons to endeavour peace, and the second, derived from it, requires, '*That a man be willing, when others are so too, ... to lay down this right to all things; and be contented with so much liberty against other men, as he would allow other men against himselfe*' (1651, Chapter 14). For Hobbes, this mutual laying down of right takes the form of covenanting to authorize a sovereign or ruler whose laws all will obey. Sovereignty is the institution 'that free and rational persons concerned to further their own interests would accept in an initial position of equality as defining the fundamental terms of their association', to adapt Rawls's (1971, p. 11) statement of his aim to Hobbes. For Rawls the outcome of the social contract is the adoption of a principle or principles of justice; for Hobbes the outcome is the authorization of a sovereign. But for both the aim of the contract is the same; Rawls's principles and Hobbes's sovereign exist to regulate our interaction for our mutual advantage. And for both we must commit ourselves to abide by our agreement – to follow the principles or to obey the sovereign.

Hobbes expresses this commitment in the third law of nature, '*That men performe their Covenants made*: without which, Covenants are in vain, and but Empty words; and the Right of all men to all things remaining, wee are still in the condition of Warre' (1651, Chapter 15). In treating it as a law of nature, Hobbes supposes that it too can be derived as a dictate of reason, and so from premisses that are morally neutral. And in deriving it he has introduced justice, which lies in the keeping of covenants. I shall consider Hobbes's understanding of justice at greater length presently. But here my concern is to emphasize that in introducing justice he claims to have established, and not merely to have assumed, the constraint of commitment to the outcome of our agreements – and has done so without appealing to any moral premisses. Hobbes has thus invested the bargaining outcome with moral significance. Contrary to Wolff's view, it would seem that the bare notion of rational agency is sufficient for morality, given that rational agents are motivated to escape from the prisoner's-dilemma structure of natural interaction.

But is Hobbes's argument sound? The third law is challenged by

> The Foole [who] hath sayd in his heart, there is no such thing as Justice; ... seriously alleaging, that every mans conservation, and contentment, being committed to his own care, there could be no reason, why every man might not do what he thought conduced thereunto: and therefore also to make, or not make; keep, or not keep Covenants, was not against Reason, when it conduced to ones benefit. (1651, Chapter 15)

If the Foole is right, a person is under no rational requirement to perform her covenants, except when and in so far as performance conduces to her benefit. And this extends, of course, to obedience to the sovereign and his laws, so that 'men are disposed to debate with themselves, and dispute the commands of the Commonwealth; and afterwards to obey, or disobey them, as in their private judgements they shall think fit' (1651, Chapter 29).

Suppose for the moment that we find ourselves accepting the arguments of both Hobbes and the Foole. Suppose we accept the claim that unless persons are committed to justice – to keeping their covenants and obeying the sovereign, then, as Hobbes insists, they have not escaped the prisoner's-dilemma structure of their natural condition, and are unable to gain the mutual benefits promised by society. But suppose we also accept the response that each person being judge of her own good, and reason dictating to her those actions that most conduce to that good, then her rational commitment to justice extends only so far as adherence to her covenants is to her benefit. Thus, to paraphrase and apply Wolff's account to Hobbes, it is not the case that persons, having agreed, will abide by their agreements in all situations, including those in which it is not in their self-interest so to abide (cf. Wolff, 1977, p. 17). Rational persons might be willing to make a social contract with their fellows, could they expect it to be adhered to, but it seems that they could not so expect, since rational persons would not commit themselves to adhere to it.

Wolff claims that the constraint of commitment is

> so minimal, so natural, so manifestly a constraint under which any person would consent to operate insofar as he made any pretensions at all to having a morality, that Rawls would, ... [were his bargaining argument to be successful], be in a position to say to a reader: *If you are a rationally self-interested agent, and if you are to have a morality at all, then you must acknowledge as binding upon you the moral principle I shall enunciate.* (Wolff, 1977, p. 17)

And given that this principle makes society, as a cooperative venture for mutual advantage, possible, it seems that Rawls could say more – that if you are a rationally self-interested agent, and if you are to have *society* at all, then you must acknowledge as binding the principle that would be the outcome of a rational initial bargain over the terms of interaction. But is this enough? May we not introduce Rawls's Foole, who will say that, being a rationally self-interested agent, he cannot acknowledge as binding any such principle, any more than Hobbes's Foole can acknowledge as binding his authorization of any sovereign?

I began with an interpretation of Rawls's account of morality – that moral principles would be the outcome of a bargain among self-interested persons over their terms of interaction, given their willingness to be committed to abide by those principles, even if it is not in their self-interest so to abide. To motivate the bargain I added the idea that these principles provided the basis of cooperation for mutual advantage. I then noted the parallel between this view and Hobbes's account of the laws of nature and the natural condition of mankind. But I found that according to the Foole, the same rationality that we ascribe to persons as dictating their making such a bargain, also dictates their not being committed to abiding by the outcome of their bargain except when it is in their self-interest so to abide. The rationality that would underlie making the social contract if persons were committed to adhering to it, undermines that very commitment. Looking to Hobbes seems to have led us to view it as unmotivated. The attempt to introduce morality through a self-interested agreement together with a commitment to adhere to its outcome may now seem incoherent.

For Rawls, as distinguished from Wolff's interpretation of Rawls, there is no incoherence. Although his theory is not my primary concern here, it may be worth sketching briefly why this is so. The key is to understand the real meaning of Rawls's statement that the principles of justice are those 'that *free and rational persons concerned to further their own interests* would accept' (Rawls, 1971, p. 11, emphasis added). These persons are not, as Wolff (1977, p. 16) may have thought, 'a group of individuals whose nature and motives were those usually assumed in contract theory'. Rather, as Rawls's Kantian interpretation of his theory makes clear, 'The parties [to the choice] regard moral personality ... as the fundamental aspect of the self', and 'moral personality is characterized by two capacities: one for a conception of the good, the other for a sense of justice' (Rawls, 1971, pp. 561, 563). In 'Kantian Constructivism in Moral Theory', Rawls (1980, p. 525) relates these two capacities, or 'moral powers' as he there calls them, to 'two corresponding highest-order interests in realizing and exercising these powers. ... moral persons are said to be moved by [these] two highest-order interests' so that 'whenever circumstances are relevant to their fulfilment, these interests govern deliberation and conduct'. The principles of justice are, then, chosen by persons, not on the basis of a self-interested calculation as we should ordinarily understand it, but on the basis of a calculation of what will best serve the two highest-order interests in realizing and exercizing a conception of the good and a sense of justice. To be sure, each is concerned with her own highest-order interests, so that as Rawls (1971, p. 147) insists, the parties to the agreement are 'assumed to take no interest in one another's interests'. But the nature of these interests ensures that the commitment to abide by the principles is effectively assured by the correct choice. Provided the persons choose those principles which best enable them to realize and exercise a sense of justice, then that sense of justice will motivate them to comply with the principles.

Indeed, I may now make sense of Rawls's insistence that in the choice of principles 'the parties have no basis for bargaining in the usual sense'

(1971, p. 139). For this may be related to his claim that 'unanimous agreement [or the principles] is best expressive of the nature of even a single self' (1971, p. 257). In rational bargaining the parties reach unanimity, but as a compromise. But for Rawls, 'The nature of the self as a free and equal moral person is the same for all', and 'the members of a community participate in one another's nature', so that 'relations of justice that conform to principles which would be assented to by all are best fitted to express the nature of each' (1971, p. 565). We began, or so we thought, with a need for principles of justice to enable persons to escape the generalized prisoner's dilemma of unconstrained interaction. But we find now that according to Rawls's Kantian interpretation, the real need for principles of justice is to enable persons best to express their nature as moral persons in social union with their fellows. It would seem that Rawls's argument involves what Wolff (1977, p. 13) took him to seek to avoid, 'the mere positing of substantive moral claims'.

I noted earlier that Rawls (1971, p. 11n) mentions Hobbes's *Leviathan* as raising 'special problems'. I speculate that these problems turn on Hobbes's very different understanding of the interests persons seek to serve in agreeing to the social contract. Rawls's insistence that 'The parties [to the choice] regard moral personality ... as the fundamental aspect of the self' gives him a very different response to the problem of commitment, as raised by Hobbes's Foole, than any response available to Hobbes. Hobbes, unlike Rawls, seeks to derive justice from the rational agreement of persons who have no prior moral concerns, and who view preservation as fundamental, not moral personality.

But if Rawls is able to bypass the 'special problems' raised by Hobbes's account, we are not. With Hobbes's Foole, we should be unpersuaded by an appeal to moral personality in the *premisses* of the contract argument. And so the problem of commitment remains. If we are to relate morality, or more specifically justice, to rationality, we must show not only the rational basis for agreeing to justice by making the social contract, but also the rational basis for adhering to justice by committing oneself to abide by the contract. It seems that if each person has the general formal aim of maximizing the fulfilment of her material or substantive aims, then each would rationally make the contract were adherence also rational, but will not commit herself to adhere to it. But is this so? If justice is, as Hobbes says, the performance of one's covenants, is it in conflict with rationality? I want now to turn to Hobbes's quite complex answer to this question.

For Hobbes as for Rawls, agreement is constitutive of justice. But whereas Rawls's concern is primarily with the justice of social institutions, which is determined by their conformity with the principles persons would accept in an appropriate initial agreement, Hobbes's concern is primarily with the justice of persons and of actions, which is determined by conformity to the agreements persons make. Actions are just or unjust in so far as they constitute the performance or non-performance of covenant. A person is just in so far as 'his Will is ... framed by the Justice ... of what he is to do', and not 'by the apparent benefit'; he is just in so far as 'he ... taketh all the care he can, that his Actions may be all Just'. A person is just not because he in fact acts justly, but because he is disposed to act justly; for Hobbes, this is to speak of his 'Manners, or manner of life'. And Hobbes insists against the Foole that to attribute justice either to a person in virtue of his manners or disposition, or to an action as the performance of a covenant, is to 'signifie ... Conformity ... to Reason' (1651, Chapter 15).

Why? I shall quote Hobbes's best answer to the Foole at length:

> he which declares he thinks it reason to deceive those that help him, can in reason expect no other means of safety, than what can be had from his own single Power. He therefore that breaketh his Covenant, and consequently declareth that he thinks he may with reason do so, cannot be received into any Society, that unite themselves for Peace and Defence, but by the errour of them that receive him; nor when he is received, by retayned in it, without seeing the danger of their errour; which errours a man cannot reasonably reckon upon as the means of his security: and therefore if he be left, or cast out of Society, he perisheth; and if he live in Society, it is by the errours of other men, which he could not foresee, nor reckon upon; and consequently against the reason of his preservation; and so, as all men that contribute not to his destruction, forbear him onely out of ignorance of what is good for themselves. (1651, Chapter 15)

In this response Hobbes directs the Foole, not to the advantage or disadvantage of particular actions, but to the advantage or disadvantage of manners or dispositions. The person whose will is not disposed to justice, who believes that he may with reason ignore the justice or injustice of his particular actions to consider only their advantage or disadvantage, is unfit to be a partner in society – unfit, we may say, to be a participant in the social contract. He must therefore expect to be excluded from the contract and from the benefits realized by the society that it creates. Since such exclusion is disadvantageous – indeed fatal, in Hobbes's view – it is as unreasonable to be unwilling to abide by the social contract as to be unwilling to enter into it. The reason that each person has to bargain with his fellows about the terms of their interaction, is also the reason he has to dispose himself to comply with the agreed terms. The commitment to abide by one's agreement, is not, as the Foole treats it, an extraneous unmotivated addendum, but an essential and intrinsic part of each person's passage from nature to society, a passage each recognizes as rational in virtue of his formal aim, of maximizing the overall fulfilment of his material or substantive aims whatever these may be.

As I noted previously, Wolff interprets Rawls's moral theory as Rousseauean. For Rousseau the social contract effects 'a moral transformation', giving each individual 'the opportunity for the first time to have or exercise a general will' (Wolff, 1977, p. 14). Such a transformation is, I believe, present also in Hobbes's account, and provides an important if implicit part of his argument against the Foole. This transformation is effected by the authorization of the sovereign, in which the subjects 'submit their Wills, every one to his Will, and their Judgements, to his Judgment. This is more than Consent, or Concord; it is a reall Unitie of them all' (Hobbes, 1651, Chapter 17). The unity is one of *reason.* In his account of reason in *Leviathan*, Hobbes argues:

> And therfore, as when there is a controversy in an account, the parties must by their own accord, set up for right Reason, the Reason of some Arbitrator, or Judge, to whose sentence they will both stand, or their controversie must either come to blowes, or be undecided, for want of a right Reason constituted by Nature; so is it also in all debates of what kind soever. (1651, Chapter 5)

The subjects, in authorizing the sovereign, commit themselves to accept his reason in place of their own. Thus in replying to Bishop Bramhall, Hobbes insists:

> because neither mine nor the Bishop's reason is right reason fit to be a rule of our moral actions, we have therefore set up over ourselves a sovereign governor, and agreed that his laws shall be unto us, whatsoever they be, in the place of right reason, to dictate to us what is really good. (1841, p. 194)

For Hobbes natural right is coextensive with natural reason. In the natural condition of mankind each supposes that she may do whatever seems to her most reasonable given her ends. In authorizing the sovereign, the subjects agree to limit their right by his reason. Thus the commands of the sovereign are the civil laws, *'those Rules, which the Common-wealth hath Commanded* ... [to every subject], *to make use of, for the Distinction of Right, and Wrong'.* Lawyers agree that these laws can never be against reason, 'but the doubt is, of whose Reason it is, that shall be received for Law. It is not meant of any private Reason; ... but the Reason of this our Artificiall Man the Common-wealth' (1651, Chapter 26). And one of the great diseases that infect actual societies is the view '*That every private man is Judge of Good and Evill actions.* This is true in the condition of meer Nature .... But otherwise, it is manifest, that the measure of Good and Evill actions, is the Civill Law' (1651, Chapter 29).

Hobbes's Foole takes for granted that each individual is and remains judge of the reasonableness of her own actions. But in the passages just quoted Hobbes makes clear that he rejects this presupposition of the Foole's argument. Thus against the Foole's appeal to natural reason to support the rationality of injustice, Hobbes may appeal to the right reason of the sovereign to support the rationality of justice. And this is not an arbitrary appeal. In authorizing the sovereign, each of us willingly and rationally subordinates her natural reason to the sovereign's reason as made manifest in civil law. So Hobbes can insist in replying to Bramhall, that 'this *right reason*, which is the law, is no otherwise certainly right than by our making it so by our approbation of it and voluntary subjection to it' (1841, p 193).

The moral transformation present in Hobbes's account is to be identified with this voluntary subordination of natural reason to the right reason of the sovereign. The sovereign's reason, establishing in law a common rule for distinguishing right and wrong, and a common standard for evaluating good and evil, corresponds to the Rousseauean general will. 'Morall Philosophy', Hobbes tells us, 'is nothing else but the Science of what is *Good*, and *Evill*, in the conversation, and Society of mankind' (1651, Chapter 15). This science must be based on the laws of nature, which each person's natural reason suggests as a basis for agreement. But to make the laws of nature effective, they must be the commands of the sovereign to whom natural reason is subordinated. As Hobbes says, 'For in the differences of private men, to declare, what is Equity, what is Justice, and what is morall Vertue, and to make them binding, there is need of the Ordinances of Soveraign Power' (1651, Chapter 26). In overcoming 'the differences of private men', the sovereign makes it possible for them to converse of good and evil. In supplanting those differences by a common standard of right and wrong, he gives them, as Wolff puts it, the opportunity for the first time to have or exercise a general will.

I asked what invests the bargaining process that results in the social contract with moral significance. Initially I found an answer in the idea that the contract establishes justice – the commitment to adhere to one's agreements. But Hobbes's argument in support of justice proved suspect. In considering how Hobbes defends it, I have been led to a deeper answer – in the social contract persons morally transform themselves by subordinating their natural reason to law, which is the expression of sovereign reason. But is this truly a *moral* transformation?

Hobbes begins with a morally neutral conception of rational agents, exhibits the prisoner's-dilemma structure of natural unconstrained interaction among such agents, establishes the rationale for each agent to agree with her fellows to accept mutual constraints on their interaction, and the rationale for her to dispose herself to abide by their agreement. Their wills now framed to justice, rational agents have become moral persons. Hobbes would seem to have had an idea even lovelier than Rawls – the idea that morality can be developed within a rational choice framework by considering only the structure of unconstrained interaction. But we are unlikely to accept Hobbes's idea in the form he presents it. To become a moral person by subordinating one's will and judgement to a sovereign, accepting his reason as right reason supplanting one's own natural reason, would be to acquire morality at the price of autonomy. Could this truly be morality? Hobbesian subjects may perform just acts, but do they become just persons? Do they develop and exercise a general will, or do they instead resign their wills to the sovereign? It may seem that rather than acquiring moral personality, they give up their initial status as rational agents.

Let us look more closely at Hobbes's account of the subordination of the subject to the sovereign. In authorizing the sovereign, persons would seem to create and accept both an *external* constraint on their interaction and an *internal* constraint. An external constraint affects the circumstances of interaction, either by altering the possible actions from which agents choose, or by altering the characteristics of the states of affairs that agents would expect to bring about by their possible actions. An internal constraint affects either the agents' preferences over outcomes, while leaving unchanged their beliefs about the characteristics of those outcomes, or the rules by which agents pass from these preferences to the evaluation of their possible actions.

To illustrate this distinction between external and internal constraint and to apply it to Hobbes's argument, consider two ways in which a person might come to perform just actions. First, she might, as Glaucon suggests in the *Republic*, consider injustice to be in itself more profitable or advantageous than justice, but nevertheless perform just acts because she expects to be punished for unjust ones. Punishment serves as an external constraint on her choices. It affects her beliefs about the possibilities open to her. It does not change her preferences, but makes one preference – for successful injustice over justice – irrelevant, while bringing another – for justice over unsuccessful or punished injustice – to bear on her choice. But second, she might, to use Hobbes's language, come to have her will framed by justice, so that she comes to choose among actions not by considering only their costs and benefits, but by considering also their justice or injustice. Here a commitment to justice serves as an internal constraint on her choices, affecting not her beliefs about the possibilities open to her, but her way of evaluating those possibilities.

Hobbes does not make clear the distinction between internal and external constraint as I have done. He seems to suppose that persons accept an internal constraint on their choices, subordinating their reason and will to that of the sovereign, but he may really believe that they accept only an external constraint, created by the power of the sovereign to compel their obedience. He acknowledges parenthetically the ineffectiveness of internal constraints when he says, 'That which gives to humane Actions the relish of Justice, is a certain Noblenesse or Gallantnesse of courage, (rarely found,) by which a man scorns to be beholding for the contentment of his life, to fraud, or breach of promise' (1651, Chapter 15). And he makes explicit appeal to the coercive power of the sovereign when he says:

> But as men, for the atteyning of peace, and conservation of themselves thereby, have made an Artificiall Man, which we call a Common-wealth; so also have they made Artificiall Chains, called *Civill Lawes*, which they themselves, by mutual covenants, have fastned at one end, to the lips of that Man, or Assembly, to whom they have given the Soveraigne Power; and at the other end to their own Ears. These Bonds in their own nature but weak, may neverthelesse be made to hold, by the danger, though not by the difficulty of breaking them. (1651, Chapter 21)

If this passage represents Hobbes's considered view, then authorizing the sovereign effects no moral transformation, or assumption of moral personality, but it also involves no real subordination of one's natural reason to the sovereign's reason. Talk of the law as right reason is mere window-dressing. What matters is the power of the sovereign to enforce his commands, and this power addresses each person's natural reason, making the disadvantage of disobedience evident.

But my concern about whether Hobbes provides a place for moral transformation does not rest on dismissing the idea that law serves as an internal constraint on each person's reason and will. Let us suppose that Hobbes does genuinely appeal to such a constraint – not exclusively, of course, but in addition to the external constraint created by the sovereign's power to punish. My concern rests on the character of this internal constraint. It arises in the act of authorizing the sovereign, in which one says '*I Authorise and give up my Right of Governing my selfe, to this Man*' (1651, Chapter 17). This is an act of surrender; each subject must *give up* her right to govern herself, accepting the sovereign's will as her will, his judgement as her judgement, his reason as her reason. Authorization is conversion, as Jean Hampton (1986, pp. 208–20) argues. Recall that among the diseases of society, private judgement of good and evil is prominent. Recall that the differences of private men and women make it necessary for the sovereign to declare what is justice. And recall that 'we have … set up over ourselves a sovereign governor, and agreed that his laws shall be unto us, *whatsoever they be*, in the place of right reason, to dictate to us what is *really good*' (Hobbes, 1841, p. 194, emphasis added). Treating the sovereign's laws, whatsoever they be, as right reason is indeed incompatible with moral personality, in so far as it requires each person to give up her initial status as an independent rational agent.

Hobbes tells us that 'the true doctrine of the Lawes of Nature, is the true Morall Philosophie' (1651, Chapter 15). It would seem that he is wrong, and that he has not succeeded in realizing the lovely idea that morality can be developed within a rational choice framework by considering only the structure of unconstrained interaction. What rational persons, faced with the state of nature, agree to is not morality, but captivity. They internalize the laws of nature, not as moral principles, but as sovereign commands:

> in the condition of meer Nature ... [the laws of nature] are not properly Lawes, but qualities that dispose men to peace, and to obedience. When a Common-wealth is once settled, then are they actually Lawes, and not before; as being then the commands of the Common-wealth; and therefore also Civill Lawes: For it is the Soveraign Power that obliges men to obey them. (1651, Chapter 26)

The laws of the sovereign, even considered as internal constraints, are chains.

My title is 'Between Hobbes and Rawls'. Rawls allows moral personality to enter the premisses of his contractarian derivation of the principles of justice. Hobbes's contractarian derivation of sovereignty effectively denies moral personality. Should we conclude that the social contract itself effects no moral transformation, that the bargaining of persons, each seeking to advance her own interests, has no moral significance? Or can we steer between the positions of Hobbes and Rawls, and find the emergence of moral personality within a contractarian understanding of morality as rationally agreed constraint? I think we can.

Begin again with the rational agent. Mindful of the costs of unstructured interaction with her fellows, mindful also of the potential benefits from cooperation, she comes to an awareness of the laws of nature. She recognizes that rationally she must be willing to agree to certain constraints on her initial freedom of action, provided others are also willing, and then to commit herself to abide by the agreed constraints. She does not give up her judgement of good and evil, but she commits herself to a common standard of judgement, provided by the laws of nature, and she is guided by that standard to seek mutual benefit rather than her individual advantage. In this way she exhibits what we may call, following Rawls, a sense of justice – or, following Hobbes, having her will framed by justice. She takes on moral personality, while retaining her authority as a rational agent, because she internalizes the laws of nature as rational requirements in her deliberation and action. She does not subordinate her reason, as to a Hobbesian sovereign, but, through the laws of nature, coordinates her reason with that of her fellows.

But there is a further dimension to moral personality as understood from a contractarian perspective. Among the particular laws of nature that Hobbes derives from the first two, are these: *'That every man acknowledge other for his Equall by Nature'*, *'That at the entrance into conditions of Peace, no man require to reserve to himselfe any Right, which he is not content should be reserved to everyone of the rest'*, and that *'if a man be trusted to judge between man and man, ... that he deale Equally between them'*. Their rationale is that 'If Nature therefore have made men equall, that equalitie is to be acknowledged: or if Nature have made men unequall; yet because men that think themselves equall, will not enter into conditions of Peace, but upon Equall termes, such equalitie must be admitted' (1651, Chapter 15). Each person must acknowledge the equality of her fellows, and so acknowledge that they enjoy the same rights that she claims for herself. Although as I have noted the right of nature is morally empty, signifying only the lack of any constraint on seeking preservation and well-being, the rights that each reserves are not, since they signify the agreed extent of one's liberty to seek one's ends without hindrance from others. Thus in acknowledging the equality of one's fellows, one recognizes them as moral persons.

Although Wolff treats the commitment to abide by the terms of agreement as exogenous to rationality, I have viewed it endogenously, as an essential part of rational interaction. But a person can have reason to commit herself to abide only by an agreement that it is rational for her to make, and as Hobbes insists it is rational for her to make an agreement only on terms that recognize her as equally rational with her fellows. Each must then be accorded the rights that the others would demand, were they in her position. Each person assumes moral personality in accepting obligations that constrain her pursuit of her own good, but in doing this each demands that others accord her moral personality in being recognized as exercising rights, equally with her fellows, that allow the pursuit of that good.

Moral personality does not play the presuppositional role in this account that it does in Rawls's; there is no suggestion that 'The parties [to the choice] regard moral personality ... as the fundamental aspect of the self' (Rawls, 1971, p. 563). But it is as moral persons that we are parties to the social contract. We can understand neither the equal recognition that each gives to her fellows, nor the commitment that each undertakes to comply with the terms of agreement, if we treat moral personality as a mere epiphenomenon of rational interaction.

Under the guise of discussing Hobbes and Rawls, I have been sketching my own conception of contractarian ethics as grounded in rational choice.

My implicit concern has been to respond to the charge that a contractarian theory, because it defends constraints on each individual's pursuit of her good only within the context of mutual benefit, offers only the simulation of morality. But neither recognition of the rights of one's fellows nor commitment to abide by mutually agreed principles is a simulation. If these are required for rational interaction, then, beginning from 'as narrow and morally neutral a conception of rational agency as can plausibly be drawn', we may develop an ethics that does 'not deviate wildly from ... our strongest moral convictions' and that takes 'the inviolability and dignity of moral personality as fundamental' (Wolff, 1977, p. 13). Between Hobbes and Rawls we may hope to have found the loveliest idea of all.

3

The agriculture of the mind

Martin Hollis

'I cannot forgive Descartes. In all his philosophy he would have been quite willing to dispense with God.' Pascal's remark takes one by surprise. How could the author of the *Meditations* possibly dispense with the God who is no deceiver and whose being is the basis of Reason? Yet, on reflection, the thrust is very shrewd. The new Cartesian-inspired science kept God as honorary prime mover and ultimate cause but soon dispensed with final causes for particular events and soon purged Reason of its older ties with Meaning in the order of things. In so doing, it lit a fuse under ethics, conceived as a rational answer to the old question of how one should live.

It was a long fuse. For example, Condorcet's *Sketch for a Historical Picture of the Progress of the Human Mind* declared triumphantly that 'truth, knowledge and virtue are bound by Nature with an indissoluble chain', since knowledge includes both our human goals and the objectively most rational means to achieve them, while virtue is the cultivation of suitable dispositions. As Helvetius put it, in the phrase of my title, 'Ethics is the agriculture of the mind'. These are typical Enlightenment gestures to a naturalistic ethics, whose typical detailed manifesto is utilitarianism. I do not mean that naturalism appealed to all Enlightenment thinkers. Kant too put trust in Reason but regarded rational moral choice as conformity to a universal maxim derived from the categorical imperative and applying to all rational beings as such. The unifying theme was not naturalism but the place of Reason in ethics.

Yet Kant and the utilitarians had seen trouble in store. They intended a rational guide to moral action which would still serve even if one granted that life has no meaning outside itself. Reason, they hoped, could survive this break with tradition, since it did not depend on a covert appeal to a divinely established order. Nietzsche thought otherwise and accused them of cowering in the shadow of a dying God. Once God is dead, he added, reason demolishes rational ethics, since, in the words which David Gauthier (1988b) quotes, 'as the will to truth ... gains self-consciousness, ... morality will gradually perish' (see page 8 above). More recently emotivism, as diagnosed for instance by Alasdair MacIntyre, has undermined the claim of reason to give any cognitive guidance to ethics. If life has *no* meaning outside itself, there is nothing for reason to discover and its office is only to destroy our illusions. How can we forgive Descartes?

Gauthier's *Morals by Agreement* is a clever and ambitious attempt at forgiveness. Although the moral meaning, which life aspires to, is internal, rather than external, and constructed, rather than unearthed, reason still has business in ethics. Starting only with a moral psychology where preferences motivate actions which, if rational, maximise expected utility, he tries to persuade rational agents to accept a moral point of view. If he succeeds, we shall have dispensed with God but morality will not have to perish too.

For all its grand ambitions, vivid illustrations and technical complexities, the book's key line is austerely neat. It is an answer to Hobbes's 'foole who hath said in his heart there is no god' and 'questioneth, whether Injustice ... may not sometimes stand with that Reason which dictateth to every man his own good'. What Reason dictateth, in Gauthier's view, is an oblique and conditional strategy. Each of us does best by acquiring a disposition to treat others justly if and only if they have acquired the same disposition. Once convinced of this, each rational agent will choose to acquire the disposition, in the knowledge that each other rational agent will have done the same. 'Justice', for these purposes, marks whatever distribution of utilities is for the best, as judged from an impersonal, impartial and universal Archimedean standpoint, achievable in theory through rational bargaining.

Of many possible themes, I shall fasten on one to do with rational motivation and the moral psychology of Gauthier's agents. They are bidden to practise the agriculture of the mind, thus binding knowledge and virtue with an indissoluble chain forged by an act of rational will. But, at least until the closing chapters, they remain the individual utility maximisers of neoclassical economics, able to switch the moral point of view on or off as occasion demands. They combine as partners, yet still think as accountants. Can a contractarian theory blend commitment and calculation in this delicate way? *Morals by Agreement* makes a truly tempting offer but, I shall argue, one which its brand of individualism cannot sustain. It is rational to be moral only if 'rational' is taken in an expressive way which affects the identity of the agents, thus either destabilising the attractive account of 'The Liberal Individual' offered at the end of the book or undermining the crucial argument at its core.

Whatever the outcome, I should like to pay tribute to the book. Its argument is beautifully constructed, clearly deployed and rich in points which make the reader think. To tackle even this one theme I shall need to consider both Humean and Kantian moral psychology, to examine various accounts of the self and its relation to others, to juggle with instrumental and expressive notions of rationality and to forage into political philosophy. To keep discussion within bounds, I shall therefore borrow a device which Gauthier himself uses with refreshing skill, and spin a fable. This fable concerns an intellectual crisis in an Arcadia, where the more enlightened inhabitants have taken *Morals by Agreement* to heart but are about to wonder whether they have been living in a foole's paradise.

The small town of Arcadia straggles along a valley in the middle of nowhere. At its older and tackier end stands a statue of its founder Thomas Hobbes, who organised what was then a handful of lawless homesteads and became the first sheriff. In the resulting time of peace the town grew and, as you stroll along the single main street past Hume Corner, a marked air of commodious living sets in. At the newer end stand solidly middle-class homes with sundials in their cultivated gardens and burglar alarms over their double garages. The street comes to rest at the Church of Reflective Reason, whose notice boards tell of Weenie roasts and subscription concerts and whose enlightened congregation can be admired on Sundays as they gather round the lychgate shaped like a needle's eye.

The commodious atmosphere of the upper end is both symbolised and partly explained by the existence of a neighbourhood watch scheme, which supplements the sketchy policing provided by the sheriff's department. The scheme demands an investment of one night a month by each householder and is well worth it, given the dispositions of the Arcadians at the tacky end of the town. Indeed even above Hume Corner (the limit of its scope) people still have a self-love which impels every man to extend his acquisitions as far as possible and is not altogether checked by reflection on the advantages of peace and public order. So, being surrounded by neighbours who, since they are neither honest nor dishonest by nature, still tend to lapse into self-love when it pays, each property-holder willingly puts in a night a month as part of a small patrol.

All this is very frustrating for Jack, a sensible knave and professional burglar, dwelling at the tacky end. The watch scheme stops him operating above Hume Corner, and, although his own neighbours do not have a watch scheme, they bolt their doors, sleep with loaded shotguns and, anyway, they do not have much worth stealing. Luckily, however, the Church of Reflective Reason is in missionary mood and has just distributed free copies of *Morals by Agreement* throughout the town. Jack has thus discovered that he lives among Straightforward Maximisers (SMs), who are riddled with the free-rider problem, whereas those above Hume Corner are constrained maximisers (CMs) who have licked it. This has given him an idea.

What if he and a hand-picked few of his cronies can convince all the tacky-enders that Gauthier is right? Then a huge flock of repentant SMs can turn up at the church one Sunday and, having all put a hefty sum in the collection (no forged notes or negative contributions, please), propose an extension of the watch scheme to the whole town. Perhaps further evidence will be needed, like hosting a communal barbeque or selling flags for charity. But, essentially, it is a tempting proposal as it will reduce each CM's nights on watch duty to six a year. Indeed Jack might even persuade everyone that if *everyone* is a CM, then the watch scheme is a deadweight loss and should rationally be abandoned. No, on reflection, that is to overstate the transparency possible or, from Jack's point of view, desirable. A better idea is to have the scheme continue with one of the bi-monthly patrols consisting of him and his cronies. A regular night's research will tell them what is worth burgling and how to elude the patrol on some other night when they go after it.

Jack's plan relies on a general suspicion that *Morals by Agreement* attempts the impossible in taking over the Kantian idea of autonomy, while holding on to a Humean moral psychology (e.g. pp. 236, 344). Arcadians living above Hume Corner have acquired a disposition to behave justly towards one another, and that might seem an obstacle to free-riding. But they remain individuals motivated by their passions, in accordance with a philosophy of mind where Reason simply advises that their passions will be better served thereby. They have not been transmuted into Moonies, so to speak. The name of the church is 'Reflective Reason', not 'General Will', and its congregation have not sunk self in community. Their passions remain what they were, not necessarily selfish, of course, but still 'self-interested' in the standard sense (cf. p. 7). Such individuals remain distanced from their dispositions, thus giving Jack an opening.

There would be no such opening, if the only way to seem sufficiently like a CM was to be one. But (for reasons which will emerge) some gap between what persons are to themselves and what they seem to others is endemic in the nature of individual agency, and Gauthier is definite that CMs are translucent rather than transparent. There is always some probability that an apparent CM is an SM in cunning disguise. In that case, Jack reckons, there is a practical question of costs and benefits. Individual free-riding may well be too costly and prone to detection. That is no doubt a sound reason for having groups on watch patrol rather than single individuals, since top-end Arcadians did not become rich by being innocent. But the calculation changes abruptly, if he can secure a whole patrol of sensible knaves.

That, at any rate, is how Jack has put it to his cronies. They are to treat each other as CMs, thus aiding the pretence that each is what he seems to outsiders. It is, of course, in the back of his mind that he might occasionally manage a second level of free-riding by exploiting his cronies too. But they will have had the same thought and, in general, the more nearly transparent they are to each other, the better they will fare in fooling outsiders. So he has put the idea of a positional good within a positional good onto the back burner for the moment. Meanwhile he believes that he has got the number in the cartel about right, so as to match Gauthier's nicely judged distinction between transparency and translucency. It is all a matter of calculation – and quite right too, when it comes to joining a church which still sings the old Victorian hymn, known affectionately as 'the pawn-broking hymn':

> Lord, whate'er I lend to Thee
> Repaid a thousandfold will be;
> So gladly will I lend to Thee.

Jack therefore helps spread the message of *Morals by Agreement* to all and sundry and one Sunday a large group of converts turns up at the church, offers to join and proposes that they be included in the watch scheme. The top-enders are, of course, suspicious, but cannot easily object when confronted with the very line of thought which made them CMs in the first place. They even consider the threat of a hidden cartel but, being unsure whether it involves a misunderstanding of Gauthier, put it aside until they have reviewed the central account of the moral psychology of individuals in *Morals by Agreement.*

The presence of Humean and Kantian elements makes this no easy task. At first sight the structure is two-tier, with passions or first-order preferences below and conditional imperatives or second-order preferences above. But, on reflection, it is more complex, especially when the Archimedean point is taken into account. There is clearly a bottom tier, resting on simple preferences of the kind which economists start from. Arcadians have their various tastes and derive orderable utilities from satisfying them. Some prefer apples to pears, others pears to apples. Still on the bottom tier there are also desires which depend heavily on beliefs. For instance those who prefer gold bath taps to silver ones would not do so unless they believed their neighbours to be more impressed by gold. This preference, however, needs to be seen as an expression of an underlying desire for, say, status as a source of utility, so as to fit it in to the complete and consistent preference order which economic notions of rationality demand.

There is also a higher tier of preferences ranging over preferences. A CM has a dispositional preference for just and honest dealing with fellow

CMs. But two distinct elements are involved in it. On the one hand there are specific properties of first-order goods, for instance that of having been honestly acquired. This is not a first-order property in Gauthier's account, since it is reason rather than passion which makes it motivating. Yet reason alone cannot be a motive to any action of the will. So a CM's disposition to act morally needs a motive capable of overriding preferences on the bottom tier, as with Hume's (1748) distinction of moral duties into 'those to which men are impelled by a natural instinct or immediate propensity which operates on them, independent of all ideas of obligation' and 'such as are not supported by any original instinct of nature but are performed entirely from a sense of obligation, when we consider the necessities of human society'. But CMs do not act automatically on their 'sense of obligation'. They remain capable of acquiring goods which they know to be stolen and are ready to play rough when dealing with SMs. So they will often need to weigh the attractions of what they would prefer, were only first-order preferences involved, against what they would prefer were they to 'consider the necessities of human society'. Even if second-order preferences can motivate, they do not do so automatically.

Hence there is a third tier, introduced by thinking in terms of a disposition to behave justly to the just. This disposition is not a precommitment of the kind which bound Ulysses to the mast. A CM is not like an alcoholic who locks the cellar and throws away the key, nor a psychiatric patient who signs away his power to discontinue the treatment. A CM retains the options of playing the CM or the SM strategy, and hence of playing SM against a presumed CM. Yet a CM also chooses a disposition whose effect is, allegedly, that he will not in fact play SM against a presumed CM even when the move would pass undetected. Two sharp questions arise, one about the choice and the other the disposition.

The choice, being prior to 'morality', is instrumental. It is not made solely by reflecting that, if everyone were dishonest, it would be worse for everyone. For, although this sort of reflection might carry conviction after one has rationally adopted the Archimedean standpoint, it cannot get one there. In so far as a reason is involved, it is an external reason until the agent's internal motivational set has been adjusted to receive it, an adjustment guided not by Reason alone but by reference to the utility of satisfying existing preferences. In a Humean moral psychology only internal reasons can motivate. Which of Jack's existing preferences will be furthered by becoming a CM? Since he is a knave, the answer seems to be those preferences best served by pretending to adopt the Archimedean standpoint. There is as yet no sense in which he has a reason to acquire preferences which could be satisfied only by becoming a genuine CM. So the question remains what exactly the choice of a CM disposition is instrumentally directed towards, so as to make it a rational choice.

Secondly, since the disposition to be a CM leaves the agent the option of overriding it, what exactly keeps him loyal to it? Gauthier's final answer is given in the immensely attractive Chapter XI, titled 'The Liberal Individual'. But that chapter is on the far side of Chapter VIII, 'The Archimedean Point'. Approaching the question from the earlier chapters, one needs to be able to demonstrate that conditional maximising pays someone whose desires are independent of all ideas of obligation. That is partly why I introduced a cartel of sensible knaves, who together possess the sort of power which might be denied a single individual and thus prise open any crack held shut by considering only individual costs and benefits. But there was another reason, to do with the self and social relations. So far, guided by Hume, we have been asking questions about what Jack wants and whether *Morals by Agreement* tells him how to get it. If we are to reach the uplands beyond Chapter VIII, however, we need also to explore his needs as a person.

Jack does not keep much of what he steals. It is risky to put silver cream jugs on the table and boring to gloat over them in the cellar. Mostly he converts them into cash to buy what he values himself, together with a legitimating (if specious) title to ownership thereof. Some of these purchases may be material objects which tickle his tastes. But most also have a symbolic dimension, and many have little to do with their physical composition. To cut the story short, suppose that Jack wants to be *someone* in his small town. Being at heart still more of a foole than a sensible knave, he at first translates this desire into the trappings of status and goes after whatever will make him a cut above average in the eyes of Arcadians. His car is opulent, his wife bejewelled and his dog pedigree. When he presently discovers that ostentation is subtly a mistake, he is a quick learner, part-exchanging car, wife and dog in good time for the next mayoral elections.

He thus learns that 'goods' have much to do with shared meanings and that their value depends on where they place him in an invisible scale of shared values. But he also learns something more disconcerting. Being 'someone' is only in part a matter of public recognition by other someones. It also has an inward aspect, where recognition turns on how things are, not merely on how they seem. Inwardly speaking, he needs to be recognised for qualities he genuinely has by persons whose recognition is genuinely worth having. Admittedly the currency of respect can be genuine without being moral. Jack's fellow knaves know him for a knave and mutual respect among professionals might be enough to sustain his self-respect. But, even granting this for the moment, there is at least a psychological need for relationships which are not purely those of exchange or power and which include some insiders within the boundary drawn in general between self and others.

To generalise the point, recall William James's division of the self into '(A) the self as known, or the *me*, the "empirical ego" as it is sometimes called' and '(B) the self as knower, or the I, the "pure ego" of certain authors'. James continues:

> *A man's me is the sum of all that he CAN call his*, not only his body and his psychic powers but his clothes, his house, his wife and children, his ancestors and friends, his reputation and works, his lands and horses, and yacht and bank account. ... Properly speaking *a man has as many social selves as there are individuals who recognise him*, ... as many social selves as there are *groups* of persons about whose opinions he cares. (1962, Chapter 12, pp. 190 ff., his italics)

Jack, as a complete knave, finds that his 'Me' is built on a relation of possession between him and his wife, children, ancestors and friends, that it is symbolised by yachts and bank accounts which he has got by cheating and that it is held in place by a recognition which he does not deserve and which is therefore not worth having. Hence his 'I', 'the self as knower', is in a dilemma, arising because he is paying himself in foole's gold.

He might assuage the problem by self-deception. But suppose that he is too sensible a knave to fool himself. Then he might try to be content in the knowledge that he is cleverer than others, being the only person who knows that he is an utter knave. But there is still a snag. He wants, or perhaps even needs, a wife who loves him for himself and friends who are truly friends. These relationships are not to be had by cheating. They hold only between persons who know each other as they are, not as they wish to seem. They are not relations of possession, as with his lands and his horses, but of expression. The clear-eyed self as knower does not mistake outward and visible signs for inward and spiritual graces.

What started as a psychological point is becoming more interesting. There are relationships which cannot be modelled as exchanges, because they extend the boundaries of self to include others as partners. In contractarian terms, they involve a wider angle of vision whose idealised case is the moral point of view.

Thus friendship, I presume, shares the feature of morality which insists that a moral agent keeps his word even when it would pay not to. A 'friendship' constructed by both parties for instrumental reasons of mutual advantage does not make them friends. Had King David tried to make friends with Uriah the Hittite in order to see more of Bathsheba, and had Uriah responded as an avenue to promotion, both might have advanced their wishes. But they would not have become friends. Similarly, Gary Becker (1976) declares that 'a person decides to marry when the utility expected from marriage exceeds that expected from remaining single or for an additional search for a more suitable mate'. If this is Jack's instrumental approach to the mating game, he had better hope for a mate with as little idea what the game is about as he has.

The crux, however, has to do not with knaves but with utility functions. In a Humean moral psychology an individual's preferences may have any source or character but, since reason alone cannot be a motive to any action of the will, they motivate because they are his own. Interaction is rationally reconstructed by showing that, where it was freely undertaken, at least one party gained expected utility and neither lost. To represent relations like love, marriage or friendship, utility functions are mutually embedded. Romeo derives utility from Juliet's fortunes and she from his. This sounds not implausible until we ask why such relationships demand honesty. In theory Romeo will deceive Juliet, if that increases her utility and hence his by more than the disutility to him of playing false with her. Well, why not? After all, such calculations do enter into love, marriage and friendship, and it may be that total transparency is as disastrous as total mutual back-scratching. But a basic honesty is constitutive of intimate relationships, not merely prudent given the chances of detection, and expresses them rather than helps them along. Intimacy and personal commitment affect who one is, even if also affecting what one wants. A moral psychology which equates agents with their preferences cannot draw this distinction at any depth.

Gauthier does not deny this aspect of social life. 'Our theory of morality, although it makes use of the idea of economic man, is not committed to that idea as a full and adequate account of human nature... Because we real human beings share some of his characteristics, morals by agreement afford us a beneficial constraint, and because we are nevertheless not economic men and women, we can be constrained' (p. 317). There are intrinsic values, like the value of participation (e.g. p. 325). The final chapter seeks 'to show that morals by agreement are more than the morals of economic man' (p. 329), who is 'not, therefore, the human ideal' (p. 335). But he hopes to accommodate as much of this as matters for the book's purpose by having rational agents adopt a disposition (Hume) to act morally (Kant) towards other rational agents. Here are three reasons for doubting whether that will suffice.

First, the scales in which economic man weighs all options are those of utility. Use of these scales led Jack to prefer seeming honest to being honest and to prefer a disposition to act justly to the just which functions as a rule of thumb rather than a moral principle. Although it might look as if the snag arose because he is a professional knave, it has a deeper source. The rational agents who are SMs until rational reflection makes them CMs suspend utility calculations only for the sake of greater utility. They cannot grasp 'the reflective dimension of rationality' and 'the deep and difficult issues about personal identity' which arise because 'the utility function which defines a particular individual is revisable, in part through the individual's own reflective activity' (p. 343). Whatever quite the gap between economic man and real human beings, it is not one which the former can cross by reflecting on the utility function which defines him, because real human beings are not defined by utility functions.

Secondly, if moral agents are to be cast in terms of Kantian autonomy and practical reason, they need a Kantian moral psychology. Kantianly rational agents can be moved by reason alone. In understanding that there is a best reason to do *x* rather than *y*, they make that reason their own and act on it. In choosing a CM disposition, they would not be adopting a rule of thumb but recognising an imperative addressed to all rational beings. In respecting the autonomy of others and claiming it for themselves, they would be guided by rational reflection on the preconditions of moral agency and on the particular maxims which satisfy the criteria implied. It might seem that they could reach this Archimedean point by climbing a Humean ladder aided by natural sympathy and cultivated benevolence. But they would still need a Kantian moral psychology, because, having achieved the moral point of view, they will thereafter be motivated by duty, without regard to inclination or consequence.

Thirdly, however, Kantian reflections take us only so far. Kant feared (rightly) that an enlightened ethics would saw through all external supports by dispensing with appeals to the moral order of God's creation. So he made the internal supports very rigid. If it is right to keep promises, then it is invariably right; and CMs are not entitled to think twice about keeping promises, even those made to SMs. Admittedly the categorical imperative presumably allows some restrictions. 'No Parking on Weekdays' is as universal as 'No Parking', and Kant is sometimes unexpectedly consequentialist, as when justifying the institution of promise-keeping on the grounds that we would be worse off without it. But Gauthier explicitly distances himself from Kant. In taking over the Kantian notion of autonomy, he firmly rejects the Kantian apparatus, because, without some appeal to preferences or capacities, a person 'would have no basis on which to consider what person he might be' (p. 344). He also hints that Kantian theory involves 'a deep conflict between rationality and individuality' (p. 237). Although Kantian autonomy seems to me not on offer without Kantian practical reason, I take the hint. The expressive rationality, which enables and constrains the choices of 'real human beings' because of what persons they are, is more Kantian than Humean but finally eludes both modes of analysis.

For these three reasons I doubt whether *Morals by Agreement* can emerge with a 'liberal individual' who has escaped being 'a creature, taking his goals and values from a divinely established order' without becoming 'an artifact, constructed through an increasingly known and alterable process of genetic engineering' (p. 354). But I applaud the aim. Is there another angle of vision? Here we might usefully consider the difference between constitutive and regulative rules. The latter govern the choice of moves within a game, being typically rules of thumb which help players gain their objectives. The highway code regulates the highway; professional codes regulate the conduct of professions. Such codes do not constitute what they govern, however, and the reasons for action which they afford are instrumental reasons. When they are explicitly rules of thumb, they evidently leave it possible that it may be rational to break them occasionally. Where they claim to be more, as with the professional ethics of doctors, it may still be rational to break them because they sometimes conflict with their purpose.

Constitutive rules create the activities which regulative rules regulate. They define the games of social life (in a Wittgensteinian sense of 'game') by specifying the character of an activity and prescribing the essential relationships among the players. The simplest examples are of wholly artificial games, like chess, whose constitutive rules come neatly printed on the box. Games expressive of a form of life, like honour games, are not so neat or artificial, nor so completely defined in advance of play. But their very messiness is an aid to noticing the constructive or creative element in following the rules governing social interaction. For instance, the military codes which constitute the honour of 'an officer and a gentleman' are not rigid in the face of changes in the technology of war or the habits of the enemy but adapt so as to preserve their core. Whereas spying used to be dishonourable, it is now the respectable work of intelligence officers.

That leaves it unclear what is constitutive and what regulative even within a well-defined practice, witness the Church of England's efforts to decide whether it can accommodate women priests. But the difference between playing the game at all (constitutive) and playing it well (regulative) still stands, in that the latter must look to the former in monitoring new constructions. This appeal is to something more like a Kantian principle than a Humean sentiment but more like an appeal court decision on the meaning of a law than either. Crucially it is one to the *identity* of a practice, in some sense of that elusive term.

Here lies a distinctive difference between a traditional universal ethics and a postmodern-situated ethics. Traditionally there is an external question about the claim of any practice to constitute some aspect of the good life, since all particular human arrangements are judged as attempts to embody an eternal truth about how one ought to live. Thus a society which solves its coordination problems by means of a constitutive asymmetry between men and women, or owners and slaves, can be arraigned for injustice at an external and eternal bar. Conversely, to regard forms of life as beyond external reproach is to licence all those with strong bootstraps. Attempts to steer between traditional and postmodern with the help of reason turn on precisely how they take 'reason'.

Rationality in *Morals by Agreement* sets off as a regulative measure, universal in the sense that it lets us ask of any plan of action whether it leaves the agent better off than alternative plans but giving no leverage on the constitution of a better-off life. It apparently remains regulative, after morality emerges as a rational constraint on choice, with morals by agreement firmly distinct from a morality of feeling (e.g. p. 286). Yet to adopt morals by agreement is to accept moral requirements as sufficient reasons for action, thus making it partly constitutive of a good life that it be lived under the guidance of reason. Then, towards the end, rationality develops a 'reflective dimension' (e.g. p. 342) which bears directly on the choice of what person to be. The liberal individual lives by social arrangements reflectively arrived at after taking account of what persons we might rationally choose to be. Here rationality has ceased to be wholly formal, non-committal and merely the instrument of mutual benefit. As the rules of rational conduct become substantive enough to imply a conception of the good life, individual and collective, they become constitutive rules.

If that creates scope for an individual who is not 'an artifact [of] an increasingly known and alterable process of genetic engineering' (p. 354), I am all for it. But the route taken sets a hard problem about means and ends. Jack wants something for himself, finds it rational to adopt the moral point of view in order to get more of it, and thus has a measure external to even the moral point of view, namely the utility which he gains by treating morality as a means to maximising utility. The snag is that the disposition to be a CM is both constitutive and regulative, with the value of morality consisting both in the constitutive fact that moral agents do not have a further goal thus served and in the regulative claim that the further goal of maximising utility will be best served thereby. This seems to me an untenable position.

In that case we must go either forward or back. To go back is to settle for a self defined by any consistent utility function and for a Humean moral psychology, where reason alone cannot be a motive to the will. Can Jack be reasoned into adopting the Archimedean standpoint through rational bargaining? I applaud Gauthier's refusal to postulate suitable passions like natural sympathy or adopt 'a morality of feeling', thus shirking the riddle which *Morals by Agreement* is intended to solve. But, although reason can convince Jack that he needs a few allies, it cannot stop a cartel of CMs exploiting other CMs in ways not worth trying individually. Gauthier might argue that the cartel is bound to be internally unstable through lack of trust. But he cannot prove it, because the members are his disciples in their dealings with one another. If all convinced CMs were to draw Jack's conclusions, of course, there would no longer be CMs to ride free upon. But that does not disprove the conclusions. It shows at most that growing distrust will lead Arcadians to periodic clean-ups so as to attain an Archimedean point which will then be gradually undermined again. That sounds uncannily like our own world, wherever instrumentally rational translucent maximisers are in power. At any rate I do not see how a Humean moral psychology can offer more (cf. Hollis, 1988, esp. Chapter 5, and 1990).

To go forward is to flesh out the constitution of the good life in the good society and then to adjust the earlier moral psychology so that a revised self will find it lastingly rational to be a CM. A promising start is to declare some relationships, like love and friendship, essential to persons and impossible to fake because only the genuine article will serve. With a self not defined by a utility function and primary moral relations immune to contractarian analysis, the route looks easier. But I doubt whether Kantian autonomy lies at its end. It may lead to a situated ethics erected on personal ties and special duties, inimical to the universal, impersonal demands of the moral point of view. Yet some liberals are willing to risk making the self essentially social and speaking a language of community. Attempts at a liberal reading of Rousseau tread this path in the name of positive individual freedom. So, less obviously, do liberals who trace out J. S. Mill's linking of individuality to concern for others. The crux is what the difference between 'economic man' and 'real men and women' implies for moral and political autonomy. But the libertarian streak in *Morals by Agreement* discourages pursuing it here.

Meanwhile the Church of Reflective Reason is in ferment. The worry is that the existing congregation seems to have the same reason to trust the apparent converts as to trust each other, and that this threatens to be finally no reason at all. So there is a move to disband the Neighbourhood Watch and treble the police force. Extra policing costs are a deadweight loss, however, unless Arcadia is indeed currently a foole's paradise, or, to add an ironical twist, perhaps even if it is a foole's paradise which works well enough. Yet faith in Gauthier, although shaken, is not destroyed. There is still warm admiration for his captivating attempt to save the Enlightenment project by showing it rational to be moral even in a world where human life has no meaning beyond itself. *Morals by Agreement* is still on the syllabus at the local College of Agriculture. But moral education classes have been suspended, while he answers urgent questions about moral psychology.

4

Practical reason, collective rationality and contractarianism

Julian Nida-Rümelin

Gauthier's theory of morals by agreement starts from the problem of cooperation paradigmatically exposed in the Prisoner's Dilemma. Within the economic paradigm of rational choice, rational individuals do not act cooperatively in the Prisoner's Dilemma, and thus individual rationality leads to Pareto-inferior outcomes. For Gauthier, the problem of cooperation is the basic problem of morals in general (while the market, in not giving rise to Prisoner's Dilemmas, is a morally free zone (pp. 13–14 and Chapter 4); thus the solution of the cooperation problem constitutes the core of ethical theory. Gauthier searches for a solution within the economic paradigm of instrumental rationality: he sets out to 'develop a theory of morals as part of the theory of rational choice' (pp. 2–3). He keeps to the 'weaker', maximizing conception of practical rationality and takes 'the onus of proof to fall on those who would defend universalistic rationality' (p. 8). The thesis of this chapter is that an adequate solution of the cooperation problem is not possible within the maximizing theory of practical rationality. If you take the supplement of the maximizing conception of practical rationality as essentially Kantian, I defend a Kantian conception; but if apriorism and rationalism are taken to be essential features of Kantian rationality, I do not want to defend a Kantian conception.

The argument is developed in several steps. After some preliminary remarks, I examine the relation between practical reason and collective rationality and show that there is no adequate solution of the cooperation problem within the paradigm of maximizing rationality. Finally I draw some conclusions for the contractarian project and for the theory of practical rationality in general.

1 Practical reasons

On the doors of the trains in the London Underground you can read: 'Obstructing the doors causes delay and can be dangerous'. Apart from the fact that this kind of information seems rather strange to a German visitor, who might have expected a sentence like 'Obstructing the doors is not allowed' or 'Do not obstruct the doors', as a philosopher one is confronted with some additional problems.

Does the sentence 'Obstructing the doors causes delay and can be dangerous' mean that I *should not* obstruct the doors, or does it *inform* me of a certain causal relation? If it is to be interpreted as a factual statement, it nevertheless could give a reason not to obstruct the doors. Essentially, there are four different possibilities of how the factual statement above could provide a reason for not obstructing the doors:

1. The singular action interpretation. It is certainly a good reason for not obstructing the doors if the *singular action* of obstructing the doors is dangerous for the person who obstructs them (1a). It is also a good reason for not obstructing the doors if that singular action is dangerous, not only for the obstructing person, but also for other persons (1b).
2. The rule interpretation. Perhaps the information given by the sentence is different, and the sentence has to be interpreted as: *in general* (the singular act of) obstructing the doors is dangerous for the obstructing person (2a). This might give you a reason never to obstruct doors in the Underground. This interpretation resembles rule utilitarianism, or more exactly rule egoism. Or: in general (the singular act of) obstructing the doors might be dangerous not so much for the obstructing person, as for other people (2b). This interpretation is closer to rule utilitarianism, and might again give you a reason never to obstruct doors in the Underground.
3. Possibly the term 'obstructing' refers to *obstructing in general* (to the generic action obstructing – the type, not the token). Then again, it could be dangerous for the obstructing person (egoistic generalization: 3a), or for other people (utilitarian generalization: 3b).
4. Theoretically, there is a fourth alternative: the sentence could be understood as predicating some attribute of the generic action 'obstructing the doors', which makes obstructing the doors bad in itself or *intrinsically* bad.

If we assume that the sentence tells the reader not to obstruct the doors, then according to these four possibilities there are different normative contents, which can be associated with the above sentence:

1. The normative content might roughly account for the following: the actor as a straightforward maximizer should know that the singular action of obstructing the doors does not maximize her subjective value function even if she is self-oriented (1a), or at least if she takes the interests of other people into consideration (1b).
2. Nobody should perform a singular action which in general has negative results for the actor herself (2a), or for people in general (2b).
3. Nobody should perform a singular action which generally performed has bad results – for the actor herself (3a), or for people in general (3b).
4. Nobody should perform a singular action which belongs to an action type which is intrinsically bad.

These normative contents all are of a kind, which one could call the 'action-oriented kind'. There are other kinds, of which the most important are the disposition-oriented ones such as the so-called virtue ethics. Indeed, the sentence 'Obstructing the doors causes delay and can be dangerous' could also be an appeal to dispositions. Perhaps the reader is assumed to have a disposition to choose that singular action which maximizes her own well-being (1a), or that of people in general (1b); or she is assumed to have a disposition to do that singular action, which in general has good results for herself (2a), or for people in general (2b); or she is assumed to have a disposition to do that singular action which generally performed has good results for herself (3a), or for people in general (3b); or she is assumed to have a disposition to do a singular action whenever it belongs to a class of actions which is intrinsically good.

What does the Underground advice have to do with Gauthier's theory of contractarian ethics? There is a basic problem in Gauthier's theory – his conception of practical reason. The various possible interpretations of the Underground advice correspond to different conceptions of practical reason. We need to examine the relation between maximizing behaviour, rational constraints and dispositions within a coherent conception of practical rationality.

Gauthier writes:

> We pay a heavy price, if we are indeed creatures who rationally accept no internal constraint on the pursuit of our own utility, and who consequently are able to escape from the state of nature, in those circumstances in which externalities are unavoidably present, only by political, and not by moral devices. (p. 164)

I perfectly agree with this statement. And, like Gauthier, I think that even if one accepts the possibility that a rational person acts on the basis of well-justified moral constraints, this does not show that the institutional framework, endowed with sanctions *in foro externo*, would become obsolete. However, I think that this idea of rational moral behaviour is in a deeper conflict with economic rationality than Gauthier apparently assumes. If we agree that there is a need for a coherent and universal theory of practical rationality, then we cannot accept Gauthier's thesis that 'the only serious candidate for an explanatory schema for human action is, as we noted previously: choice maximizes preference fulfilment given belief' (p. 56).

In my view, the alternative is not to return to an objectivist theory of value, which Hume, McIntyre, Mackie, Gauthier and others have forcefully criticized, but rather to develop a theory of practical rationality based on a revised relation of action and subjective value. Gauthier's theory of constrained maximization is already a major contribution to this undertaking, in so far as it gives an attractive account of collective rationality in cooperative interactions.

What is the relation between economic rationality and constrained maximizing in Gauthier's view? He says: 'Our argument identifies practical rationality with utility-maximization at the level of dispositions to choose' (p. 187); but in what sense does one choose dispositions? Dispositions become objects of choice only under special and rare conditions. I would even claim that it is an essential attribute of a rational person to be relatively free from dispositional determinants. The ideal rational actor is free to choose that singular action, which has the best reasons in its favour. He is not forced to choose a (rational) disposition first and then to act in accord with that disposition. It is my impression that this is also Gauthier's view. Certainly, it is one criterion of rational choice to choose a singular action only if it fits into a type of behaviour which might be called constrained maximizing. But if dispositions do not bind the rational actor, then the rational actor who acts in accordance with constrained maximization is consciously *not* maximizing – since the primary object of choice is the singular action.

An essential part of Gauthier's conception of practical reason is the claim that a population of constrained maximizers would be rationally stable: no one would have reason to dispose himself to straightforward maximization. This seems to be a reconciliation of constrained maximization and usual (economic) maximization. But in fact there are only three possibilities.

The first possibility is that in the singular case it is not maximizing to follow the principle of constrained maximization. Then there is no stability in a society of constrained maximizers.

The second possibility is that a singular action in accord with the principle of constrained maximization is (for every singular action and under the special conditions of a society consisting only of constrained maximizers) also maximizing. Then these actions do not constitute constrained maximizing behaviour in the ideal moral society. (Nevertheless, constrained maximizing might still be necessary for developing this ideal moral society.)

The third possibility is that Gauthier's use of the term 'dispose' profoundly modifies our understanding of rational choice, limiting the freedom of choice in an essential way. This understanding of dispositions seems not to be in accord with an attractive concept of a rational person. Furthermore, it is hard to conceive how dispositions understood as psychological constraints on choice could ever be in accord with a principle like that of minimax relative concession. This attractive principle of justice has all the features of a piece of rational advice rather than of a psychological disposition, which we can acquire in the same sense as we can acquire the disposition to get up at 7.30 (if we can acquire such a disposition at all).

These remarks show that it is necessary to have a closer look at the relation between practical reason, collective rationality and the role of contractarianism.

2 Practical reason and collective rationality

Traditionally there are two questions for ethical debate. First: what is worthwhile; to which goals should people devote their efforts; what life is good? Second: assuming we know what is good, what action is then correct? The general attitude both in the classical ethical tradition, as it was founded by Plato and Aristotle, and in the economic theory of rationality, is that the second question can be trivially solved once the answer to the first question is known. For economic theory this trivial solution is the maximization of expected utility. I think the opposite is true: answers to the second question are in great part independent of answers to the first question; and an answer to the first question does not make the answer to the second question trivial.

To show this, it is useful to introduce the concept of *collective rationality*. Collective rationality is to be defined in terms of a relation of 'collectively better than': a collective action a (understood as an n-tuple – or list – of individual actions) is collectively irrational if there is another collective action a′ which is collectively better than a. It is reasonable – at least within a subjectivistic context – to postulate Pareto-inclusiveness of any collective better relation. Therefore any collective action which is not Pareto-efficient is also collectively irrational. This is only a necessary condition for collective rationality, but for the following considerations of practical reason it is not necessary to have a sufficient condition. It is not necessary to give a more detailed account of collective rationality. To do this we would need second-order rules upon which the members of the respective group could agree.

Whereas collective rationality is an attribute of *collective* action, practical reason is an attribute of *individual* action. However, collective rationality and practical reason are closely related. *Practical reason requires that individual actions fit into a system of rules of behaviour which the agent can accept rationally*. The main, but not exclusive, subject of practical reason is the coordination of individual actions. Although we do not assume that coordination of individual actions is a sufficient criterion for moral rightness, it is at least a necessary criterion. And it is hoped that with some further qualifications which go beyond the relation to collective rationality, practical reason could be made into a sufficient criterion for moral action. Behaviour which is in accord with practical reason will be called *reasonable*.

Certainly a fully developed theory of practical reason would consider not only personal interests and moral valuations, but also rights, dispositions, and virtues of the interacting persons. For the present purpose, however, we can limit our analysis to subjective preferences. Within this limited analysis there is a close relation between collective rationality based on personal interests and practical reason: any system of rules of behaviour has to allow for collective actions which are collectively rational. A system of rules of behaviour is in accord with collective rationality if there are no circumstances under which it prescribes a collective action which is collectively irrational. So we have a negative criterion for practical reason: one should never act in such a way that there is no system of rules of behaviour in accord with collective rationality allowing that act (see Nida-Rümelin, 1987, 1988).

In the 'miniature world' of the prisoners in their dilemma, in which there are no external effects with moral relevance for the situation, the collective action consisting of both prisoners taking their maximizing actions (that is, confessing) is collectively irrational. Therefore, in that miniature world it is not in accord with practical reason to act uncooperatively. So in some situations of interaction, maximizing behaviour on the part of the participants leads to an outcome which is worse for everyone than if the participants had not behaved in a maximizing way. The classical economic theory of rationality defends uncooperative behaviour in problematic situations as rational. (The term *problematic social situation* is due to Raub and Voss, 1986). It is defined as a situation of interaction in which individually rational behaviour by strategically interdependent actors leads to outcomes which are not Pareto-efficient. This type of situation is sometimes called a 'generalized Prisoner's Dilemma'.)

Contemporary economic theory of rationality, however, has not been satisfied with this analysis and has tried to find ways in which cooperative behaviour in such problematic situations could count as rational.[1] Undoubtedly there are situations which seem to be problematic but in fact are not. The iterated Prisoner's Dilemma is such an example if some further conditions are fulfilled. Likewise, altruistic motivations can undermine the problematic structure of a game. But all these attempts to show that cooperative, or more generally, 'collectively rational' behaviour is also maximizing do not solve the problem if there is at least one problematic situation in which cooperative behaviour can be considered as rational. And certainly there are many.

Let us assume that two actors decide to follow the cooperative strategy in an apparently problematic two-person situation. We will consider this state of affairs as requiring explanation. Both actors apparently have not behaved according to the maximization principle. Yet this behaviour seems to be advantageous because the outcome reached is better for each than the outcome they would have obtained if they had maximized their expected pay-offs.

We may distinguish four different types of explanation of such cooperative behaviour:

The irrationality solution. Cooperative behaviour is explained by the participants' lack of knowledge of the actual consequences of the alternatives, or by the low intelligence of the participants preventing them from understanding the situation's structure, or by the spontaneity of the participants' decisions, and so on – in short, by information deficits, epistemological irrationality, or inconsistency of subjective valuations.

The Shaftesburian solution. Cooperative behaviour is explained by the fact that, beside egoistic motives (in the Prisoner's Dilemma: to spend as little time behind bars as possible), there are also altruistic motives, such as not to cause the other person too much harm, and similar considerations which contribute to the actors' decisions.

The Hobbesian solution. One assumes that there are sanctions in society which deter non-cooperative behaviour. (In the Prisoner's Dilemma, for example, each criminal would have to expect certain consequences from the world of organized crime if he acted as chief witness in the other criminal's prosecution.)

The Kantian Solution. The persons base their behaviour on collective rationality or, in a more Kantian formulation, they act in such a way that they can wish that the maxim of their action can be made into a general law. In the 'little world' of the Prisoner's

Dilemma, only cooperative behaviour, and not uncooperative behaviour, satisfies this criterion.

There is a special commonality among the Shaftesburian and Hobbesian solution. While the irrationality and Kantian solution do not deny that the interaction situation of the prisoners has a problematic structure, for the Shaftesburian and Hobbesian solution, the situation is, in fact, not a problematic one.

The competing claims of the Shaftesburian and Kantian solution are of special interest for the following reason. No one disputes that there is irrationality or that, in many cases, cooperative behaviour results from lack of information, poor consideration, or acting out of habit. No one disputes, either, that in many cases there are legal sanctions and sanctions which arise out of everyday moral sensitivities which induce people to avoid uncooperative behaviour. But if there is some cooperative behaviour that cannot plausibly be explained either by irrationality or sanctions, we must ask which of the remaining alternatives can provide an adequate explanation.

There are only two possibilities to save rational actors in problematic situations from behaving with collective irrationality. Either one must claim that rationally they should not maximize (the generalized Kantian solution), or one must claim that cooperative behaviour is also maximizing (the generalized Shaftesburian solution).[2] My claim is that *rational actors should not maximize in every problematic situation.* Gauthier agrees with this claim, but he postulates a coincidence between it and a kind of overall maximization. He tries to reconcile three equally attractive ideas: the maximization concept of rationality, the idea of collective rationality, which has to be guaranteed by constraints, and the idea of free moral choice. The conjunction of the last two ideas implies moral and not merely political constraints. In order to make the first idea consistent with moral constraints, Gauthier makes use of the concept of rational dispositions. Later in this chapter I shall discuss this concept, but first we have to look more closely at the relationship between practical reason and collective rationality.

In order to show that rational people should not maximize in every problematic situation, we will take a look at the contrary assumption and its counterintuitive implications. If rational behaviour in the broader sense were a 'manifestation' of preferences – if rational behaviour maximized the numerical function which represents the actor's preferences over outcomes – then we would be able to find preferences for problematic situations which would lead to reasonable (that is, collectively rational) behaviour via maximization. And indeed the search for those until now hidden preferences has been undertaken: this strategy, taken up by Sen

(1974),[3] can be called the *metapreference approach*. I think it is a desperate attempt. But if it succeeded, the idea of practical rationality as maximizing behaviour would be saved. On the other hand, if it does not succeed, I do not see any other strategy which could save maximizing rationality as the general paradigm of rational action.[4]

The idea of the metapreference approach is to gain a better understanding of morality by conceiving preference relations which would lead to cooperative behaviour qua maximization. If people acted on the basis of those morally superior preferences, they would refrain from non-cooperative behaviour in some real problematic situations. Sen originally introduced two new games on the basis of the Prisoner's Dilemma – the *Assurance Game* and the *Other-Regarding Game*.

The preference structure of the Prisoner's Dilemma may be written as follows:

Prisoner's Dilemma

A: $[D, C] \succ [C, C] \succ [D, D] \succ [C, D]$

B: $[C, D] \succ [C, C] \succ [D, D] \succ [D, C]$

(A and B are the actors in the Dilemma; [D, C] denotes that prisoner A defects and prisoner B cooperates, and similarly for [C, C], [D, D] and so on; $\succ$ stands for the relation 'is preferred to'.) With this preference structure, whatever a person expects the other to do, she prefers not to behave cooperatively. In a consequentialist interpretation: whatever the other person does, the outcome of (individually) behaving non-cooperatively is preferred. Thus, Prisoner's Dilemma preferences lead to the outcome [D, D].

Sen's other two games have the following structures:

Assurance Game

A: $[C, C] \succ [D, C] \succ [D, D] \succ [C, D]$

B: $[C, C] \succ [C, D] \succ [D, D] \succ [D, C]$

Other-Regarding Game

A: $[C, C] \succ [C, D] \succ [D, C] \succ [D, D]$

B: $[C, C] \succ [D, C] \succ [C, D] \succ [D, D]$

In the Assurance Game, so long as the other person behaves cooperatively, each individual prefers to behave cooperatively too. If the other person does not behave cooperatively, then each individual prefers to behave non-cooperatively. Realization of the cooperative outcome [C, C] depends on mutual assurance that the two players will behave cooperatively. In this game, there are two equilibrium outcomes: [C, C] and [D, D]. But because each individual's decision depends on what is expected of the other, there is no guarantee that an equilibrium will be the outcome. Only when the participants have the same subjective expectations of the other's decision will an equilibrium outcome result. A fundamental feature of the Assurance Game is that a cooperative outcome can be reached through an agreement which would not require external sanctions. There would be no reason for the participants to act contrary to any agreement as to their intended actions, because each prefers the cooperative solution to any alternative. If there is mutual assurance of the other's willingness to cooperate, the collective decision [C, C] is collectively rational, not only with respect to the Assurance Game preferences but also with respect to the Prisoner's Dilemma preferences. Thus, if the prisoners were to behave as if they had Assurance Game preferences and if they were to act on the assumption of a mutual willingness to cooperate, they would reach the collectively rational outcome of the Prisoner's Dilemma – whereas they would reach a collectively irrational outcome by basing their behaviour on Prisoner's Dilemma preferences.

In the Other-Regarding Game, the mutual assurance condition for cooperation is not necessary, since the cooperative outcome [C, C] is dominant. Furthermore, this solution is collectively rational both with respect to Assurance Game preferences and to Prisoner's Dilemma preferences. Thus the prisoners might be still better off if they behaved as if they had the preferences of the Other-Regarding Game.

With respect to Assurance Game and Other-Regarding Game preferences, the collective outcome [C, C] is the best outcome for each prisoner. Although [C, C] is not the best outcome for the individual with respect to Prisoner's Dilemma preferences, it is a better outcome for each individual than [D, D], which would have been reached had the prisoners followed their Prisoner's Dilemma preferences. Assurance Game preferences guarantee the collectively rational outcome with respect to Prisoner's Dilemma preferences on the epistemological condition that there is mutual assurance of cooperative behaviour, and Other-Regarding Game preferences guarantee the collectively rational outcome even without any epistemological condition.

Thus, there are situations of interaction in which individual rational behaviour leads to a collectively rational outcome when that behaviour is based on preferences other than those that actually constitute the situation. Does it therefore make sense to determine a moral ordering of preferences and to secure collective rationality by maximizing behaviour relative to those preferences? If the answer is 'yes', then the Other-Regarding Game preferences would rank above the Assurance Game preferences, and the Assurance Game preferences would rank above the Prisoner's Dilemma preferences.

Sen argues for metapreferences in the sense of a moral ordering of the possible individual preference orderings. Whereas the individual preference orderings are defined over the set of possible outcomes, the moral ordering is defined over the set of possible individual preference orderings. The interpretation of this moral preference ordering is, however, obscure. If I wish for moral reasons to have other preferences than in fact I have, this may motivate me to undergo some training to change my actual preferences. So the most simple interpretation of the metapreference approach is that morality consists in modifying actual preferences in such a way that maximizing those preferences[5] yields good results. This implies a moral preference for those preference relations that ensure that problematic situations do not arise. This interpretation of the metapreference approach fits quite well into the economic paradigm of rationality. It is attractive because, if it worked, there would be a new kind of reconciliation of the moral and economic aspects of rationality. But its inadequacy becomes clear if one tries to carry through the enterprise.

Other interpretations are possible. Moral metapreferences might be interpreted as advising actors in problematic situations to behave *as if* they had certain preferences, even though they actually do not have those preferences. But then the actors would not maximize their actual preferences and we would have to assume some other, non-maximizing conception of practical rationality. Moral metapreferences might also be understood as constituting a purely moral evaluation of outcomes on the basis of given preferences. And indeed I think this is an important object of ethical theory. But in this case, too, people who acted on their metapreferences would not maximize their actual preferences. We may therefore concentrate our analysis on the first interpretation.

So the metapreference approach seems to be in a deadlock as long as one confines the analysis to a uniform concept of preference. But if we get rid of the idea that there is at any time only one kind of preference, which has an empirical, non-metaphysical status in so far as it is revealed by behaviour, the metapreference approach gains plausibility. Metapreferences have to be understood as *second-order preferences*: on the basis of certain known preferences of one kind, there is a subjective ranking of preference relations of another kind. This interpretation is based on the assumption that there are different kinds of preferences and that it is acceptable to ascribe different kinds of preferences to a single person in a given situation. Within this wider conceptual framework, it is possible to define problematic situations by referring exclusively to the actors' *subjective interests*. In this interpretation, metapreferences rank either one's revealed preference relations or one's subjective moral preference relations.

In both cases the evaluation is based on the given structure of subjective interests.

An interaction structure in terms of subjective interests, or *interest structure*, is – by analogy with the normal form of a game in game theory – determined by the number of players, their possible strategies, and their subjective interest functions over the set of outcomes of the game. When these functions merely represent individuals' (interest-based) preferences over the set of possible outcomes, they are ordinal; when they represent preferences which satisfy all the rationality conditions of expected utility theory, they are real-valued and unique up to linear transformation. In this scheme, the sometimes postulated dichotomy between revealed preferences and interests is made explicit: an individual's evaluation of consequences cannot be inferred from her behaviour.[6]

The morally recommended individual behaviour and the associated revealed preferences on the one hand, and the morally good preferences on the other, are not as closely associated with each other as ethical theory normally assumes. Typical questions relevant for the subjective moral preference relation are: which distribution of goods (determined by various collective decisions) is just? What is a fair compromise between individuals' interests in the interaction situation? And so on. So this second-order interpretation is obviously twofold: We can consider metapreferences either as evaluating *revealed preferences*, which via decision theory and game theory guide the actual behaviour of maximizing persons, or as a ranking of the *moral judgements* of the actors which are represented in their subjective moral preference relations. It is clear that only the first fits into the maximizing conception of practical rationality. A thorough analysis of it shows quite clearly that maximizing in problematic situations is not rational in all circumstances.

A two-person Prisoner's Dilemma is an interaction situation with four strategy combinations or collective decisions: [D, D], [C, D], [D, C], [C, C]. We assume that the outcomes, which are relevant for the individuals' subjective valuations, are unambiguously determined by the strategy combinations. Each individual has $4! = 24$ possibilities for ranking the four collective decisions. Altogether there are $24 \times 24 = 576$ possible individual preference ordering combinations. If we require symmetry, the number of logically possible preference structures of one type is reduced from 576 to 24.

The Prisoner's Dilemma structure of problematic situations is given in terms of an interest structure. A's interest to sit as short a term as possible behind bars is best satisfied if A confesses and B does not: [D, C] satisfies his interests best, followed by [C, C], [D, D] and [C, D]. Symmetrically for B: [C, D] satisfies his interests best, followed by [C, C], [D, D] and [D, C]. These ordinal evaluations or *interest rankings* can thus be represented by four numbers: 4 for the highest value, 3 for the second, and so forth. In order to facilitate the analysis we characterize the outcomes, or equivalently, the collective decisions by the corresponding ranks:

		B's decision: D	B's decision: C
A's decision	D	2, 2	4, 1
	C	1, 4	3, 3

Since the actors not only have interests, but also have moral values and revealed preferences, which via expected utility maximizing guide the actual decisions of the actors (according to the model of economic rationality), we have a large number of possible combinations of these other two types of preferences given the invariant structure of subjective interests. We will concentrate here solely on revealed preferences. Then the originally vast variety of preference structures is reduced to 24.

Twelve of these 24 preference structures respect the rule: Follow your own interest as long as no foreign interest stands in the way, that is, maximize your own well-being if this does not detract from the well-being of any other person. This rule implies a relation between action-guiding preferences and personal interests: the action-guiding preference has to be Pareto-inclusive in relation to personal interests. We begin with those preference structures that satisfy this condition of *Pareto inclusiveness*, or PI.

1. Revealed preferences are based on personal interest. One can call such revealed preferences egoistic preferences. They would have the following form:

   $$\text{A:}\quad (4,1) \succ (3,3) \succ (2,2) \succ (1,4)$$

   $$\text{B:}\quad (1,4) \succ (3,3) \succ (2,2) \succ (4,1).$$

   The 'tragedy' of the egoists (and the essence of the Prisoner's Dilemma) is that with these preferences the egoists end up with the outcome (2, 2). Thus their own interests are not very well served when they form their revealed preferences egoistically.
2. Revealed preferences are strongly influenced by a sense of justice. Those outcomes which have the same position in both individuals' interest rankings are given a high priority in the revealed preference ordering, as long as that priority does not conflict with PI; outcomes which are Pareto-better with respect to the interest rankings are given an even higher revealed priority; but when from the moral point of view there is no difference between two outcomes, one prefers the

outcome which makes one personally better off:

$$A: (3,3) \succ (2,2) \succ (4,1) \succ (1,4)$$

$$B: (3,3) \succ (2,2) \succ (1,4) \succ (4,1).$$

These preferences, however, do not guarantee collective rationality. With this strong sense of justice, A chooses the non-cooperative behaviour D if he expects B to choose D. (It is possible that B chooses D, since C is not dominant for B.) [D, D] is an equilibrium point in this case with respect to these revealed preferences, but there is also the additional equilibrium point [C, C]. If the interaction situation is not *transparent* (that is, if the actors cannot predict one another's behaviour), then maximizing behaviour can result in any one of the four strategy combinations [C, C], [C, D], [D, C] or [D, D].

3. Even when a sense of justice is combined with altruism and we get the following revealed preferences:

$$A: (3,3) \succ (2,2) \succ (1,4) \succ (4,1)$$

$$B: (3,3) \succ (2,2) \succ (4,1) \succ (1,4),$$

the collectively rational outcome cannot be guaranteed for the same reasons as described in case 2.

4. Revealed preferences of a completely opposite orientation to justice-based preferences could be interpreted as the expression of a strong anti-egalitarianism:

$$A: (4,1) \succ (1,4) \succ (3,3) \succ (2,2)$$

$$B: (1,4) \succ (4,1) \succ (3,3) \succ (2,2).$$

These anti-egalitarian revealed preferences have two equilibrium points [C, D] and [D, C]. Again, if the interaction situation is not transparent, acting maximizing can result in any one of the four strategy combinations.

5. If, however, altruism supersedes justice in the form of the following revealed preferences (which correspond with those of the Other-Regarding Game):

$$A: (3,3) \succ (1,4) \succ (4,1) \succ (2,2)$$

$$B: (3,3) \succ (4,1) \succ (1,4) \succ (2,2),$$

the collectively rational outcome [C, C] is finally guaranteed: this is an equilibrium point of dominant strategies. But some doubt arises as to the inner consistency of these preference relations because $(4,1) \succ (2,2)$ is neither altruistic nor just, but rather egoistic, while $(1,4) \succ (4,1)$ is extremely altruistic.

6. But a purer altruism also guarantees the collectively rational outcome:

$$A: \quad (1,4) \succ (3,3) \succ (2,2) \succ (4,1)$$

$$B: \quad (4,1) \succ (3,3) \succ (2,2) \succ (1,4).$$

   [C, C] is the only equilibrium for these pure altruistic preferences and for both actors C is the dominant strategy.

7. The following preference structure could be understood as expressing a weakened altruism:

$$A: \quad (3,3) \succ (1,4) \succ (2,2) \succ (4,1)$$

$$B: \quad (3,3) \succ (4,1) \succ (2,2) \succ (1,4).$$

   These preferences have their only equilibrium point in the outcome [C, C], and thus they still guarantee collective rationality.

8. The following revealed preferences correspond with Sen's Assurance Game:

$$A: \quad (3,3) \succ (4,1) \succ (2,2) \succ (1,4)$$

$$B: \quad (3,3) \succ (1,4) \succ (2,2) \succ (4,1).$$

   A person with Assurance Game preferences will behave cooperatively as long as he can be assured that the other person will behave likewise. The collectively rational outcome [C, C] is an equilibrium point for these preferences; but so also is [D, D]. Neither of the actors has a dominant strategy. In this case, collective rationality depends on mutual assurance of cooperation.

The remaining four PI preference structures are difficult to interpret. The following preferences guarantee collective rationality, with [C, C] being a dominant strategy solution:

9.

$$A: \quad (3,3) \succ (4,1) \succ (1,4) \succ (2,2)$$

$$B: \quad (3,3) \succ (1,4) \succ (4,1) \succ (2,2).$$

In each of the following two preference structures, there are two equilibrium points, [C, D] and [D, C]:

10.

$$A: \quad (1,4) \succ (4,1) \succ (3,3) \succ (2,2)$$

$$B: \quad (4,1) \succ (1,4) \succ (3,3) \succ (2,2).$$

11.

$$\text{A:}\quad (4,1) \succ (3,3) \succ (1,4) \succ (2,2)$$

$$\text{B:}\quad (1,4) \succ (3,3) \succ (4,1) \succ (2,2).$$

Without transparency, maximizing behaviour can result in any one of the four strategy combinations [C, C], [C, D], [D, C] or [D, D]. Finally, the following preference structure guarantees collective rationality:

12.

$$\text{A:}\quad (1,4) \succ (3,3) \succ (4,1) \succ (2,2)$$

$$\text{B:}\quad (4,1) \succ (3,3) \succ (1,4) \succ (2,2).$$

I shall not go into the details of the preference structures which do not satisfy PI, but a short overview will complete the picture. The only non-PI preference structure which guarantees collective rationality could be interpreted as masochistic:

13.

$$\text{A:}\quad (1,4) \succ (2,2) \succ (3,3) \succ (4,1)$$

$$\text{B:}\quad (4,1) \succ (2,2) \succ (3,3) \succ (1,4).$$

Thus self-hate – like pure altruism (6) and weakened altruism (7), like the rather oddly motivated Other-Regarding Game preferences (5), and like (9) and (12) – guarantees the collectively rational outcome [C, C]. It is interesting that a non-PI preference structure – one in which the actors prefer a Pareto-inferior outcome to a Pareto-optimal, that is, collectively rational, outcome – can guarantee collective rationality.

The opposite case of sadistic revealed preferences:

14.

$$\text{A:}\quad (4,1) \succ (2,2) \succ (3,3) \succ (1,4)$$

$$\text{B:}\quad (1,4) \succ (2,2) \succ (3,3) \succ (4,1)$$

also fails to satisfy PI. Whereas egoism in the Prisoner's Dilemma was not successful (trying to fare better, the actors fare worse than if they had not tried to fare better at all), this preference scheme, oriented towards bringing the other as much harm as possible, does succeed – due to the symmetrical efforts of both parties. But, nevertheless, the equilibrium point [D, D] is collectively irrational in terms of individual interests.

Three non-PI preference structures (15, 16 and 17) have [C, C] and [D, D] as equilibrium points, and three (18, 19 and 20) have [C, D] and [D, C] as equilibrium points:

15.

$$\text{A}: \ (2,2) \succ (3,3) \succ (4,1) \succ (1,4)$$
$$\text{B}: \ (2,2) \succ (3,3) \succ (1,4) \succ (4,1).$$

16.

$$\text{A}: \ (2,2) \succ (3,3) \succ (1,4) \succ (4,1)$$
$$\text{B}: \ (2,2) \succ (3,3) \succ (4,1) \succ (1,4).$$

17.

$$\text{A}: \ (2,2) \succ (1,4) \succ (3,3) \succ (4,1)$$
$$\text{B}: \ (2,2) \succ (4,1) \succ (3,3) \succ (1,4).$$

18.

$$\text{A}: \ (4,1) \succ (1,4) \succ (2,2) \succ (3,3)$$
$$\text{B}: \ (1,4) \succ (4,1) \succ (2,2) \succ (3,3).$$

19.

$$\text{A}: \ (1,4) \succ (4,1) \succ (2,2) \succ (3,3)$$
$$\text{B}: \ (4,1) \succ (1,4) \succ (2,2) \succ (3,3).$$

20.

$$\text{A}: \ (1,4) \succ (2,2) \succ (4,1) \succ (3,3)$$
$$\text{B}: \ (4,1) \succ (2,2) \succ (1,4) \succ (3,3).$$

Thus, without transparency, six out of the twelve non-PI preference structures allow a collectively rational outcome, but do not guarantee it.

Five of the non-PI preference structures inevitably lead to collective irrationality. One of these structures is the sadistic one (14). The others are:

21.

$$\text{A}: \ (2,2) \succ (4,1) \succ (3,3) \succ (1,4)$$
$$\text{B}: \ (2,2) \succ (1,4) \succ (3,3) \succ (4,1).$$

22.

$$A: \quad (4,1) \succ (2,2) \succ (1,4) \succ (3,3)$$
$$B: \quad (1,4) \succ (2,2) \succ (4,1) \succ (3,3).$$

23.

$$A: \quad (2,2) \succ (4,1) \succ (1,4) \succ (3,3)$$
$$B: \quad (2,2) \succ (1,4) \succ (4,1) \succ (3,3).$$

24.

$$A: \quad (2,2) \succ (1,4) \succ (4,1) \succ (3,3)$$
$$B: \quad (2,2) \succ (4,1) \succ (1,4) \succ (3,3).$$

The task of a second-order normative metapreference theory is to determine the best ordering of the possible individual revealed preference orderings. For the case of the Prisoner's Dilemma, symmetrical revealed preference structures can be separated into three types, each of which contains both PI and non-PI preferences. The first type contains those preference structures which guarantee collective rationality. The second type contains those preferences which (if there is no transparency)[7] allow collective rationality, but do not guarantee it. The third type contains those preference structures which inevitably lead to collective irrationality.

Thus, there are three possible results of behaviour which is individually maximizing with respect to revealed preferences. A strictly outcome-based normative metapreference theory would not be able to distinguish any further moral difference. Each of the first type of revealed preference ordering would be better than each of the second or third types, and each of the second type better than each of the third type. To this extent, at least, the idea of a normative metapreference theory is successful: we have found a method of strict outcome-based moral evaluation of individual preference relations. But the euphoria of success disappears when one takes a closer look at this moral evaluation of preferences. In the first priority grouping of the moral metapreference scheme one finds not only honourable altruistic preferences (6 and 7) but also Other-Regarding Game preferences (5), non-PI masochistic preferences (13), and two other implausible preference structures (9 and 12). In the middle moral group one finds preferences which express a sense of justice (2 and 3), which intuitively seem morally superior to some of the preference relations which the moral metapreference scheme ranks in the highest priority grouping. But also in the middle group are preferences which take predominant consideration of one's own interests (8), quite immoral anti-egalitarian preferences (4), and six preference structures which fail to satisfy PI and therefore should not be recommended at all. In the group which is given the lowest ranking by moral metapreferences one finds, as one might expect, egotistic (1) and sadistic (14) preferences, as well as three quite implausible non-PI preference structures (22, 23 and 24).

The idea of outcome-oriented moral metapreferences may appear convincing when the analysis is limited to a small group of seemingly adequate examples of preference structures. But if one considers the outcomes of the Prisoner's Dilemma in relation to *all* the possible symmetrical structures of revealed preferences, it becomes clear that collective rationality cannot be secured by maximization with respect to morally recommended preferences. Thus, the conflict between individual rationality and collective rationality is not resolvable by an outcome-oriented change in preferences, when preferences are understood to guide behaviour via maximization. It is not possible to reconstruct reasonable behaviour as maximizing an adequate subjective value function.

3 Practical reason and contractarianism

Now there are different possibilities of action which are in accord with practical reason. First, one might 'invent' institutions which influence the actors' behaviour. It could be reasonable to introduce sanctions which would prevent the prisoners from confessing. The actors themselves might under certain circumstances vote for such sanctions out of their own personal interest: this is Hobbes's solution. Second, it could be reasonable to change one's own subjective valuations to escape Prisoner's Dilemma situations. But such changed subjective valuations could not eliminate all Prisoner's Dilemma situations, and in the remaining cases there would still be a need for practical reason. But even more important, there seems to be no plausible subjective valuation which guarantees collective rationality as the result of maximization, even if we take vicarious effects into account. It is, for example, not very plausible to infer from the fact that prisoner A decides not to confess when there are no external sanctions, that A ranks the outcome [C, D] higher than the outcome [D, D] or [C, C] higher than [D, C] for reasons of altruistic or moral sentiments. If the prison term is long enough, it cannot realistically be assumed that vicarious effects play such an important role that they induce cooperative behaviour via maximization. So in cases where there is no Hobbesian solution, the Shaftesburian solution for both of the above reasons does not seem to be sufficient either.

What remains is the solution I have called 'Kantian': the persons act reasonably. In the Kantian solution, individual behaviour can no longer be characterized as maximizing behaviour relative to a given individual preference relation – except in a purely formal sense. In a purely formal sense, the von Neumann–Morgenstern axioms tell us that, even for a Kantian agent, there exists a subjective valuation function which that agent is maximizing. But for a Kantian agent, such a subjective valuation function would not represent any axiological judgements or attitudes concerning the outcomes of the interaction situation: it would be a merely formal representation of the agent's actual behavioural preferences.

Now I do not assume that the Kantian solution is empirically the most widespread; there is some evidence that this solution is not only possible for human agents, but that it is in fact empirically relevant (see Rapoport and Chammah, 1965; Kern and Räder, 1988). The assumption that there is only the Hobbesian or the Shaftesburian solution for problematic social situations is due to a widely accepted model of human motivation. This model is intentionalist in the sense that human action is understood as an instrument of the agent to achieve some of his goals. Despite forceful criticism within the philosophy of ordinary language and within philosophical action theory, this model is still implicitly taken for granted in scientific research which relies on the economic paradigm of rational action.

There is no good reason to reject 'behaving according to a certain rule' as a possible motive for action. If this is accepted there is, furthermore, no reason to reject practical reason as a possible motive for action. And certainly there is a possibility of weakening the Kantian claim in so far as one might develop a disposition to act according to certain rules of behaviour which guarantee collective rationality. This can be seen as the essence of virtue ethics (see Foot, 1978). But whereas the Hobbesian solution changes the outcomes of the game and the Shaftesburian solution changes the subjective valuations of the outcomes, a disposition to behave reasonably should not be interpreted as maximizing a new kind of preference over outcomes. That interpretation would lead to the same problems as before.

For Gauthier, the task of morality is to develop a system of constraints on the pursuit of individual interests. Since a theory of morals serves a useful purpose only if it can show that 'all the duties it recommends are also truly endorsed in each individual's reason' (p. 1), Gauthier chooses a contractarian account of these moral constraints. Essentially these constraints have the task of making possible cooperative behaviour in problematic situations. But there are different possibilities as to how these contractarian constraints become practically relevant. Again there is the Hobbesian, the Shaftesburian and the Kantian way.

The Hobbesian way to behaviour in accord with contractarian constraints is based on a sanctioned system of rules which guarantees that under the new conditions of the institutionalized system of constraints, maximizing behaviour is cooperative. The problematic situations typical of the state of nature disappear in civil society; the only cause of this change is the system of external sanctions. In this narrow sense Gauthier is not a Hobbesian: for Gauthier, reason guides behaviour even if there are not sanctions to punish deviation.

The second way to reconcile maximization and practical reason as it results from rational contract is the Shaftesburian. Sanctions *in foro interno* – the internal sanctions of conscience – ensure that rational maximizers behave cooperatively in problematic situations. Indeed Gauthier seems to think that the missing link between maximization and practical reason is formed by dispositions: contractarian constraints become practically relevant not only by legal and other external sanctions but also by certain dispositions. The rational agent wishes that the behaviour of others were guided by certain dispositions; and he might possibly even wish that his own behaviour were guided by the same dispositions.

Now there are two serious problems for this bridge between maximization and morality. First, certainly I can wish for reasons of rational self-interest to develop certain behavioural dispositions. But a priori it does not seem very probable that these rationally recommended individual dispositions will meet moral criteria such as justice or the Lockean proviso. And second, if these dispositions have to be understood as some kind of sanctions *in foro interno*, Gauthier's *Morals by Agreement* contains an inadequate theory of moral agency. The moral agent decides rationally on the basis of the given personal interests of all participants in the game, accepting certain reasonable constraints which lead to cooperative behaviour in problematic situations. The rational and moral agent, then, will not always maximize, and in so far as he acts in accord with certain rules or constraints which he rationally accepts as guidance for everybody in society, he is a Kantian agent. His criterion for a system of rules is its conceivability as the result of a contract between rational persons. The Kantian agent does not wait until he has internalized these constraints as 'dispositions'. Otherwise, to use Gauthier's words (pp. 1–2), reason would again be 'impotent in the sphere of action' and 'no more than the handmaiden of interest'; we should indeed have to conclude that 'the moral enterprise – as traditionally conceived – is impossible'.

Notes

1. See Axelrod (1981, 1984), Elster (1979, 1983), Opp (1983), Voss (1985), and Kliemt (1985, 1986a, 1986b).

2. For further discussion of this problem, see Axelrod (1980, 1984) and Diekmann and Mitter (1986).
3. See Sen (1974). The idea of metapreferences must be seen in the broader context of widening the economic paradigm of rationality. For similar proposals see, for example, Frankfurt (1971), Jeffrey (1974), Schelling (1978, 1980, 1984), Hirschmann (1982, pp. 66–71), McPherson (1982), George (1984), and Raub and Voss (1986, 1988).
4. In order to exclude a possible misunderstanding, I should emphasize that the word 'general' is essential in this thesis, because the economic paradigm of rational action might nevertheless be adequate in some broad ranges of research. One of these ranges is certainly the phenomenon of cooperation between self-oriented maximizing actors, as Axelrod and others have shown.
5. The expression 'maximizing one's preferences' is to be read as an abbreviation for 'maximizing the expected value of that real-valued function over the set of outcomes, which represents the subjective preferences of the actor'.
6. One may ask how it is possible to identify an actor's interest-based preferences. As in conventional decision-theoretic models, we may imagine the actor facing choices over various lotteries, but then ask which lottery the actor would choose in regard to his personal interests alone.
7. If instead we assume transparency, the second type has to be divided into one subgroup where the outcome may be either collectively rational or collectively irrational (the equilibrium points [C, C] and [D, D]) and another subgroup with two asymmetrical, but not collectively irrational outcomes (the equilibrium points [C, D] and [D, C]).

5

Justice, social union and the separateness of persons

Albert Weale

Fundamental to the contractarian enterprise is the task of showing how in appropriate circumstances social order can arise from the operation of individual rationality. The terms of the social contract are intended to state the basic principles of the social order, including the distribution of property rights, the scope for democratic participation and the freedoms and responsibilities of individuals. Yet, within the contractarian tradition, these terms are conceived as the product of negotiation between rational individuals none of whom need be endowed with an essential sociality. Thus, the idea of a social order may be understood as a set of rules and practices within which individuals can pursue their own ends whilst respecting the rights of others to pursue their own ends.

Such a conception of political society has been dominant within recent restatements of the liberal tradition, but it is by no means the only conception within that tradition. Against the idea of a social order we may set the idea of what Rawls (1971, pp. 520–9) has termed a social union, defined as an agreed scheme of conduct in which the excellences and enjoyments of each are complementary to the good of all and in which each member of society shares with all other members certain common final ends. Whereas a liberal social order is defined by reference to a set of social practices within which individuals can pursue their own ends, the idea of a social union relies upon a claim that there is sufficient sociality in human life for individuals to hold to shared ends.

If it is difficult to see how social order can arise by a process of rational negotiation among individuals located in a state of nature, it is even more difficult to see how a social union might arise. However, I shall argue that, at least in respect of his theory of economic justice, David Gauthier's work has to be interpreted as offering a theory of social union and not merely a theory of social order. Gauthier's work in general is distinguished by the attempt to take the most difficult version of the contractarian problem, namely showing how rational individuals, knowledgeable of their own circumstances, could none the less negotiate a binding social contract. Moreover, many of the essential elements of the social contract that Gauthier hypothesises reproduce the basic elements of the social morality of a commercial society, of which promise-keeping when it is to one's own disadvantage provides a paradigm case. However, in *Morals by Agreement*, Gauthier also offers a distinctive theory of economic justice, and it is in respect of that theory that I shall consider the relationship between the principles of individuality presupposed by the rational choice foundations of social contract theory and the principles of a social union.

The essence of the problem of economic justice, as it has been considered in recent theories, can be stated as follows: Assuming that there is sufficient social order for markets to function reasonably effectively across a wide range of economic activity, what grounds might there be for the state to redistribute resources from those who do well in the market allocation to those who do badly? Clearly, the general form of contractarian answer to this question will be that there are such grounds as rational individuals would consent to in the making of a social contract. However, for a contract theorist, the possibility of redistribution from market outcomes provides a particularly daunting challenge, since market arrangements are so frequently taken as an example of a liberal social order in which individual ends are not subordinated to a collective vision of some social good. Contrary to this libertarian strand of liberalism, and despite his depiction of the market as a morally free zone, Gauthier wishes to argue that a contractarian theory of economic justice does not simply endorse market outcomes, but instead provides grounds for economic redistribution. To understand the logic of his position, we need to locate his arguments in the more general debate about social justice.

Among the many controversial topics in the theory of justice, one issue has been of central importance in recent discussions. Is an allocation of resources to be regarded as just in virtue of some structural property that it possesses (for example that it possesses the property of minimising inequality) or is it to be regarded as just in virtue of the process by which the allocation arose (for example that it results from exchange among persons entitled to their initial holdings none of whom used force or fraud)? In addressing this issue different theorists take competing attitudes. Egalitarians, Rawlsians and those whom Sen (1982, p. 19) refers to as 'welfarists' stress the need for an allocation to satisfy certain structural properties. Libertarians, by contrast, stress the need to examine the process by which an allocation arose to see if it contains elements that might invalidate its claims to be just and, according to libertarians, free market exchange provides a paradigm of a just process at work. Of course, those who are convinced of the need to look at structural properties will disagree among themselves as to what precisely these are, just as libertarians differ as to what exactly makes for a free exchange. None the less, each species of answer seems quite distinct, even if both are home to more than one genus.

The reason why this dispute is central is not far to seek. If an allocation must satisfy some structural property in order to be just, then it will be morally permissible, and perhaps even morally required, for the state, as the social agency with the responsibility for social justice, to bring about a specific allocation of resources, and of course the state will need to be provided with the powers to fulfil its responsibilities. On the other hand, if the only condition that an allocation needs to satisfy is that it arose from a previously just allocation by a morally legitimate process, the moral permissibility of redistribution by any agency, including the state, is thereby called into question.

Much of this dispute has been played out between the competing conceptions of economic justice offered by Rawls (1971) and Nozick (1974). For many it has seemed that if we accept the particular form of contractarianism offered by Rawls, then it would be natural to favour a conception of justice that requires essential reference to the structural properties of an allocation that was to be appraised. Deprived of the knowledge of their own talents and abilities behind a veil of ignorance, there seems little for individuals to focus upon except the structure of an allocation, especially if those individuals are ignorant of their own conception of the good. On the other hand, it has also seemed to many that Nozick captured a central moral intuition in any political culture influenced by Kantian liberalism, when he argued that respect for persons precludes our thinking about them merely as place-holders in an allocation whose only just-making characteristics are defined structurally. For a number of years now the centrality of this dispute has been matched only by its apparent insolubility.

When theoretical disputes are so deep and pervasive, it is likely that we are dealing with fundamental intuitions some elements of each of which need to be incorporated into any adequate theory of justice. One way of appreciating this point is to note the ambiguity contained in the contractarian understanding of society as a cooperative enterprise of individuals for their mutual advantage. If the emphasis is placed upon the *cooperative* nature of the enterprise, then the idea of a social union is being invoked, and it would seem plausible that certain structural conditions will need to obtain in the distribution of economic advantage if the cooperative nature of the venture is to be respected. On the other hand, if the emphasis is placed upon the *individuals* who are party to the enterprise, then the workings of the social order will need to respect the rights and individuality of those individuals. The implication is that any adequate theory of justice will have to strike a justifiable balance between the principle of the separateness of persons on the one hand and the ideal of a social union on the other.

In considering various ways in which the balance may be struck I shall examine a series of views, each of which would place limits upon the extent of redistribution by distinguishing between the alienable and the non-alienable assets of persons. In the next section, I seek to show why the question of alienable and non-alienable assets is so central to the debate of economic justice, and then, in the subsequent section, I shall offer a Rawlsian interpretation of the problems involved derived from *A Theory of Justice*. The reconstructed Rawlsian position I shall expound in that section brings it close to the position that has been expounded by David Gauthier, although Gauthier offers a quite distinct rationale and justification of its underlying premisses. My concluding argument will be that the reconstructed Rawls/Gauthier position inevitably takes us beyond the logic of individual instrumental rationality. However, before embarking on this argument, I must first set the background by explaining some of the moral difficulties to which the practice of economic redistribution has been thought to give rise.

1 Some taxing questions

One example that has served to focus the debate between structural and process theories of justice has been the case of Wilt Chamberlain. Suppose, says Nozick (1974, pp. 160–4), you claim that a particular structural allocation is just, and suppose that you have the power to allocate resources according to the pattern or structure that you believe to be just. Then allowing people the liberty to use the resources you have allocated to them will quickly upset this pattern. This can happen in a number of ways, but let us suppose it happens as follows. Suppose that in a society resources are allocated in accordance with a particular structural principle. The highly esteemed basketball player, Wilt Chamberlain, signs a contract with a team by which he receives 25 cents of each ticket sold. His fans are keen to see him, and willingly pay the extra 25 cents from their own resources to attend the matches in which he plays. By the end of the season Wilt Chamberlain has amassed a considerable income, and the pattern or structure that defined a supposedly just allocation of resources at the beginning of the season has now been upset by allowing people freely to trade.

Although Nozick sees the main conclusion of the example as being that liberty upsets patterns, it is clear that this claim is part of a larger attack upon schemes of economic redistribution on the grounds that such schemes deny the 'separateness of persons'. This notion is never clearly analysed by Nozick, but it appears that it is intended to capture our intuitions about justice to the effect that persons should not be used merely as means towards the attainment of some collective goal. Thus, in criticizing Rawls's assumption that the distribution of abilities is to be thought of as a collective asset, Nozick notes that some people will complain of this assumption that it 'does not take seriously the distinction between persons', a charge that Rawls notoriously levels against utilitarianism (Nozick, 1974, p. 228; Rawls, 1971, p. 28).

Part of the force of the Wilt Chamberlain example derives from its according with some widely shared intuitions. One of these is that persons own their own abilities, and it is therefore up to them as to how they use their own abilities. Since Wilt Chamberlain has the ability to play basketball, it is up to Wilt Chamberlain, on this view, to decide whether and how to use this ability. From these assumptions, it would appear to follow that Wilt Chamberlain is entitled to keep the value of any incentive that has to be used to motivate him to exercise his abilities, since, as the 'owner' of these abilities, Wilt Chamberlain has an entitlement to whatever is necessary to persuade him to exercise them. Of course, the notion of persons owning their own abilities is metaphorical. The exercise of abilities does not deplete their value, as the use of land or capital depletes its value, and persons cannot transfer their abilities to one another as they can transfer their property. The metaphor is therefore standing duty for the principle that persons are entitled to keep the value of what they have received in free exchange for the exercise of their abilities. We may call this the principle of reward for free exchange.

This principle of reward for free exchange is compatible with the principle that justice requires persons to receive the value of their marginal product in the economy, but the two principles are not identical nor are they simple logical equivalents. Thus, in holding to the principle of reward for free exchange, it is not necessary to assume that the system of exchange satisfies the conditions of a fully competitive market where the equilibrium will yield every economic agent his or her marginal product. Indeed, according to Nozick (1974, pp. 156–7), the rule that economic value should be distributed by reference to marginal product is another example of a structural or patterned principle, since it does not allow for entitlements arising from voluntary unilateral transfers.

This lack of logical equivalence is, of course, clear. Yet the connection between the principle of reward for free exchange and the marginal product principle is closer than Nozick allows. The argument that gifts and charitable donations do not conform to the marginal product rule would be good against a conception of justice in which people would receive *only* their marginal product, but it is irrelevant against the principle that persons are entitled to receive *as much as* their marginal product. A system of free exchange that conforms to the conditions of a competitive equilibrium will allocate resources in accordance with the marginal product of individuals, so that under these conditions the principle of reward for exchange and the principle of marginal productivity will characterise extensionally equivalent states of affairs. Moreover, both the free exchange principle and the marginal product principle provide a reason for restricting economic redistribution, and it can be argued that the underlying reason in each case is that both are grounded in the concept of persons owning their own abilities from which it follows that any attempt at redistribution fails to take seriously the differences between persons. To see how this might be so, it is useful to consider the ways in which redistribution involves a pooling of abilities.

One reply to Nozick's claim that liberty upsets patterns is to say that any proposed just-making structure should describe a Pareto-optimal allocation in the economy. In a competitive economy the point of equilibrium will be in the set of Pareto-optimal allocations. This has implications for the Wilt Chamberlain example, for the structural theorist who is also committed to Pareto-optimality will now say that the just-making structure is one that should obtain after trading has taken place, and not before. Liberty will not upset this pattern since although individuals in a competitive equilibrium are free to dispose of existing resources by trade, they have no incentive to do so, and therefore will not use their liberty in order to do so. Nozick's example may therefore be taken to show not that liberty upsets patterns, but that any pattern theorist must also be a Paretian (Yaari, 1981).

However, although this conclusion offers a reply to the claim that liberty upsets patterns, it does not show that schemes of redistribution fail to take seriously the distinction between persons. To see why this issue is problematic we have to consider how any particular pattern might be secured in the competitive equilibrium of the economy. The first fundamental theorem of welfare economics tells us that the allocation of resources at a point of competitive equilibrium is Pareto-optimal; the second fundamental theorem tells us that every Pareto-optimal allocation is a competitive equilibrium for some initial endowment of resources. It is this second theorem that allows pattern theorists to believe that their preferred patterns can be in the set of Pareto-optimal allocations arising from market processes. In order to achieve a specified pattern, all that is necessary is to assign initial endowments in such a way that the competitive equilibrium will attain the preferred result.

In a pure exchange economy this initial assignment of endowments can take place by means of an appropriate allocation of commodities. In an economy with production, on the other hand, the situation is more complicated, since a major contribution into the productive output of the economy will consist of the labour, skills and talents that individuals possess. In this sort of economy, if we wish to secure an allocation having a specific pattern from among the Pareto-optimal set, we may well find that we have to impose a lump-sum tax on ability upon some individuals. In effect, highly skilled and talented people whose services are going to be in high demand will find themselves saddled with a debt before they even begin their productive lives, and they will be obliged to pay off this debt from their earnings. Conversely, those whose skills and talents will be in low demand will find themselves possessed of a capital endowment which they will have to deplete over their (non-)working lives and which will sustain their consumption.

Since a lump-sum tax upon ability does not distort relative prices in the economy, it does not lead to the sort of efficiency losses that we might expect from the marginal taxation of earnings. Unlike taxes upon earnings, lump-sum taxes on ability are not a disincentive to productive effort. Thus, when faced with a tax upon earnings, those with highly marketable skills may simply choose to withdraw their supply of labour from the market, whereas faced with lump-sum taxes upon ability, there is a spur to productive effort provided by the need to pay off the debt. For the welfarist, then, concerned both with redistribution and efficiency, lump-sum taxes upon ability, if they were feasible, would be superior to the taxation of earnings. Yet, although the welfarist is not embarrassed by the lack of incentive effects with lump-sum taxation, other proponents of redistributive justice will be, in exactly the form that Nozick alleges against Rawls. For Rawlsians, among others, are supposed to believe both in redistribution to the advantage of the least well-off and in an ethic that respects the separateness of persons. Constructing a system of taxes on ability that leaves the highly skilled with no choice as to whether they work or not hardly seems compatible with according respect to persons; instead it seems simply to be a form of indentured labour. Thus, this form of taxation would appear to be, to borrow Nozick's (1974, p. 169) phrase, 'on a par with forced labour'.

Nozick's characterisation of taxation as being on a par with forced labour is commonly objected to as untrue to the facts. Taxation does not force people to work; it merely stipulates the conditions under which they are entitled to work. This is true of conventional schemes of taxation on marginal earnings. What the proposal for a lump-sum tax on ability brings out clearly is that a simultaneous concern both for efficiency and for patterned redistribution will limit the labour choices of those with skills in high demand. The problem, then, is not that liberty upsets patterns; it is that if any particular pattern is to be established, without losses in efficiency, it would appear to involve significant restrictions upon liberty, and thereby a denial of the separateness of persons.

But what does respecting the separateness of persons involve? The difficulty I have identified so far is that efficiency-preserving schemes of redistribution appear to require a situation in which the exercise of abilities by those with highly valued skills may be used to advantage persons other than those who possess those skills. Nozickians and those who support the marginal productivity principle regard the pooling of ability implicit in efficiency-preserving schemes of redistribution as violating the principle of the separateness of persons. For both groups, this principle is interpreted to mean that persons own their own abilities and they are thereby entitled to keep the full proceeds they receive from free exchange within the economy. However, it is not clear that the principle of the separateness of persons has to be interpreted to imply the principle of reward for free exchange. Both Rawls and Gauthier, for example, accept a version of the principle of the separateness of persons, but both resist a simple process account of justice and both deny the justice of the principle of either the marginal productivity principle or the principle of reward for free exchange. Rawls's position on these issues is somewhat ambiguous, as I shall seek to show in the next section where I offer a particular reconstruction of his theory. Gauthier's account resembles my proffered reconstructed Rawlsian account, but goes beyond it by trying to derive key assumptions from a contractarian method rather than treat them axiomatically. To see the measure of Gauthier's achievement, we need first to investigate the Rawlsian position.

2 The Rawlsian framework

It may seem strange to suggest a discussion of Rawls in this context, since Rawls has been attacked by Gauthier precisely because his assumption that abilities should be thought of as forming part of a common pool seems at variance with a duty to respect the individuality of persons (p. 254). From this point of view there would appear to be no rational limit that could be placed upon the redistribution of the benefits of unequally distributed abilities. If abilities should be thought of as forming part of a common pool, then how can we relate persons and their abilities in a structural theory of justice?

In reply to this question I shall draw attention to those aspects of Rawls's theory that seem to point in a quite different direction to what is here implied. The position that Gauthier attacks is not, I shall argue, part of the fundamental thrust of Rawls's theory, although it might appear to follow from Rawls's decision–theoretic rationale for the difference principle, and his references to the pooling of abilities. None the less, the overall approach of Rawls has a quite different rationale.

Rawls's general conception of justice is easily stated: all social values are to be distributed equally unless an unequal distribution of any, or all, of these values is to everyone's advantage (Rawls, 1971, p. 62). If we ask how an inequality might work to everyone's advantage, then the obvious answer is that the inequality is a necessary condition for securing the advantage. Hence within the general conception of justice we need to know what is 'necessary' in order to secure an improvement in the position of the least well-off. One of the morally acceptable grounds for an inequality, according to Rawls (1971, p. 78), is the provision of incentives to productive effort. An incentive, I shall assume, provides a person with a reason for free action. Thus, if incentives are accepted as necessary to motivate free and rational persons to productive effort, this must carry the implication that the more productively endowed should only be expected to exercise their abilities when they receive sufficient reason for doing so. In other words, the most productively endowed would seem to be able in a Rawlsian framework to veto the attainment of particular social states.

The picture we now have of the Rawlsian framework is as follows. All social primary goods are to be distributed equally unless an unequal distribution is to everyone's advantage. The distribution of *abilities* is not a matter of social primary goods, however. These are natural primary goods, which are thereby excluded from the scope of principles of justice (Rawls, 1971, p. 62). Since the provision of incentives is explicitly allowed among those circumstances in which an unequal endowment of primary goods is necessary to improve the position of everyone, it follows that those with highly valued natural abilities are entitled to an incentive if they are to exercise their abilities. But if such incentives are allowed, indeed even required within the Rawlsian theory of justice, it cannot be claimed that Rawls is simply ignoring the separateness of persons in advancing the difference principle.

Yet, this leaves us with a puzzle. In what sense at all can there be a pooling of abilities in Rawls? How can Rawls say, for example, that the difference principle represents an agreement to regard the distribution of natural talents as a common asset the benefits of which are to be shared among the members of society? (Compare Rawls, 1971, p. 101.) The requirement for incentives seems to provide highly endowed individuals with a veto over the attainment of some social states, but this conclusion seems at odds with the assumption that the distribution of abilities should be looked upon as a common asset. How are we to resolve this paradox?

One way of resolving the paradox is to distinguish the different stages of Rawls's argument. The general conception of justice that Rawls advances requires an initial presumption in favour of equality in the distribution of primary goods which may then be rebutted by appeal to considerations of the general advantage. The claim that abilities are to be thought of as part of the common pool might therefore be thought to underlie only the initial presumption of equality, with a concern for individual freedom allowing individuals to benefit from the exercise of their own abilities, provided that in doing so their activities benefit everyone else.

This is undoubtedly a possible interpretation of Rawls's general conception of justice, but it is by no means the only one. An alternative and more successful resolution, I should like to suggest, lies in distinguishing two separate components of an economic incentive (compare Weale, 1978, pp. 40–4). The first component is that which it is necessary to pay someone if they are to exercise their abilities freely. This sum will have to be more than the sum which would be necessary to compensate someone for the exercise of their abilities (since this latter sum will merely leave the person as well off as they were before); it must also supply an incentive that will leave suppliers of labour better off than they would have been had they not chosen to exercise their abilities. However, such incentives will, in general, be less than the wage rate that suppliers of labour would receive in a competitive market, since in competitive markets the wage rate is set by the demand for the marginal worker.

This, then, identifies the second component of a Rawlsian incentive, namely economic rent. Rent is here defined as the positive difference between the income that individuals are paid and the generally lower income they would need to be paid in order to perform the same job. Note that this rental component of income is not a feature of the income of a few highly paid individuals in an economy; it is a pervasive and widespread aspect of market exchange. All intra-marginal workers will be in receipt of a rental component to their income (Bergson, 1967, pp. 662–3). They would do the same job for less income, but since they are all being paid for their marginal product they will not be paid less.

Rawls collapses the distinction between the rental and the non-rental component of an economic incentive and hence the presuppositions of the difference principle remain confused. Since the rental component of an individual's incentive is not strictly required for the exercise of his or her abilities, it might seem that this rental component could form the basis of the pooling of abilities to which Rawls appeals. This is clearly a reinterpretation of the Rawlsian position, but it is a plausible reinterpretation. In adopting such an approach we should in fact be taking the principle of the separateness of persons as axiomatic and imposing it as a constraint upon schemes of redistribution. The imposition of this constraint might be regarded as producing an acceptable compromise between the principles of individuality and social union. And yet such an approach remains without any deep theoretical justification.

One way of overcoming this problem would be to ground the distinction between the rental and the non-rental component of incomes in some deeper logic. Within this reconstructed Rawlsian framework the principle of individual self-ownership and the distinction between social and natural primary goods enter as axiomatic constraints on morally acceptable requirements of justice. Can they be rationalised in some way? In the next section I turn to a discussion of the most impressive attempt to date to offer a rationalisation, namely Gauthier's *Morals by Agreement.*

3 From Robinson Crusoe to market exchange

In *Morals by Agreement* Gauthier aims to defend a version of the separateness of persons. In particular, he aims to derive the right to use one's own mental and physical capacities to one's own advantage, provided that one does not thereby worsen the situation of another. Gauthier, like Rawls, is a contractarian, but he is a radical contractarian. Unlike Rawls, he does not impose the device of a veil of ignorance on the contracting parties. In Gauthier's version, contractors strike their bargains in full knowledge of their own capacities and preferences. The task of the theory is to specify what bargains it would be rational to make in these circumstances, and to use this understanding to derive normative principles of social and political choice. This general programme is worked out in some detail in relation to the right to use one's own talents and abilities, a right that seems to be at the heart of the moral claims about the separateness of persons. Gauthier's strategy is to show how such a right would arise through a process of rational bargaining.

The starting point for this derivation involves considering the position of a solitary Robinson Crusoe figure. Alone on her island she is free to use her capacities in whatever way will best fulfil her preferences given the external circumstances in which she finds herself. The extent of her capacities limits her fulfilment, but Gauthier denies that this is a limitation upon her freedom, since on his account of freedom a person is free in so far as she is able, without interference, to direct her capacities to the service of her preferences. Moreover, since Crusoe may cease her productive efforts at any time that she chooses, she has only herself to blame if marginal effort exceeds marginal gain. In short, in this solitary situation, Crusoe's position is one of freedom, absence of externalities and optimality. According to Gauthier, Crusoe in this situation is in a 'morally free zone' (pp. 90–2).

The importance of this example is that Gauthier wishes to claim that a fully competitive market is a morally free zone in the same sense (pp. 83–112). The capacities, preferences and productive activities of others provide a set of conditions for economic agents within which each person seeks maximum benefit. If persons are fully entitled to the fruits of their productive efforts in the Crusoe case, it might seem as though market participants were entitled to the full fruits of their productive efforts and mutually beneficial exchanges. The control over her own capacities that Crusoe exercises in isolation might seem to warrant a commitment to the separateness of persons in exchange relationships. Yet clearly this is not an argument, it is only an analogy, and Gauthier recognises this by distinguishing between the inferences that can be drawn from the situation of the solitary Crusoe and the inferences that can be drawn from the workings of the competitive market.

There are two features of the market in particular for which Gauthier wishes to advance claims. The first is that rational individuals would subscribe to the rights to self-ownership implied in the principle that persons ought to be provided with an incentive to forgo the opportunity cost of their next preferred productive activity. The second is that rational individuals would not subscribe to the principle that economic agents should retain the rental component of their income (pp. 257–67). This combination of claims comes close to the reconstructed Rawlsian position that I identified in the previous section, but there are two principal differences.

First, Gauthier differs from Rawls on the principles that would emerge from rational negotiation. Rawls argues that primary economic goods should be distributed in accordance with the difference principle, whereas Gauthier thinks that persons are entitled to the fruits of their own independent labour but should accept a principle that distributes the product of a cooperative surplus in accordance with minimax relative concession. Secondly, Gauthier wishes to claim that his principle of economic allocation is a unique solution to a bargain struck between rational individuals. To sustain this latter position, Gauthier needs to demonstrate the truth of two propositions: rational individuals would concur in the right of persons to the exercise of their own powers without hindrance from others; and persons cannot rationally claim rent as a justified return for the free exercise of their powers in market interactions.

Clearly the second of these propositions presupposes the first, so we shall need initially to look at the claim that rational individuals would concur in a right of persons to exercise their own powers without hindrance from others. There is one crucial difference between Crusoe's isolation and any situation that involves interaction with others. When there is interaction there is labour power for use in a way that there is not in the

Crusoe situation. Since we are presupposing no moral constraints, we may think of individuals as being in a Hobbesian state of nature with respect to one another, and, as Hobbes says, every person in a state of nature 'has a right to everything; even to one another's body' (Hobbes, 1651, Chapter 14; quoted by Gauthier, p. 159). If Gauthier is to demonstrate the rational basis for a right to control and dispose of one's own abilities, then he has to show that rational individuals in a Hobbesian state of nature would concur in a right to control one's own capacities. This he tries to do. His strategy is to formulate a version of Locke's proviso on the acquisition of property, and then seek to demonstrate that rational, self-interested individuals would respect the proviso.

Locke's (1690, Second Treatise, Chapter 5) proviso on the acquisition of property says that persons acquire goods as property when they mix their labour with those goods, *provided* they leave 'enough, and as good left in common for others'. As is well known, this proviso is impossible to satisfy literally as long as resources are scarce. For the person who is precluded by the proviso from acquiring property because his or her acquisition will not leave enough and as good for others has had a right of acquisition eliminated by the previous activities of others. But those previous others, by the same token, did not satisfy the Lockean proviso, and so by a process of backward induction we can infer that at no stage in the chain of acquisition did any person satisfy the Lockean proviso, taken in its literal sense. Moreover, as Gauthier points out, if you are stronger than I am, then your claim to your body's resources will not leave enough and as good for me: I should be better off with a half share in our joint resources than a full share in my own. Gauthier, therefore, decides to follow Nozick (1974, pp. 174–82) in reinterpreting Locke's proviso to mean that in appropriating resources the appropriator should ensure that the position of others is not worsened thereby. In this verson, the Lockean proviso prohibits bettering one's situation through an action that worsens the situation of another.

Why would rational individuals, originally placed in a Hobbesian state of nature, choose to assent to the Lockean proviso? Gauthier's argument runs as follows. Let us define a person's 'basic endowments' as those resources a person could use and which cannot be used without that person. Thus the baseline for my interaction with others is constituted by my basic endowments. If other people are present, then I can better my situation and worsen theirs by seeking to use their endowments if they do not use mine; or I can worsen my situation by allowing them to use my endowments without using theirs. However, if I continue to use my abilities, and refrain from using the abilities of others, then I may fail to better the position of others but I do not worsen their position.

> Thus the proviso, in prohibiting each from bettering his situation by worsening that of others, but otherwise leaving each free to do as he pleases, not only confirms each in the use of his own powers, but in denying to others the use of his own powers, affords to each the exclusive use of his own. (p. 209)

If we suppose that there are considerable disadvantages to all participants in a situation in which everyone is laying claim to the abilities of others, then it is clear that the deficiencies of this situation can be overcome by an agreement in which everyone will lay claim only to their own abilities. What this shows is that an exclusive rights-assignment may be Pareto-superior to a situation in which everyone lays claim to *all* of the abilities of others. However, it does not show that such an assignment is Pareto-superior to a situation in which some people lay claim to *part* of the abilities of others. Perhaps the physically strong but intellectually weak will realise the disadvantages of seeking to get much productivity out of the clever by slavery (especially if they have Hobbes's thought that in this context the most relevant form of human equality is the ability of persons, even when physically weak, to kill one another). But why should they not seek to institute a scheme of redistributive taxation in their favour as a form of 'protection money', and hence, in effect, obtain more than they could do by the exercise of their own abilities? Thus, the claim that a rights-assignment which confirms everyone in the exclusive use of their own abilities fails to be a uniquely rational solution to the bargaining problem as posed. There is, therefore, no reason on these grounds to make a sharp separation between alienable and inalienable assets.

Let us suppose, however, that it may be possible to reconstruct an argument for this exclusive right of persons to their own abilities. What might follow from such a demonstration? Surprisingly perhaps, in view of the general tenor of his theory, Gauthier does not adopt either the marginal productivity principle or the reward for free exchange principle, but insists that the right to one's capacities only entails the right to receive one's share of the surplus generated by factor rent in accordance with the principle of minimax relative concession (p. 274).

The basic rationale for cutting the inference from self-possession to the right to full factor rent is that each person, as a contributor to social interaction, shares in the production of the benefit represented by factor rent. Thus the ice hockey player, Wayne Gretzky, has talents which command factor rent because they are scarce, but their scarcity is not a characteristic inherent in his talents, but is instead a function of the conditions of supply and demand. Gauthier supplements this argument with the claim that we cannot use Crusoe's situation on the desert island as a paradigm for entitlements in a market in this respect. Although allocating the benefits of factor rent interferes with liberty, it does not interfere with the sort of liberty that is any part of the freedom of a solitary being: the rental surplus arises *only* through interaction, and so cannot be one of the entitlements of the natural freedom enjoyed by a Robinson Crusoe.

An important point to make about this argument is that it is not intended to rest upon a basic moral intuition about the priority of social union over individuality in the principles for distributing the product of a social surplus, but rests instead upon a claim about the rationality of social cooperation. For Gauthier the distribution of the cooperative surplus deriving from factor rent, according to the principle of minimax relative concession, is the only rationalisable basis of distribution, in the sense that it is the only principle that could secure universal consent in a hypothetical contract among rational individuals.

Given this requirement of rationalisability, can Gauthier cut the inference from personal self-ownership to the principle that economic value should be allocated according to marginal product? Such a severing of inference is needed if individuals are to be denied their full factor rent, since in a competitive economy, in which individuals bargain with one another over the supply of labour, individuals, as producers, are normally able to secure their full factor rent.

The consistency of three claims is at issue here:

1. Persons have a right to the full exercise of their powers without hindrance from others.
2. Persons cannot rationally claim rent as a justified return for the free exercise of their powers.
3. The market is a morally free zone.

I shall now seek to show that in a competitive market (1) and (2) are inconsistent, so that either (2) has to be dropped or the market is not morally free.

Consider then a corollary of (1). Define an incentive as a device for motivating persons that is not a form of compulsion or a hindrance. Thus, monetary incentives in a market are typically the contrary of a hindrance: they motivate persons to action without compulsion. Since the right to an exercise of one's powers involves the choice not to exercise one's powers without sufficient motive, we can derive the following corollary from (1): Persons may refuse to exercise their powers unless they are provided with sufficient incentive.

Note that this corollary, taken on its own, is compatible with proposition (2). Since rent is defined as the positive difference between the earnings a person receives in exchange for working and the sum that would be sufficient to induce a person to do the same work, it follows by definition that one would have sufficient incentive to perform one's work even in the absence of full factor rent. Since proposition (2) is compatible with a corollary of proposition (1), it follows that, taken on their own, propositions (1) and (2) are compatible.

What happens when we turn to bargaining over labour supply in a market, however? In a competitive market the application of the corollary of proposition (1) will lead to suppliers of labour receiving their marginal product including full factor rent. Jean Hampton (1988, p. 339) has shown how this arises in the Wayne Gretzky case. As a result of a series of offers or potential offers, the club for which Gretzky plays has to offer him sufficient inducement to prevent his moving. If the Edmonton club were to pay him less, Gretzky would be losing the opportunity to earn more with other clubs if he stayed with Edmonton.

The conclusion from this argument is that in a competitive market producers will receive their marginal product identified by the opportunity-cost of their chosen activities. Hampton also wishes to assert that this means that Gretzky is not receiving rent, but this does not follow. Suppose that ice-hockey clubs, as representatives of the fans, could collude with one another so that none of them had to pay individual players more than a given wage. If this agreement could be made to stick, then Gretzky's potential earnings would be reduced. However, provided they did not go below a certain level, Gretzky would still prefer to play ice hockey rather than take up another occupation and the savings in wage bill secured by the club would be passed on to the fans in the form of lower prices for the tickets. If earnings are the only determinant of Gretzky's choice of club, then the collusive arrangement would have enabled his club to extract some portion of his producer's surplus and transfer it to the fans.

The point about competitive markets, of course, is that collusive arrangements of this sort to transfer the producer surplus from potentially high-income workers cannot be made to stick. There are the familiar problems of free-riding that any cartel faces in fixing the terms of trade and the transactions costs involved in fixing agreed maximum levels of price between clubs and players are considerable (and become more considerable if non-wage factors enter into a player's choice of club). A competitive market is analogous to a situation in which individuals bargain with one another about their share of a joint product. Looked at as a problem of bargaining in this way, the core of an economy is one in which there is no coalition of individuals – that is, a subset of those bargaining – who, for a given allocation of resources, could do better with their own allocation than they could do in the proposed overall allocation (Arrow, 1984, p. 188). In the absence of externalities and increasing returns to scale, the core of an economy shrinks to the competitive equilibrium, provided that the number of individuals is large (Weintraub, 1974, pp. 29–39).

The circumstances of a competitive market economy are counterparts for Gauthier of the circumstances that make Crusoe's situation a 'morally free zone'. Just as Crusoe takes natural circumstances as given, so in an economy with a large number of individuals persons have to take the terms on which they are able to bargain with one another as given. Since, in the limit, the results of rational bargains coincide with the terms of trade that are set by prices in a competitive market, rational individuals will be able successfully to negotiate their marginal product. Thus, with an indefinitely large number of individuals, Gretzky cannot face a cartel (he can always find someone else with whom to bargain) and so he is able to secure the value of his full marginal product, including the factor rent.

The conclusion that follows is that in the market, if persons may as a matter of right refuse the exercise of their powers without sufficient incentive, then they may rationally claim their full marginal product and this will inevitably involve a rental component. Hence propositions (1) and (3), when conjoined, involve the rejection of the proposition that persons cannot rationally claim rent as a justified return for the free exercise of their powers.

There are at least three ways in which Gauthier can respond to this dilemma. In the first place, he could give up proposition (2) and say that rational individuals can justifiably claim the full factor rent as a return for their work effort. Since this would imply the principle of marginal productivity, and not minimax relative concession, as the outcome of rational bargaining, I assume that this is an unattractive option, for it would mean using one standard of rationality in one part of his theory and not in other parts.

A second line of defence is to give up the principle that persons have a right to the full exercise of their powers, at least in so far as that principle involves the corollary that persons may refuse the exercise of their powers unless they are provided with sufficient incentive. On this second view persons may be required to exercise their powers and the state imposes duties upon individuals precisely to overcome the collective disadvantages that would arise from the rational pursuit of rational self-interest. In this conception persons cannot claim rent as the justified price for the exercise of their labour, or, as R. H. Tawney (1921, p. 220) once put it, the soldier who rouses the company to danger does not spend the next day collecting the capital value of the lives he has saved. The implication of this approach is that social duties may constrain persons in the full exercise of their powers, preventing them from extracting all the advantages they could secure by rational individualistic bargaining. Again I assume that this would be an unattractive approach from Gauthier's viewpoint, since the social duties that constrain individual rationality have no deeper grounding in the logic of contractual negotiation.

The third alternative would be to accept that in the standard conditions of competitive market equilibrium the marginal product rule is appropriate but to deny that those standard conditions hold in the world in which rational individuals bargain.Thus, maybe Kenneth Arrow's (1984, p. 188) conjecture is correct that 'in some deep sense there are increasing returns to scale', so that there are significant gains to social interaction over and above what individuals and subgroups can achieve on their own. Underlying this view there is a belief in the value of specialisation both in the economy and society at large, so that the complementarities of individual role performance in society provide a context in which all are better off than they would be in socially atomised production and living. One example of how there can be increasing returns to scale is provided by the institution of limited liability. The possibility of limited liability for firms depends upon their operating in an economy of a certain size, for limited liability enables large losses to be widely spread because the failure of one business leads to small losses among all the creditors rather than large losses among a small number of shareholders (Atiyah, 1979, p. 566).

My conjecture is that this third way is the natural one for any contractarian theorist to go who wishes to defend the legitimacy of redistribution from market exchanges. From this third perspective what matters is not so much the contribution that individuals make to the total social product, but the common contribution that all individuals can make to maintaining the social institutions that a large economy needs to secure increasing returns to scale. These institutions include the system of property rights and division of social obligations upon which the successful functioning of market exchange rests, as well as the moral dispositions towards truth-telling, promise-keeping and the like that contractual exchange requires. Respect for these institutions and practices is essential if the benefits of the cooperative surplus are to be realised at all and the case for redistribution therefore rests upon the principle that, if all need to restrain their behaviour in order to maintain these institutions, then all should benefit from some portion of the cooperative surplus that is thereby produced. In essence, this is to assert that social union is the condition for individual advantage rather than a derivative from it. In the final section, I shall seek to explore the implications of this approach for the type of contractarian enterprise that Gauthier favours.

4 Social union and individual rationality

The aim of the contractarian enterprise is to provide a rational reconstruction of moral dispositions and social practices. For Gauthier this aim has urgency because he holds that present generations are living off the moral capital built up over previous generations under the influence of now discarded metaphysical and religious assumptions. *Morals by Agreement*, Gauthier (1988b, p. 385) has written,

> is an attempt to write moral theory for adults, for persons who live consciously in a post-anthropomorphic, post-theocentric, post-technocratic world. It is an attempt to allay the fear, or suspicion, or hope, that without a foundation in objective value or objective reason, in sympathy or sociality, the moral enterprise must fail.

He might well have added that the social practices that sustain society as a cooperative enterprise could fail as well in the face of the same challenge. And yet Gauthier presents us with a theory of economic justice which, through its principle that economic rent should be shared, offers the vision not simply of a social order but also of a social union. From the metaphysical rubble of the collapse of a view of value as objective there arises a strong theory of economic justice in which redistribution from the highly skilled to the less skilled is rationally required.

If the theoretical interest of Gauthier's project is to be sustained, then these conclusions will have to be derived from 'a weak and widely accepted conception of practical rationality' (p. 17), namely the instrumental conception of rationality we find in decision and game theory. Yet, in saying that rental income is not a characteristic inherent in individual talents but arises only through social interaction, Gauthier has posed an insoluble problem for this conception of rationality. Although the maintenance of the social practices underlying a market order require general, if not universal, adherence to certain social norms, no one individual, or small subset of individuals, in a large economy is required for that economy to work. Hence no one individual has any bargaining power; no one can trade his or her compliance for a share of the cooperative surplus. When the cooperative surplus of a society is large, people are on the outside struggling to get in (as migratory patterns in the world currently show) not bargaining for an increased share in order to be induced to stay.

Where individuals are redundant in this sense, what reason can be given, within an instrumental conception of rationality, for individuals to contribute to the maintenance of the norms and social practices that underlie a market order? From the viewpoint of individuals, such norms and social practices cannot be regarded as the product of the sum of individual actions, in which each person plays a part, but they have instead an objective existence requiring individual conformity. It would seem that the only conception of rationality capable of moving individuals to conformity in this context is not one that rests upon the practical advantages to individuals of conformity, but is one which instead appeals to the rationality of being able to will only that which could be rationally willed by all. Whether Durkheim and Kant can be so invoked to succeed where Hobbes and the theory of games fail is of course an open question, and Gauthier has every right to say that he would like to see the enterprise attempted, just as he has attempted the task with his Hobbesian conception of rationality. Yet, within the spirit of the contractarian enterprise there is room for more than one conception of rationality, and, if my arguments have been correct, necessity for something other than the currently dominant instrumental view if the principles of social union and respect for persons are to be adequately combined.

6

Right constraints?[1]

Percy B. Lehning

1 Reason and morals

The intent of Gauthier's project is to satisfy the standards of morals and of reason at the same time. His main concern is to validate 'the conception of morality as a set of rational, impartial constraints on the pursuit of individual interest, not to defend any particular moral code' (p. 6). From the start of his argument it is clear that 'morality' is conceived as being equivalent to 'impartiality', that 'impartiality' is equivalent to justice, understood as 'a just distribution', that the quintessential meaning of morality or impartiality or justice is, for Gauthier, 'not taking advantage', and that the general constraint on interaction, the proviso, is also defined as 'not taking advantage'. I shall argue that this conflation of concepts leads to problems.

Gauthier's claim is:

> that in certain situations involving interaction with others, an individual chooses rationally only in so far as he constrains his pursuit of his own interest or advantage to conform to principles expressing the impartiality characteristic of morality. (p. 4)

The core of Gauthier's proviso is a moral and a rational requirement. The proviso establishes a structure of rights that is both rational and impartial. But not only is it a moral (that is, impartial) requirement, it is also a just one: 'We do claim that justice, the disposition not to take advantage of one's fellows, is the virtue appropriate to co-operation, voluntarily accepted by equally rational persons. Morals arise in and from the rational agreement of equals' (p. 232). The norms of justice are, we are told, identical with rational *and* impartial choice. In this chapter we shall ask: Is Gauthier's theory indeed impartial and, if so, is it also just?

One should realize that Gauthier's project is, in fact, a double project. First, he wants to show what is the strategic choice from the perspective of the *real* individual actor. The second part of the project is a moral analysis of choice from the perspective of the *ideal* actor. Or, as Gauthier formulates this double point of view: 'Moral theory offers an Archimedean point analysis of human interaction. The theory of rational choice offers an analysis from the standpoint of each interacting individual' (p. 266).

The upshot of Gauthier's project is to reconcile reason and morals. Ultimately, the impartial perspective of the ideal actor should cohere with the perspective of rational individuals actually engaged in strategic choice.

In this project there are at least two important steps: first, the description of *the initial bargaining position*, and second, *the bargaining problem proper*.

2 The initial bargaining position

The initial bargaining position defines what persons bring, so to speak, to the bargaining table. What they bring with them will, of course, determine the outcome of the bargaining process, through Gauthier's principle for the distribution of the cooperative surplus, the 'principle of maximin relative benefit'. So the description of the initial bargaining position is of the utmost importance. If unfairness exists in the initial position, it is likely to influence the bargaining process, and it will be transmitted by the bargaining process to the outcomes (Coleman, 1988, p. 315). The importance of a correct or acceptable description of the initial bargaining position becomes clear from Gauthier's remark that 'fair procedures yield an impartial outcome only from an impartial initial position' (p. 191).

In this initial bargaining position, rights provide the *basis for* agreement, and are not the *object of* agreement (p. 199, note 8). Therefore, Gauthier's theory is not contractarian in the sense that it takes rights as grounded in a contract as, for instance, in the theory developed by Buchanan (1975). In Gauthier's theory, the primary candidates for justification by contractarian agreement are *constraints* – constraints on the rights persons have, which are necessary if they 'are to cooperate voluntarily and ... if the outcome of such voluntary cooperation is to be divided among the cooperators in a manner to which they would at the outset voluntarily consent' (1982, p. 442).

The question to be answered now is: What does each person bring to the bargain that underlies a cooperative arrangement? First of all, this initial position must be, according to Gauthier, non-coercive.[2] But also: 'each individual's endowment, affording him a base utility not included in the co-operative surplus, must be considered to have been initially acquired by him without taking advantage of any other persons – or, more precisely, of any other co-operator' (p. 201). The leading idea here is that 'not taking advantage' is 'a reasonable and fair constraint that natural interaction must satisfy in so far as its outcome provides an initial position for bargaining'. This constraint is based on a modification of Nozick's interpretation of Locke's proviso. Gauthier contends that Locke's constraint on acquisition is expressed as a proviso 'that simultaneously licenses and limits the exclusive rights of individuals to objects and powers' (p. 201). This gives each person a sphere of exclusive control, partly protected from the interference of others. The proviso 'prohibits worsening the situation of others except where this is necessary to avoid worsening one's own position' (p. 203).

According to Gauthier, there is an essential distinction between worsening someone's situation and failing to better it. The proviso prohibits the former, but not the latter. The base point for determining how I affect you, in terms of bettering or worsening your situation, is determined by the outcome that you would expect *in my absence*.[3] The central formulation Gauthier gives of the proviso is as follows:

> We interpret the Lockean proviso so that it prohibits worsening the situation of another person, except to avoid worsening one's own through interaction with that person. Or, we may conveniently say, the proviso prohibits bettering one's situation through interaction that worsens the situation of another. This, we claim, expresses the underlying idea of not taking advantage. (p. 205)

The proviso constrains natural interaction to determine 'an initial position from which a fair and optimal outcome may be attained' (p. 208). Its role is thus basic in Gauthier's theory: it introduces a rudimentary structure of rights into natural interaction.

The justification of these rights or basic endowments is the following:

> Each person, in the absence of his fellows, may expect to use his own powers but not theirs. This difference is crucial. For it provides the base point against which the proviso may be applied to interaction. Continued use of one's own powers in the presence of others does not in itself better one's situation; use of their powers does better one's own situation. Refraining from the use of one's own powers worsens one's situation; refraining from the use of others' powers fails to better one's situation but does not worsen it. (p. 209)

Basic endowments are defined as what a person can make use of, and what no one else could make use of in his absence. It comprises his *physical and mental capacities*. Each person identifies with those capacities to which he has direct access, 'and we see that this identification affords each person a normative sense of self, expressed in his right to those capacities' (p. 210).

The application of the proviso affords, first, each person exclusive right to the use of his body and its powers, his physical and mental capacities. Second, the proviso requires *full compensation*, which leaves a person without any net loss in utility: one worsens the situation of another in not giving her full compensation for the effects of one's actions on her. However, it should be stipulated that although the proviso affords a right *in* the fruits of one's labour and so to full compensation, it is 'not a right *to* those fruits and so to market compensation' (p. 211).

The final step which defines the full endowment of each individual introduces exclusive rights to land and other goods:

> Exclusive rights of possession may afford benefits to all, because they give individuals the security needed for it to be profitable to themselves to use the resources available to human beings in more efficient and productive ways. They transform a system in which each labours on a commons to meet her own needs into a system in which each labours on her own property and everyone's needs are met through market exchange. Individual self-sufficiency gives way to role specialization. The division of labour opens up a new way of life, with opportunities and satisfaction previously unimagined. Thus the mutually beneficial nature of exclusive rights of possession provides a sufficient basis for their emergence from the condition of common use which is the final form of the state of nature. (pp. 216–17)

The proviso ensures that at every stage in interaction, each person is left as much as she could expect from the previous stage. Advantage is thus not taken, but equality is not assumed. Indeed, the proviso allows for inequality. This is a consequence of the fact that the proviso 'determines the initial endowments of interacting persons, taking into account the *real* differences among those persons as actors' (p. 220, emphasis added).

Here we get to the core of Gauthier's reasoning for the content of the proviso:

> Each human being is an actor with certain preferences and certain physical and mental capacities which, in the absence of her fellows, she naturally directs to the fulfilment of her preferences. This provides a basis, in no way arbitrary, from which we may examine and assess interaction, introducing such conceptions as bettering and worsening. A principle that abstracted from this basis would not relate to human beings as actors. A principle that did not take this basis as normatively fundamental would not relate impartially to human beings as actors. (p. 221)[4]

We see that individual rights are identified with the factor endowments that each individual has. They provide the *starting point* for agreement. They are built into the proviso, and assert the moral priority of the individual to society and its institutions. The prospect of mutual advantage brings rights into play, as constraints on each person's behaviour. The proviso reflects the equal rationality of persons who must constrain their natural interaction in order to enter into a mutually beneficial social relationship.

Let us recapitulate: we have been concerned with a description of the initial bargaining position, examined from the perspective of the individual actor, choosing strategically. The individual actor brings to the bargaining table a knapsack filled with the natural assets which he eventually will bring to society. There has been no bargaining on the content of the knapsack: its content is not a product of agreement. This basis – this difference in natural assets, this *unequal* starting point – is, according to Gauthier, so 'normatively fundamental', that, without having taken it into account, one could not speak of 'impartiality' or of 'not taking advantage'.

Quite clearly, when developing a contractarian argument, one needs some point at which to begin. Assumptions about rights are, of course, moral assumptions and can give such a starting point. In Gauthier's analysis, rights are based on persons' natural assets: these provide the 'normatively fundamental' starting point. Constraints on these rights are justified by contractarian agreement.

Gauthier himself insists that:

> the idea of morals by agreement may mislead, if it is supposed that rights must be the product or outcome of agreement. ... [T]he emergence of either co-operative or market interaction, demands an initial definition of the actors in terms of their factor endowments, and we have identified individual rights with these endowments. Rights provide the starting point for, and not the outcome of, agreement. (p. 222)

Still one may wonder whether, in a theory of 'morals by agreement', the content of rights should not be the subject of contractarian agreement. Does not this non-contractarian 'initial definition' of rights fit oddly into Gauthier's theory? Should not the content of rights themselves be founded on a prior agreement? Why not develop a 'pre-market' and 'pre-cooperative' agreement to set up market and cooperative interactions? That would result in an agreement on an *ex ante* distribution of rights.[5]

Gauthier's project would have gained in strength if it had been built on two stages of contractarian agreement: first, an agreement on the initial bargaining position, in which rights are defined, and second, an agreement in the bargaining situation proper, in which principles of social cooperation are agreed on – principles that give an answer to the question how the social product should be divided. The lack of a contractarian argument for the initial bargaining position is all the more problematic because the way the starting point is described permeates the whole of Gauthier's theory. In fact, all that follows in his theory is just a specification of the proviso and of the initial bargaining position.[6]

One of the central aspects of Gauthier's theory is the role played by basic endowments or natural talents. The formulation of the proviso is deeply influenced by Gauthier's view on how to deal with the differences between persons in regard to their talents. As we shall see in Section 4, this view emerges in Gauthier's presentation of his disagreement with Rawls.

3 The Archimedean point: the perspective of the ideal actor

We now turn to the second perspective, the moral one, which is characterized by impartiality. If Gauthier's project is to be a success, this perspective must cohere with the perspective of rational individuals actually engaged in strategic choice. And, as we shall see, basic endowments once again play a central role.

From this moral point of view, we deal with the choice of an ideal actor, aware of her individuality but not of its particular context. The ignorance of the ideal actor extends only to her inability to identify herself as a particular person within society:

> [A]lthough ignorance of one's identity precludes any display of positive partiality in one's choice, this is insufficient to guarantee equal rationality. Impartiality in choice is found, not in the absence of concern for those affected, but in the presence of equal concern. And this is assured by the ideal actor's maximizing aim. Although she may identify with no one, everyone may identify with her. The impartiality of the ideal actor is thus exhibited in the fully representative character of her choice. (p. 236)

However, some pages further on, we learn how 'equal concern' should be interpreted. It is not a predisposition of the actors, but a property of the choice situation itself:

> In choosing the proviso, the ideal actor exhibits no altruistic or even impartial concern for her fellows. She has no interest in refraining from taking advantage of them, no desire not to better her position by worsening theirs, should this prove the most effective way to maximize her own utility. But the conditions of Archimedean choice prevent the ideal actor from choosing principles of interaction that would permit her to indulge her single-minded concern with maximizing her own utility, when this could be achieved only at the expense of others. In choosing to benefit herself through interaction, the ideal actor can only choose mutual benefit. (p. 259)

The conditions of choice are such that impartiality is guaranteed: '[T]he Archimedean point nullifies the biasing effects of individuality while retaining the idea, not merely of individual choice, but of choice by an individual concerned to advance his own interests' (p. 237).

Remember that the Archimedean point requires total ignorance of identity: '[T]he individual intents, and the capacities and preferences on which they rest, are excluded from moral consideration, not because they are arbitrary, but because they are partial. The Archimedean point neutralizes their effect' (pp. 256–7). Now the terms 'nullifies' and 'neutralizes' should not be misunderstood. These terms are meant to mean that no one can tailor principle to his advantage. It does *not* mean that the choice made excludes the *effects* in real life of the differences in natural talents or basic endowments. On the contrary, the choice made should do exactly this.

The ideal actor reasons from the conditions common to all individuals. Her answer to the normative question of how she should choose is first, that she chooses to interact only if she expects to benefit. And so to minimize the occasions *on which she must interact whether she will benefit or not*, and to maximize the opportunities for beneficial interaction, she chooses a basic freedom of action in relation to her fellows – a freedom to advance her own interests as she sees fit, in so far as others remain free to choose whether or not to interact with her:

> If interaction is to be mutually beneficial, then it must preclude the unilateral imposition of costs by one person on another. ... Supposing the possibility of mutual benefit, the ideal actor must choose to prohibit the unilateral taking of advantage. No one may better himself through interaction that worsens the position of another, where *the base point in relation to which we determine bettering and worsening is the absence of the other party to the interaction.* And so the ideal actor must choose the proviso as one of the principles of interaction. (pp. 258–9, emphasis added)

Thus the ideal actor, reasoning from the Archimedean point of view, chooses the same proviso as the actor who makes a choice from the perspective of strategic choice.

Having established the initial position from which market competition and cooperation proceed, the ideal actor must consider the principles for that interaction. And now not only mutual benefit, but also optimality will be the object of Archimedean choice.

4 The Archimedean point: Rawls and Gauthier

As we have stated earlier, a core idea in Gauthier's theory is that the proviso determines the basic endowments of persons, taking into account the *real* differences between them. Rights of persons, identified with the basic endowments each person has, are provided by and protected by the proviso. The role and influence of this starting point can be illustrated by contrasting Gauthier's view with that of Rawls. Indeed, Gauthier himself elaborates on Rawls's theory when discussing the Archimedean perspective. We shall follow Gauthier's arguments closely.

According to Gauthier, Rawls argues that 'from the Archimedean point, it is just to maximize the minimum amount of utility, *without distinguishing the portion of it that constitutes the co-operative surplus*' (p. 247, emphasis added).[7] This, of course, runs directly against Gauthier's point of view. Gauthier wants to make a distinction between what a person can get without cooperation and the additional amount that she can get by cooperating.[8] For Rawls on the other hand, it does not make any sense to talk about producing in a situation without cooperation and then to compare this situation with one of cooperation. Rawls is not concerned with determining 'anyone's contribution to society, or how much better off each is than they would have been had they not belonged to it, and then adjusting the social benefits of citizens by reference to these estimates' (Rawls. 1978, p. 62).

In Gauthier's interpretation of Rawls, this is taken to mean that 'no person is entitled to any benefit except as a member of society, and no person is entitled to any benefit as a member of society in virtue of his contribution to the production of goods, whether in market or in co-operative interaction' (p. 248). According to Gauthier, Rawls's theory makes clear

> that the more productive are not entitled to a greater share of goods in virtue of their greater contribution. If giving them a greater share increases their contribution, and if this in turn raises the social minimum, then they are to receive that greater share. But their rewards are purely instrumental, means to the goal of maximizing minimum utility, and not a recognition of entitlement based on contribution. (p. 248)

Gauthier takes it that Rawls rejects the notion of an *individual's* contribution to productivity: 'We must then take Rawls to be simply asserting that an individual's contribution does not entitle him to any return from society' (p. 249).

This, however, is *not* a correct interpretation of Rawls's view of cooperation for mutual advantage. There *is* in Rawls's theory a recognition of entitlement based on contribution. The criterion that is used for this recognition is the system of public rules that specify the scheme of cooperation. The more productive are entitled to a greater share in virtue of their greater contribution, *as long as they use their endowments for the general good.* As Rawls himself formulates it: 'We have a right to our natural abilities and a right to whatever we become entitled to by taking part in a fair social process' (1978, p. 65).

Be this as it may, Gauthier would still object that Rawls does not require that people are *fully* compensated for the basic endowments that they bring to society. A closer look at the two theories, comparing the way reasoning goes behind the veil of ignorance, will make this even more clear.

Behind the Rawlsian veil of ignorance, 'No one knows his situation in society nor his natural assets, and therefore no one is in a position to tailor principles to his advantage' (Rawls, 1971, p. 139). And Rawls elaborates:

> If a knowledge of particulars is allowed, then the outcome is biased by arbitrary contingencies. ... [T]o each according to his threat advantage is not a principle of justice. ... The arbitrariness of the world must be corrected for by adjusting the circumstances of the initial contractual situation. (1971, p. 141)

Now compare this with Gauthier's idea of Archimedean choice:

> [A]lthough the ideal actor is not aware of her identity, she is aware that she has an identity. It then seems reasonable that she choose with this in mind, and consider her claim on the fruits of social interaction given that identity. She would then choose a principle to regulate interaction in such a way that the particular, natural characteristics of each person, in so far as they affect what he accomplishes, will enter into the determination of the distribution of benefits. And these particular characteristics constitute the person's natural assets. Thus we should expect, contrary to Rawls's assertion, that in Archimedean choice natural assets but not social contingencies would be taken as part of one's unknown but real identity. One brings the former to society; they enter into the formation of one's preferences, and they determine one's social contribution. They do not seem to be morally arbitrary in any sense that would or could exclude them from being taken into account in impartial choice. What the Archimedean point excludes is tailoring principles to favour one's particular assets. But why need or should it exclude tailoring principles to relate the distribution of the social product to the way in which each person's assets are exercised in production? (p. 251)

We see now very clearly that, although in *both* theories the purpose is to prevent tailoring principles to one's advantage, or to favour one's particular assets, the crucial distinction lies in the way 'taking advantage' is defined and in the role that basic endowments play in this definition.

This distinction can be illustrated by Gauthier's interpretation of the difference principle, the principle that plays such an important role in Rawls's theory, 'Justice', Gauthier remarks,

> is the disposition not to take advantage of one's fellows, whether as a free-rider or as a parasite. It appears that the ... difference principle licenses

> those with lesser natural talents to take advantage of those naturally more fortunate, requiring the latter to use their abilities, not primarily for their own well-being, but to maximize the minimum level of well-being. But to criticise Rawls in this way we must suppose that each individual may be defined independently of social interaction, so that he brings his talents and aptitudes, attitudes and preferences, into society as part of a natural endowment. We must suppose that each person's characteristics, in enabling him to make a certain contribution to the social product, also provide him with a claim *to a certain share of that product.*
>
> This is precisely what Rawls rejects, and his rejection leads him to a very different view of what justice requires. The person who takes advantage of her fellows is not the less talented individual who benefits from the maximin principle, but the more talented individual who uses her talents solely for her own benefit. For she diverts to her exclusive use an undue portion of the total assets of society. She robs her fellows of what rightfully is theirs. (p. 252, emphasis added)[9]

This is, to put it mildly, not a fair or even correct interpretation of the Rawlsian project. First, we have to remind ourselves that we are talking about choice from the Archimedean point of view. In this prospective view, the parties make an agreement in good faith, with the intention of honouring it, and in the belief that they can reasonably do so. The derivation of principles behind the veil of ignorance is one in which the prospective view prevails with the intention that the retrospective view coheres.

Second, in Rawls's view *no one* is taking advantage, neither the less-advantaged nor the more-advantaged. For Rawls, society is a cooperative venture for *mutual advantage*, and the difference principle is a principle of *reciprocity*. Implicit in this idea for reciprocity is that social institutions are not to take advantage of contingencies of native endowment, or of initial social position, or of good or bad luck over the course of life except in ways that benefit everyone, including the least favoured.

Finally, it is true for Rawls's system, just as it is for Gauthier's, that each person's characteristics, in enabling him to contribute to the social product, provide him with a claim to a certain share of that product.

The main difference between the two views concerns what 'a certain share' means. In Gauthier's interpretation, it is based on the 'real' contribution persons make to the social surplus: each individual should be fully compensated, as the proviso requires, so as to be left without any net loss of utility. In Rawls's theory, both parties – the less- and the more-advantaged – are compensated. The essential element of the difference principle is that it is a principle of *compensating inequalities*. The basic structure should be arranged in such a way that natural contingencies

> work for the good of the least fortunate. Thus we are led to the difference principle if we wish to set up the social system so that no one gains or loses

> from his arbitrary place in society, without giving or receiving compensating advantages in return. (Rawls, 1971, p. 102)

We are talking about reciprocal advantages. One needs one another: the point is not that the more favoured fail to get what they have a right to – 'full compensation' in Gauthier's words – but rather that both parties are compensated. Their talents, *all* talents, are effective only in social cooperation. Gauthier seems to recognize this point at some places in his work himself:

> The co-operation that justice makes possible, considered both in terms of what it brings about, and in terms of the participatory activity that it involves, is not a second-best way of realizing what could, but for some particular obstacles, better be realized in some other way. In co-operating we make the most effective use of our powers to attain ends that would otherwise lie beyond our individual capacities. (p. 345)[10]

Despite this acknowledgement, however, we have to note that Gauthier would still insist that people should be fully compensated for using their powers, as required by the proviso.

The purpose of developing the two perspectives, the impartial perspective of the ideal actor and the perspective of rational individual actors engaged in strategic choice, has been to show that, in the final analysis, both lead to the same principles. We have seen that in both perspectives the same proviso is formulated. One may wonder, however, how strong the justifications are in the two perspectives. It seems that in both cases one should rather speak of a *petitio principii* than of a conclusive argument.

At this point we just want to stress Gauthier's lack of doubt about the content of the principles agreed to – a lack of doubt that the chosen principles would, indeed, reflect the differing abilities of the persons. The question is, of course, *how* those principles reflect those inequalities.

5 Gauthier's liberalism and neutrality

Modern liberal theories share at least one common fundamental principle: that the state and its laws should remain *neutral* with respect to the varying conceptions of the good life held by individuals.[11] This neutral concern is a principle of anti-perfectionism. Neutrality is seen as a political ideal: it governs state policies and institutions, the *public* relations between persons and the state, and not the *private* relations between persons and other institutions.

The justification of constitutional neutrality is based on the wish to show everyone equal concern and respect. All persons are due equal respect by virtue of their capacity to work out their own conceptions of the good life. On this view, all persons should have equal freedom to pursue their own conceptions of the good life, and the state is denied the right to implement any specific conception of it. The fundamental political principles assign to persons rights and duties and define the appropriate distribution of the benefits and burdens of social cooperation: these principles are the principles of social justice. They are liberal principles because of their neutrality with regard to conceptions of the good.

How does Gauthier's liberal individual fit into this conception of neutrality? Gauthier seems to underwrite this conception, understood as anti-perfectionism. For instance, he remarks that:

> we deny that justice is linked to any substantive conception of what is good, either for the individual or for society. A just society has no aim beyond those given in the preferences of its members. ... [It] is concerned only to enable each person to realize the greatest amount of her own good, on terms acceptable to all. (p. 341)

But the conception of liberal neutrality has, according to some theorists, a second component, distinct from the idea that the state should be neutral with respect to the varying conceptions of the good life held by individuals. As Raz (1986, pp. 123–4), for example, formulates it: 'The conflict in which the state is supposed to be neutral is about the ability of people to choose and successfully pursue conceptions of the good.' With this conception of neutrality, the state can be neutral *only* 'if it creates conditions of equal opportunities for people to choose any conception of the good, with an equal prospect of realizing it'.

So, according to this argument, equal freedom of choice and political neutrality have to go hand in hand. Now Raz's formulation of 'neutrality' as the *equal* prospect of realizing one's conception of the good is a rather strong one. I do not want to elaborate on this point, but simply will assume that we are talking about a reasonable opportunity for each citizen to realize his or her conception of the good. Or, following Rawls's formulation of this neutrality of aim of the state, we will understand it to mean that the state ensures for all citizens equal opportunity to advance any permissible conception of the good. (In Rawls's case: those conceptions that respect the principles of 'justice as fairness' (1988, p. 262).)

The equal freedom of each person to lead a good life of his own choice requires that citizens have an adequate range of options. On this interpretation of the liberal idea of neutrality, the state has a duty to ensure for all persons a reasonable opportunity to pursue the good of their own choosing. The fundamental question then becomes how to create conditions of equal opportunity for people to choose any (permissible) conception with a reasonable prospect of realizing it.

Different answers are formulated on how to create those conditions of equal opportunity without abandoning liberal principles, and especially without abandoning the idea of self-ownership.[12] These answers are concerned with, for instance, the problem of what to do with differences in talents, in mental and physical capacities (and the fruits thereof), and in external resources. In the remainder of this chapter, we will analyse where Gauthier stands with regard to self-ownership and with regard to internal and external resources.

As we have already seen, Gauthier's formulation of the proviso affords each person an exclusive right to use his body and its powers – to use his physical and mental capacities. It also affords him a right in the effects of his labour. It determines the initial endowments of interacting persons, taking into account the real differences between persons as actors (p. 220). In regard to both internal and external resources, Gauthier seems in agreement with Nozick. We will first elaborate on Gauthier's ideas about *internal* resources, the natural capacities of persons.

6 Gauthier and internal resources

The inequalities allowed for by the proviso are, in Gauthier's view, not an indication of partiality. Remember that the proviso is supposed to be an impartial constraint on interaction. Remember also that for Gauthier, just as for Rawls, society is a cooperative venture for mutual advantage. But with regard to the question of how to treat natural talents, Gauthier and Rawls part company. Gauthier uses Rawls's discussion of talents as a specific example of Rawls's general view on how the capacities of persons should be regarded by society and on how they should be dealt with.

Rawls (1971, p. 74) holds that '[t]here is no more reason to permit the distribution of income and wealth to be settled by the distribution of natural assets than by historical and social fortune.' In his theory, the difference principle represents:

> an agreement to regard the distribution of natural talents as a common asset and to share in the benefits of this distribution whatever it turns out to be. Those who have been favored by nature, whoever they are, may gain from their good fortune only on terms that improve the situation of those who have lost out. ... No one deserves his greater natural capacity nor merits a more favorable starting place in society (1971, pp. 101–2)

Gauthier's interpretation of this is that, for Rawls, 'morality demands the giving of free rides; no other interpretation can be put on the insistence that talents be treated as a common asset' (p. 220). Gauthier continues:

> We may agree with Rawls that no one deserves her natural capacities. Being the person one is, is not a matter of desert. But what follows from this? One's natural capacities determine what one gets, given one's circumstances, in a condition of solitude. One's natural capacities are what one brings to society, to market and co-operative interaction. Why should they not determine, or contribute to determining, what one gets in society? How could a principle determine impartially how persons are to benefit in interaction, except by taking into account how they would or could benefit apart from their interaction? (p. 220)[13]

The essential question for Gauthier is, as we have noted before, how to distribute the cooperative surplus. According to Gauthier, one should make a distinction between the value that would be obtained without social cooperation and the value that is created by cooperation. Each person seeks to maximize his gain over the outcome of non-cooperation, and so is concerned with his share of the value produced by cooperation. However, even if each were to receive some portion of the cooperative surplus, each could not expect to benefit in the same way as his fellows.

In contrast, Rawls is of the opinion that talking about 'a condition of solitude' does not make any sense. One is born into society, which is an ongoing scheme of fair cooperation over time, without any specified beginning or end taken as relevant for political justice. The question is how social institutions work now, or should work now. Gauthier's idea of asking what one would have got in a state of nature, and then deliberating on how to divide the cooperative surplus, plays no role in 'justice as fairness'. For Rawls, what would happen in the state of nature is unknowable, or of no significance.[14]

Rawls's idea that the distribution of natural talents should be treated as a common asset is interpreted by Gauthier (and others)[15] as a denial of self-ownership in regard to talents and natural endowments. Several objections to the idea of 'talent-pooling' have been raised.[16] One objection, developed by Nozick (1974), is derived from Locke's theory of property rights. The argument here is that talent-pooling necessarily violates people's entitlements by forcibly depriving them of the right they have to their own natural capacities. In Nozick's view, and one should add, also in Gauthier's view, basic endowments come into the social world tied to particular individuals. These individuals then have a right to what follows from these endowments. Rawls, however, strongly rejects the idea that talent-pooling forcibly deprives persons of their right to use their own talents in their own way. As he remarks: 'greater natural talents are not a collective asset in the sense that society should compel those who have them to put them to work for the less favored' (1974, p. 145).

Another objection against talent-pooling is the argument that it is impossible actually to redistribute natural capacities. But the object of pooling is *not* to achieve this. In Rawls's theory, the point is to share the advantages and disadvantages that *result* from the natural talents that different individuals have. Rawls never says that personal talents themselves are to be regarded as collective property. What he says is that the distribution of native endowments – that is, the differences among persons – are to be regarded as a common asset.[17] Differences in talent consist not only in the *variation* of talents of the same kind but also in the *variety* of talents of different kinds. This variety can be regarded as a common asset. The difference principle is formulated as an acceptable principle for *all* members of society, and it uses the distribution of endowments as a common asset in the sense mentioned above. This argument is also based on Rawls's view that only in society does it make sense to talk about entitlements to a certain amount of the social product.

Gauthier, then, has not shown convincingly that the idea of talents as a common asset runs afoul of self-ownership. The question is how institutions deal with the effects of the natural distribution. As Waldron (1988, p. 404) has noted, there is no sense to the idea 'that talents can simply be *exercised* by those who own them apart from any social framework whatsoever'. So, what we are talking about is a distribution problem. The nature of this problem is accurately formulated by Coleman (1988, p. 314): 'Cooperation is necessary to *produce* the surplus, which is in turn contingent upon agreement on the *division* of those gains. No agreement upon relative shares, no surplus.' It is, of course, the Rawlsian difference principle that tries to find this optimal point of equilibrium between producing and dividing the social product.

'Justice as fairness' takes the basic structure of society as its primary subject. One of Rawls's reasons for doing so is that basic institutions have a profound influence on the life prospects of persons. According to Rawls, inequalities in life prospects are affected by three kinds of contingencies: by the *social class* into which citizens are born; by the *natural endowments*, and the opportunities to develop those endowments, that citizens have; and by *good or ill fortune* over the course of citizens' lives. In a well-ordered society, life prospects are affected by these social, natural and accidental contingencies and especially by the way the basic structure responds to these contingencies to meet the requirements of 'justice as fairness'. The important question is how institutions deal with the effects of *all* of these different kinds of contingencies.

In Gauthier's theory, social institutions should take care only of specific contingencies that are determined by specific social structures. For example, a social structure in which males are encouraged to actualize capacities that are repressed in females should be considered unfair, 'because it fails to relate benefits to the contributions each person would have made had each enjoyed similar opportunities and received similar encouragement' (p. 263).

7 Gauthier and external resources

We now turn to Gauthier's view on the implications of the proviso for external resources. Gauthier illustrates his ideas with the example of the appropriation of land. As with his argument about internal resources, the essential question is whether the appropriation of land by one person worsens the situation of another. And, elaborating on that, what exactly is to count as 'worsening'? Gauthier argues that

> an individual might rightfully appropriate land or other goods previously in common use for her own exclusive use, provided the effect of such appropriation was to leave other persons at least as well off as before. The appropriator betters herself without worsening the situation of others. (pp. 277–8)[18]

Is this, indeed, the case? Is the situation of others *not* worsened by the appropriation of land? Gauthier answers: 'In making the best appropriation open to one, one does not take advantage of others simply because they now lack the opportunity that one was the first to seize' (p. 278). Again one has to ask: Is this really the case?

Earlier it was noted that Gauthier's proviso is a modification of Nozick's interpretation of Locke's proviso. In his discussion of the appropriation of land, Nozick (1974, p. 175) formulates the proviso in the following way: 'the crucial point is whether an appropriation of an unowned object worsens the situation of others.' Gauthier's line of reasoning, as well as his formulation of the proviso, is essentially the same as that of Nozick. Remember that Gauthier's example has to do with the appropriation of land *that is in common use*. One might conclude that Gauthier is right and that, starting from a situation of initial common ownership, appropriation does not worsen the situation of others. But this may be too hasty a conclusion. Gauthier seems to be aware of the point, contrary to Nozick, that external resources are not up for grabs:

> Were the world such as the Dobu have been said to conceive it, so that all goods were in fixed supply, then the proviso would indeed limit appropriation by the requirement that as good an opportunity be left for others, so that one should take only an *equal* share of land or of other goods. (p. 278, emphasis added)

Remember that Gauthier is talking about the appropriation of land. And of land there is, generally speaking, only a *fixed* supply. Following the logic of his own reasoning, Gauthier should have taken a position in which self-ownership is combined with private ownership of *initially equal parts* of the world's resources.

This 'left-wing' liberal position is defended by Steiner (1977). In the so-called 'Steiner constitution', each individual has a right to an equal share of the basic non-human means of production. Unlike joint ownership, which forbids a Nozickian (or Gauthierian) formation of unequal private property by placing all resources under collective control, the Steiner constitution institutes private property from the start. But it forbids the inegalitarian scramble by privatizing resources in an initially equal division.[19] This 'starting gate theory' can, of course, eventually lead to inequality, and probably will.

There is no reason why Gauthier should not have taken the same position as Steiner on the appropriation of land, uniting self-ownership with egalitarianism in raw external resources. But, as we have seen, Gauthier takes a different position. Defending his claim that appropriation does not take advantage of others, he uses the illustration of a race:

> The winner of a race does not take advantage of the other runners, at least if participation in the race is itself advantageous. The runners all prefer a situation in which benefit is unequal, so that there are winners and losers, to one in which all benefit equally, but there are no races. (p. 278)

Now this example is rather inapt, it seems to me, to illustrate the appropriation of external resources. In real life, this race is not between the Ovetts, Coes and Crams. It is not even a race between Ovett, Chamberlain and Gretzky. It is a race between the Coes and those who can't run at all.

If one thinks races are an adequate analogy for the problem we are discussing – the distribution of external resources, or rather the *effects* of this distribution – then the starting gate theory more accurately describes the race Gauthier is talking about.[20] In this starting-gate theory, the (track) race is conceived as one in which initial equality in external resources is combined with subsequent unequalizing competition – a competition based on the arbitrary role played by differences in skill. But even if this example is more apt to illustrate the race Gauthier wants to describe, the essential question remains the same: why, in real life, should there be losers at all?

This and the preceding section of this chapter have discussed the central idea of liberalism, self-ownership, in relation to internal and external resources. Two main conclusions have emerged. First, distributing the *effects* of differences in basic endowment need not violate self-ownership. Second, there should be at least an initial equal division of raw external resources.

8 Liberalism, neutrality and impartiality

I have argued that the idea of liberal neutrality has two components (see Section 5). The first component is anti-perfectionism. The second component requires that conditions should prevail in which each person has an equal opportunity to choose any permissible conception of the good with a reasonable opportunity of realizing it. With regard to this second component of liberal neutrality, one can raise two questions about *Morals by Agreement*. First does Gauthier himself subscribe to this conception of neutrality? Second, regardless of whether Gauthier subscribes to it, what are the implications of Gauthier's theory for the prospects of realizing this conception of neutrality?

From the foregoing discussion of Gauthier's position, it has become clear that he would challenge the legitimacy of government activity that would, for example, implement a Rawlsian conception of justice by creating equal opportunities for people to choose any conception of the good with a reasonable prospect of realizing it. However, Gauthier *does* seem to subscribe to some kind of liberal neutrality in its second interpretation. For instance, he remarks that 'the neutrality of the essentially just society, with respect to the aims of its members, is shown in its adaption to whatever their aims may be, bringing their fulfilment into optimal relative equality' (pp. 340–1).

But does Gauthier's theory realize this 'optimal relative equality'? One can have serious doubts about this. The main problem with Gauthier's conception of neutrality is that it is a *procedural* conception of neutrality. A neutral procedure is justified by an appeal to neutral values, that is, to values such as impartiality, equal opportunity for contending parties to present their case, and so on. Such values regulate fair procedures for adjusting between conflicting claims. So, although Gauthier thinks his theory to be neutral in *aim* it is, at most, only neutral in *procedure*. But is it even this?

In Gauthier's theory, each successive step in the argument is defined by impartiality. The first step, in which the *proviso* is defined as being equivalent to 'not taking advantage' or 'not worsening the position of someone', has a notion of impartiality at its core. In the second step, the *initial bargaining position*, being constrained by the proviso is a principle of impartiality. In this initial position, differences in basic endowments (but not their eventual effects) are neutralized. In the *bargaining situation proper*, procedural equality or impartiality is guaranteed by equal bargaining skills which, once again, prevent the taking of advantage. The outcome – the principles which will be used to distribute the social surplus – are then principles that do 'not take advantage', that are impartial and just.

Now at first sight this might look like a completely procedural, impartial theory, about *formal* constraints. Or, to put it another way, this might look like a theory about formal justice rather than about substantive justice. In the steps taken by Gauthier to develop his argument, however, there is one fundamental *substantive* step, and that is the first one. The definition of the proviso *is* a substantive definition. It is 'normatively fundamental', as Gauthier himself remarks. In it, 'not taking advantage', or 'not worsening the position of someone', is given a substantive meaning. But, according to Gauthier, the proviso is at the same time an *impartial constraint* on interaction.

It has become clear that 'not taking advantage' in Gauthier's theory means not taking advantage of *other persons' advantages.* Now whatever one may think of the advantages other persons have, their existence clearly means that oneself is *disadvantaged*: if there are persons with advantages, there must also be persons with disadvantages. The question, then, is how to evaluate those advantages and disadvantages. In Gauthier's theory, these are differences that, from both a rational and a moral point of view, are *relevant.* But a closer look at these advantages (and the corollary: the disadvantages) may give reason to doubt their moral relevance.

Analysing the reasons that could be given for equal access to advantages, Cohen (1989, p. 920) has argued that to be able to answer the question of whether advantages are just or not, one has to ask if someone with a disadvantage could have avoided it or could now overcome it. If he could have avoided it, he has no claim to compensation. This discussion of involuntary disadvantage and responsibility captures the problem we are dealing with. The differences between persons that, according to Gauthier, should play such an essential role in the initial bargaining situation are *involuntary* differences, based on brute luck. Such differences run contrary to a situation in which one can speak of real choice. Following Cohen's argument, this should give the disadvantaged a claim to compensation.

Because of the effects those disadvantages have in the final outcome of the bargaining process proper, we suggest (contrary to Gauthier) that no one can claim full compensation. If one is reluctant to create a real condition of equality in the initial bargaining position, then one way to redress the effects of disadvantages in that position is to turn to the outcome of the bargain situation proper and to deal with the social product in a Rawlsian way. This would be to compensate *each* individual, but not in full, according to the difference principle.

In Rawls's view, the well-ordered society corrects the arbitrariness of natural, social and accidental contingencies. In Gauthier's view, the social order should mirror the partiality of the natural order. The inequalities in basic endowment should be transmitted to the social order when talking about just benefits. Differences in talents *should* make a difference. But by not paying attention to the fact that these differences cannot be avoided, Gauthier has missed an important element of what justice is really about.

Notes

1. I am most grateful to John Rawls. Discussions with him have been enormously helpful and have led to many improvements. I would also like to thank G.A. Cohen and Albert Weale for comments on earlier versions of this chapter.
2. This is the main reason why Gauthier parts company with Buchanan (1975), especially with regard to Buchanan's idea of the initial bargaining position, as the starting point for rational cooperation. In Buchanan's theory, this position is identified with the natural distribution, or non-cooperative outcome. According to Gauthier, this starting point 'represents the effects of power' (p. 198).
3. The paradigmatic example which Gauthier uses to illustrate the distinction between worsening someone's situation and failing to better it is one 'beloved of philosophers': the difference between pushing someone into the water and failing to rescue someone who has accidentally fallen in (p. 204).
4. Baier (1988, p. 321) remarks in regard to this quotation: 'It is not arbitrariness, but obscurity, that I am complaining of in the crucial concept of presence and absence, and in the related concept of interaction.'
5. See Coleman (1985, especially pp. 92–101) for a discussion of 'pre-market' agreement to set up the market and to agree on property rights.
6. For an argument in defence of Gauthier's not taking these two steps, see Narveson (1989).
7. In fact, Rawls is not talking about utility, but about 'primary goods'.
8. Gauthier makes no attempt to discuss what the non-agreement payoff for each person would be. On this, see Barry (1989a, p. 252).
9. Note the resemblance between Gauthier's wording and that of Nozick in, for example, Nozick's (1974, p. 169) remark that '[t]axation of earnings from labor is on a par with forced labor'.
10. See also Gauthier's (1982, p. 437) remark that 'each must benefit from the presence of every other cooperator ... [A]ll benefit from the inclusion of all in social arrangements'.
11. On the conception of liberal neutrality, see Larmore (1987) and Jones (1989).
12. See Alexander and Schwarzschild (1987) for a discussion of the neutral distribution of resources.
13. Similarly, Gauthier (1974b, pp. 15–16) remarks that 'it is surely mistaken to hold that natural inequalities are undeserved. They are not deserved, they do not accord with desert, but equally they are not undeserved, they are not contrary to desert.'
14. On this, see Barry (1989a, pp. 238 and 298).
15. This interpretation of Rawls's position on natural talents can also be found in Nozick (1974, pp. 225–9) and in Cohen (1986a, p. 114; 1986b, pp. 15–16).
16. Kronman (1981) gives an overview of these objections, and argues for their rejection.
17. For this interpretation, see also Waldron (1988, p. 403).

18. See also Gauthier, p. 216.
19. As Cohen (1986b, p. 88) remarks in his analysis of Nozickian appropriation.
20. For the link between the starting-gate theory and a track race, see Cohen's (1986b, p. 95) discussion of Dworkin's interpretation of Locke's theory of acquisition.

7

Equal rationality and initial endowments

Robert E. Goodin

David Gauthier, like many before him, hopes to ground morality in something outside of itself. At the outset of *Morals by Agreement* he announces his hope of generating morality purely from the 'non-moral premisses of rational choice' (p. 4). He restates that as his central aim in his own contribution to the present volume.

Trying to derive moral conclusions from non-moral premisses amounts to no more than looking for derivations that actually do some work. An argument that smuggles its conclusions into its premisses is simply not a very strong argument. It is question-begging. It assumes what it purports to prove. All pretence of argument is a fraud, or anyway a smokescreen. All the real work that the argument purports to accomplish is not being done by the argument at all, but rather by something that was settled before the argument ever got started.

Philosophers hope they can do better than that – and not purely for the sake of philosophical purity, either. There is a practical point as well as a purely philosophical one to seeking strong arguments. They alone are capable of moving people. Or, anyway, they alone are capable of moving people in the distinctively intellectual way in which mere arguments might ever move people at all. An argument for respecting the demands of morality can get no grip on people who are not already inclined to do so in so far as it relies upon a premiss that is in itself a moralized one. The amoral, who do not feel the force of moral appeals directly, cannot be made to feel their force indirectly by recourse to arguments that presuppose morality.

Much is therefore at stake in this aspect of the argument: philosophical kudos and practical efficacy alike. Alas, at the end of the day I do not think that Gauthier's version of the argument will work to provide a thoroughgoingly non-moralized argument for morality. At crucial junctures, Gauthier – like so many others – ends up smuggling moral assumptions into the premisses of his argument for morality. Hence his theory ends up being as liable as any other to the charge of 'morality in, morality out'.

In saying this, I do not mean to suggest that the ambition is not a worthy one. Nor do I mean to suggest that anyone else has been any more successful in realizing it than Gauthier himself. Certainly John Rawls's theory of justice, for example, is guilty of the same sin. The veil of ignorance, so crucial to Rawls's derivation, is a highly moralized device; and Rawls himself admits, in the end, that people have to have a 'sense of justice' (understood as a disposition to behave justly, once the just course has through his theory been revealed to them) in order for his theory to get any motivational grip on people (Rawls, 1971, *§§* 24, 86). So too, perhaps, does John Harsanyi's (1977) analogue – the suggestion that, in judging moral matters, everyone should suppose there is an equal probability that they will experience any given outcome.[1] So if Gauthier's attempt to derive moralized conclusions from non-moralized premisses is a failure, he is in distinguished company, among contemporaries and precursors alike. Still, fail I think it does.

My discussion of these issues proceeds in two parts. First I shall discuss Gauthier's 'equal rationality' postulate. That discussion will then lead me to reconsider Gauthier's seemingly innocuous solution to the problem of specifying initial endowments. In the end, I have doubts as to whether Gauthier's position on either point is actually defensible. My principal complaint, though, is that in order to defend his position in each case Gauthier needs to appeal explicitly or implicitly to premisses of a distinctly moral sort. Those premisses may or may not be morally appealing. Whatever you say about that, the point remains that they are undeniably moral in character. And the defence of morality by appeal to morality is, of course, just what Gauthier was hoping to avoid.

1 Equal rationality

Let me begin with a few comments about what exactly it is that we seek when we are attempting to mount a case for morality. Obviously, we are looking for prescriptions for people's behaviour. Furthermore, we are looking for ones which the agents themselves are capable of internalizing and self-consciously acting upon. But, of course, not just any old prescriptions of that sort will necessarily count as 'moral' ones.

To short-circuit a long story, let me simply assert baldly my presumption that what makes propositions moral ones has something to do with their content. Specifically, what makes propositions recognizably moral is the 'impartiality' which they enjoin upon people who are in the position of assessing the competing claims of themselves and of others. That may not be the only way of filling out the basic formula, and it certainly is not all there is to the story; but at least that basic Golden Rule prescription is, on most accounts, a large part of the story.

Impartiality of that sort is what most sharply distinguishes moral from purely egoistic behaviour. It is indeed that contrast which is of most interest here. Gauthier, like so many others before him, takes egoists to be the 'hardest sell'. Arguments for morality are addressed principally to egoists (or their first cousins),[2] on the implicit assumption that if those arguments can persuade them then they can persuade anyone.

Against this background, it is clear what it means to get 'morality out' of the derivation. The derivation will have succeeded in its self-assigned task if it provides an argument – addressed in the first instance to egoists and proto-egoists, but applying *mutatis mutandis* to all others besides – for behaving impartially.

Against that background, it is also clear what would constitute loading 'morality in' at the outset of the argument. Any premiss that amounts to, or rests upon, an assumption of impartiality on the part of the rational agents making the choices that are supposed to generate morality is, on these grounds, prima facie suspicious. In watching for ways in which Gauthier and others of his ilk might be smuggling the conclusions into the premisses, this is the sort of contraband which we must be seeking.

In principle, illicit premisses might be lurking in the most innocuous of places. The best smugglers hide their contraband in the most unlikely of places. Still, it is most natural to start our search in the most obvious of places. In looking for the ways in which a theorist might be illicitly smuggling morality-cum-impartiality into his theory, it always pays to probe whatever it is in his theory that is doing the bulk of the work in getting morality-cum-impartiality out. All too often, the device that is doing the real work of the theory in this sense itself embodies a thinly veiled moral assumption of impartiality, in the first place.

Thus, for example, what makes people impartial in Rawls's derivation is the 'veil of ignorance', depriving them of all knowledge of their particular interests, tastes and preferences. What makes Rawls's derivation illicit is the fact that you must want to be impartial to put yourself behind the veil of ignorance in the first place. Real people do have a pretty clear image of what their preferences are and where their interests lie. If they are pure egoists with no prior, independent interest in impartiality, why should they pretend to forget all that they know about how best to further their interests when choosing basic structures of their society?

Or, again, what drives Harsanyi's arguments for impartial utilitarian concern for the interests of all weighed equally is the 'equiprobability assumption'. But, again, why should pure egoists (with no prior, independent interest in impartiality) make choices on the assumption that their chances of ending up in each social slot are equal, when they know fully well that they are not?

The functional equivalent to those devices in Gauthier's own theory is his notion of 'equal rationality'. The basic idea is just that each person must be impartial because, knowing that others are just as rational as he is himself, no one can expect others to agree to make relatively greater concessions than the ones which he is prepared to make himself (p. 143).

There can be little doubt that the conclusion which emerges from this argument counts as a form of morality: its impartiality, and hence morality, is perfectly plain. Instead, it is the derivation of this principle which I intend to question. Gauthier commends that conclusion to rational egoists ostensibly on grounds of pure prudence alone. Were he correct in this claim, Gauthier would indeed have succeeded in getting 'morality out' of premisses that are themselves completely non-moralized.

I do not think that this claim can be sustained, however. I shall begin by attacking the rationality of this equal rationality assumption. The rationality of behaving in accordance with that principle – at least in the way that Gauthier goes on to develop it – can be sustained only by recourse to some further assumptions about the initial baseline from which bargaining proceeds. Those assumptions, in turn, are not commended to us by pure rationality alone. They depend instead upon a warrant that is at least as much moral in character as it is rational.

No doubt it is irrational, just as Gauthier says it is, for a person to make a larger demand that 'he supposes some rational person is willing to entertain' (p. 143). But that is not simply equivalent to saying, as Gauthier goes on to say, that 'no one can expect any other rational person to be willing to make a concession if he would not be willing to make a similar concession' (pp. 143–4).

That may well be what 'equal rationality' would imply in a world in which everyone had equal power and identical preferences. But the real world is not like that. The real world is one characterized by people with differing tastes and resources.

Each of those two kinds of difference between people matter in the course of bargaining. Given our differing tastes, I am more than happy to concede my flat in the city for your house in the country, and you are more than happy to make the opposite concession. Trade would never get off the ground without a willingness of this sort to concede to others what you would not expect them to concede to you.

Likewise, given differing resources, some bargainers can drive harder bargains than can others. The better-endowed can afford to hold out longer; they are better equipped to sustain the short-term losses involved in a war of attrition. Thus, other people may well be willing to entertain demands that you would yourself reject – not because they are less rational, but merely because they are less well-endowed. *In extremis*, the poor are always going to be willing to concede what the rich would not.

Gauthier's model would attempt to solve both problems using the same device. Taking on board the fact of obviously differing tastes, Gauthier proposes relativizing 'concessions' to people's preference structures. Surely 'equal rationality' does not mean that you must be prepared to concede to me literally the very same physical object that I am prepared to concede to you. Properly understood, all that that principle requires is simply that we each be prepared to make concessions that are 'as great' as the other's. But how 'great' any particular concession is, to each person, crucially depends upon how central the things conceded are to that person's preferences.

Gauthier might attempt to take on board the point about the rich and poor in like fashion. It may well be true, Gauthier might agree, that the poor would make greater concessions than the rich in *absolute* terms: they may, in a pinch, be prepared to give up jobs, houses and educational opportunities in a way that the rich never would. But, Gauthier would emphasize, focusing upon the absolute numbers (of hours employed, rooms per occupant, years of schooling) is misleading. We must look instead at how big those concessions are relative to the preferences of the agents themselves.

Specifically, Gauthier insists that we should look at the proportion of demands that each agent is willing to forsake. This is the sense in which he claims that the assumption of equal rationality requires that each person be prepared to make broadly the same 'relative concessions', somehow calibrated, as that person demands of anyone else.

Notice what has happened here, however. The form of relativization initially under discussion was really pretty innocuous. There, it was merely a matter of relativizing to the particularity of different people's differing preferences. Varying tastes obviously lead people to cede to others what they do not want, in exchange for what they do want. The form of relativization now in view relativizes not only to preferences but also to how many other demands a person is also making at the same time.

The implicit assumption linking to two forms of relativization must, presumably, be that the more demands people have to make, the less any given one means to them. I can see good ethical grounds (along the lines of 'counting each for one and none for more than one') for acting as if this were true. I can also see good ethical grounds for not doing so. Roughly speaking: why should we regard it as equally important that someone who is already pretty near his bliss point get still closer to it as it is that someone in dire straits get proportionately nearer his?[3] But in any case, ethical reasons are precisely the sort that Gauthier eschews, hoping to get morality out without putting morality in. What he needs are grounds for this presumption that are defensible either a priori or else empirically. I can see none for that proposition – and several against it. For just one example, the linearity of the relative concession model flies in the face of empirically well-grounded notions of diminishing marginal utility, which would lead us to suppose that the last increments of a good mean proportionately less to a person than earlier ones.

Even if, for the sake of argument, we grant Gauthier his relative concession model of equal rationality, there is still a spanner waiting to fall into his works. This has to do with people's attitudes towards risks, and with the impact that such attitudes might have upon the relative concessions that they would be willing to make.

Ceteris paribus, someone who is willing to take more risks would be able to drive a much harder bargain than someone who is more averse to taking risks. The former, being willing to take more of a chance that negotiations will break down altogether, would be prepared to concede less, both absolutely and relatively. The latter, being less willing to risk a breakdown of negotiations, would be prepared to concede more, both absolutely and relatively. Differing attitudes towards risk lead perfectly rational bargainers to make very unequal relative concessions.

This point – interesting and telling against Gauthier's argument, in and of itself – becomes all the more interesting and important when we notice that attitudes towards risk are not purely idiosyncratic personal tastes. Instead they are, in part, socially structured. Specifically, it is perfectly rational – it is purely prudent – for those who have less of a protective cushion to be relatively more reluctant to take risks.[4] Being in this way rationally more risk averse, it is rational for the poor, in particular, to make relatively greater concessions than do the rich. (That is perfectly consistent with – and in many ways derives from – the observation that the poor actually run considerably more risks than the rich. My point is just that they do so out of necessity rather than out of preference. There is not necessarily some pathological culture of poverty at work here; it is not as if the poor are risk-lovers, necessarily. The more natural, and certainly the more parsimonious, assumption would be that the poor have the same relatively cautious attitude towards risks as anyone else. The poor value security as much as the next guy. But by virtue of their very poverty, they enjoy less of all goods – security included – than do their richer fellows.)

There is, it should be said, a way in which Gauthier might accommodate all this in his argument. In the standard microeconomic tradition upon which Gauthier's bargaining model rests, tastes for risks are regarded as tastes like any other. Those who are risk averse are simply said to have a stronger taste for 'security'. The fact that they would concede more to get it (paying a higher price for a safer car, for example) then fits just fine with Gauthier's relative concession model of bargaining. Those who are risk averse demand two things (safe and cheap transportation), Whereas those less averse to risks demand only one (the latter). Making similar concessions relative to their overall demands, in the way that Gauthier prescribes, would therefore entail the bargainer who has two demands conceding more in any given dimension (in terms of price, for example) than would the bargainer with demands in that one dimension alone.

That reply underwrites the rationality of equal relative concessions in the face of risk. But it does so in a way that undercuts the morality of the model that derives from it. In discussions of the rationality of choices, it is unreasonable to ask whence people's preferences arise. Tastes and preferences are themselves neither rational nor irrational. Those terms can be predicated, within standard microeconomic frameworks, only of choices made in pursuit of them.

In terms of rationality, therefore, it is quite irrelevant that some people are forced by their circumstances to be more risk averse – and forced by that fact, in turn, to make greater relative concessions. Those are their preferences, whatever the source of those preferences. The effect of such preferences, once people have internalized them, is to make it rational for agents to behave in the ways described. If it works to their relative disadvantage in bargaining games to have these preferences, then that is just their bad luck. It in no way impugns the rationality of the choices predicated upon those preferences, though.

The morals of the matter are different. The further Gauthier backs off from putting 'morality in' – the more he backs away from demanding that everyone makes the same absolute concession, the more he relativizes those concessions to their preferences and resources – the less successful he is in getting anything recognizable as morality out of his argument.

The poor are risk averse not by choice but rather by necessity. The poor are disadvantaged in bargaining, more generally, because they must perforce make demands which have long ago passed off the agenda of the rich. It may be perfectly rational for others, in bargaining with them, to take advantage of this fact. But a model that commends this course of action can hardly be said to be 'morally impartial' as between rich and poor.

The essence of impartiality is, presumably, treating like cases alike. But a model which puts on a par deep needs and mere desires fails this test of impartiality. Both generate demands in bargaining games, it is true. But in all the ways that really count, morally, they are really very different. Among other things, one can change the one in a way that one cannot change the other.[5] Necessities must be satisfied. Mere desires can be revised, in the light of experiences – among them, the experience of their proving to be too costly to satisfy.

2 Initial endowments

What concessions each party would make in the course of bargaining is only part of the story, though. Any theory of bargaining also needs to specify a baseline from which bargaining and concession-making proceeds. A baseline is sometimes conceived, in historical fashion, as that which people brought with them to the bargaining table: as a specification of what they held *before* bargaining got under way. Other times, it is conceived as a 'default option': as a specification of what each person would get, should bargaining break down without agreement being reached. In so far as the two specifications differ, it is that latter, forward-looking standard upon which rational bargainers should surely focus.

In the economic models upon which Gauthier piggybacks, there is little discussion of how this 'nonagreement point' is to be specified. Typically it is just taken as given. And in one sense, given it is, fixed by something outside the bargaining model itself. But in another sense, the nonagreement point is not at all 'given', in the sense of being fixed by forces outside the control of human agency.

How much or how little of people's initial holdings are necessarily on the table, in any given round of bargaining or in bargaining in general, is very much a question to be settled socially, albeit antecedently to any actual bargaining. Various specifications are possible here. One is a bargaining equivalent of zero-based budgeting: the rule here would be that *everything* is on the table in each round. Another is a bargaining equivalent of a limited liability corporation: only as much of people's existing holdings is on the table as they *choose* to put on the table. Another still is a bargaining rule of 'divide the surplus': the rule here would be that none of people's existing holdings are on the table; bargaining concerns only division of the new *surplus*, not previously allocated to anyone.

None of these rules is fixed somehow in the nature of things. We must instead choose one, in preference to the others on offer. That choice precedes and powerfully shapes all of the choices made in the course of rational bargaining.

There might be 'rational' considerations underlying that choice, too. They might even be considerations that are 'rational' in much the same – if not exactly the same – sense as the subsequent choices made in bargaining games that proceed from that initial choice.[6] I do not want to deny that possibility in anything I say here. Neither, however, do I want to explore it – at least not directly.

The point that concerns me here is simply this. The considerations governing the choice that has been made, in any actual society, among all these various possible baselines for bargaining will most typically have been moral considerations, at least in large part. The question is typically conceived as being one of how much people should and should not have to put on the bargaining table, in each round of bargaining. And the 'should' at work here is typically given a reading that is distinctly *not* prudential, either directly or indirectly. It is characteristically seen as a question of what is 'right', 'fair', 'proper' – rather than as a question of what is egoistically rational.

That is a comment on social practice, not on Gauthier's theory. The fact that those rules as actually cast are grounded in morality is, strictly speaking, neither here nor there for purposes of assessing Gauthier's theory. He is concerned to say how they should be set, however they actually are being set in actually existing societies.

Still, the observation that actual social choices on this score characteristically are morally impregnated should none the less alert us to a further source of danger to Gauthier's own theory. What it should tell us is that the specification of the initial baseline from which bargaining proceeds is another possible source contamination of a purely rational model by moral concerns. This is another point at which we have grounds for fearing 'morality in, morality out'.

That risk turns out to be real, I think. In specifying people's initial endowments – the baseline from which bargaining proceeds – Gauthier's solutions once again become rationally compelling only if certain moral assumptions are first built in.

Gauthier himself explicitly advocates a 'no coercion' baseline (pp. 196–7). That is to say, what people should be able to count upon, absent agreement, is as much as they could have obtained for themselves without coercing anyone else or being coerced by them. That much should not be on the bargaining table, available for social redistribution.

Gauthier argues that it is rational for people to adopt that baseline, appealing in the process to the costs of enforcement of agreements concluded from any other baseline (pp. 196–7). His argument here is simply that enforcing an agreement costs less, the greater the extent to which people are willing to comply voluntarily with its dictates. The more coercion that is required, the costlier the enforcement becomes. Gauthier's thought seems to be that if a bargaining baseline itself contains aspects of coercion, then there will be costs in enforcing any bargaining agreement based on it, right from the start; and the further solutions depart from those dictated by bargaining from a baseline of non-coercion, the more it costs to secure people's compliance with them.

But why should coercion being built into the baseline necessarily diminish the value of bargains based on it, in the eyes of purely rational egoists? Defining the baseline in terms of some coercive starting point just means calibrating it in terms of how much 'threat advantage' each has over the other– how much each could hurt the other, push come to shove. That formulation is notably counterfactual, however. It refers to what people *could* do to each other, not (or anyway not necessarily) something that people actually have done or need to do to each other before bargaining gets under way. So the costs of that coercion might be purely hypothetical, too.

Furthermore, while bargaining on that basis may start from a baseline in which some would have initially to be coercively made worse off than previously, it does not end there. The name of the bargaining game is to distribute a surplus, with the effect that all parties to the bargain are better off than they would have been at the baseline. Supposing that the surplus being distributed is big enough, and that the rules of distribution give each a big enough share of it, there is every reason to expect that each would ordinarily end up better off as a result of the bargain predicted on the prejudicial baseline than they are under the *status quo*. So even if the baseline would require coercively taking goods from people who presently possess them, the bargaining solution that proceeds from that baseline would not.

Gauthier is wrong, then, to suppose that departures from a 'no coercion' baseline will necessarily entail costs of coercively enforcing the bargains based on it – at least so far as purely rational egoists are concerned. Parties to prejudicial bargains may take moral offence, which may give rise to resistance and enforcement costs in turn. But that is a very different matter.

Beyond all that, however, Gauthier's argument on this score embodies a general presupposition that the more you have to coerce people, the more it will cost to do so. That is not necessarily so. Strictly speaking, how much enforcement will cost depends not upon how much people are coerced but rather upon how much they resist. Thanks to the law of anticipated reactions, a really big threat can – if sufficiently credible, or even if just sufficiently threatening, however incredible – actually have its desired effect without ever having to be carried out. In that case, coercion would have proven costless. The costs of exercising power do not, therefore, necessarily increase linearly with the extent of power being exercised.[7]

Furthermore, and more to the present point, what Gauthier says will be true only in so far as the downtrodden actually internalize his prescriptions. In order for what Gauthier envisages in his increasing-cost-of-enforcement argument actually to happen, people must see themselves as being coerced when Gauthier sees them being coerced; they must resent the fact, and do so increasingly the more they are coerced; and they must resist more vigorously (and indeed more efficaciously, or anyway in more costly fashion) the more resentful they become.

Psychologically, increasing resentment of and resistance to increasing coercion might be a plausible enough assumption. But Gauthier's argument, recall, deals in terms of rational choices rather than in terms of humanly understandable psychologies. For his to be a thoroughgoingly rational account, he would have to assert: (a) that it is rational to choose the baseline he proposes; and (b) that that is rational because it would be rational for people increasingly to resent and resist increasing coercion. Alas, he gives them no rational reason for doing so. His argument from rationality ends up assuming what it is meant to prove.

Be Gauthier's rationalist pretensions as they may, one assumes that what is really at work here is an argument not from the irrationality of coercion, but rather from its immorality. That, one suspects, is the argument that ends up bearing all the weight. People resent and resist coercion not because they think that it is irrational for others to try and coerce them but rather because they think that it is immoral for others to do so. It is moral offence, not rational miscalculation, that drives the model here. It is that which is crucial in generating the conclusion that costs of enforcing compliance increase, the more the baseline for bargaining deviates from Gauthier's preferred one.

But were that so, then Gauthier would have failed in his central project. What the outcome of bargaining will be depends upon the baseline from which bargaining initially proceeds. If the choice of that baseline is itself based mainly (albeit indirectly) on moral grounds, then Gauthier cannot pretend to have used his bargaining theory to derive moral conclusions from non-moral premisses. It will be a case of 'morality in, morality out', once again.

Elsewhere, Gauthier argues for a more general 'no interaction' baseline (pp. 16, 203–17). That proposal is obviously in the same spirit as that for a 'no coercion' baseline. On its face, though, this latter proposal is for a much broader specification. There are, after all, various ways in which people can 'interact' with one another without coercion.

In the arguments Gauthier actually deploys for that broader specification, however, he brings it much nearer to the narrower specification. He invokes a notion of 'not worsening' the position of others (pp. 203–8). What 'no interaction' turns out to mean, for Gauthier, is 'no harmful interactions'. That is the baseline from which bargaining is to proceed. What is to be on the bargaining table is the surplus that has been or that might be produced by productive interactions, and that alone.

That is still rather different from 'no coercion', we might note in passing. We can harm others without coercing them. The drummer, in Braithwaite's classic case, harms the violinist (and derives considerable bargaining advantage from the harm that he can do him), without in the least meaning to coerce him. So too can we coerce others without harming them, in the sense of worsening their position. Someone in a position to throw a drowning man a life preserver (or, analogously, to give a starving man a job) does not worsen his position or, therefore, 'harm' him by withholding that benefit. But he does, at least arguably, coerce him into acceding to his demands by threatening to withhold support needed to sustain life itself.[8] Certainly, at the very least, he derives very considerable bargaining advantage from his capacity to threaten to withhold such support.

More importantly from the present perspective, that notion of 'not worsening' itself turns heavily upon a moralistic distinction between two ways of harming people – one through your actions, the other through your omissions. As Gauthier himself says at this point in his argument, 'The crucial distinction that we must establish is between worsening someone's situation and failing to better it, since the proviso prohibits the former, not the latter' (p. 204). There is a dispute within moral philosophy as to whether such a distinction can be sustained at all and, if so, whether there is any moral importance attaching to the distinction. All of that can, for present purposes, safely be left as an open question.

The point at issue here is not whether the distinction is morally defensible. Rather, the point is that one has to appeal to morality to defend the distinction at all. It is simply not a distinction that would be independently defensible to a rational egoist, possessed of a purely amoral concern with prudence alone. Whatever interest we have in the act–omission distinction must, I suggest, be morally motivated.

A purely rational agent sees opportunity costs as being fully on a par with all other kinds of costs. Forgoing the opportunity to earn £100 is a cost to him, fully on a par with paying a £100 bill. (More precisely, they are identical, apart from 'income effects', for there is a genuine difference in the fact that in the one case the agent is £100 richer.) In like fashion, it would be a matter of indifference to a rational egoist whether £100 was taken from his bank account automatically by standing order or whether the same sum was taken from his bank account by direct debit, which requires the payee to undertake actions to collect the money. The one involves action in a way the other does not. But the rational egoist would regard this as a distinction without a difference. Who has to lift the phone or put pen to paper or put magnetic tapes into the post is immaterial. His position has been worsened, to the tune of £100, either way.

The implication for bargaining games should be clear. Return to the case of the man, drowning or starving, who is seeking life-saving assistance from some particular other who is (let us suppose) uniquely in a position to provide it. The existence of others who could have helped, but did not, will, by analogy to the opportunity cost argument, have made that person worse off. Gauthier's 'no worsening' baseline, in so far as it involves a distinction between acting and omitting, does not appeal to purely rational egoists. For them, not harming is helping, and not helping is harming.

Notice, furthermore, that Gauthier cannot easily reformulate the 'not worsening' clause to take these points on board. At least he cannot without putting everything – or else nothing – on the bargaining table. For the effect of the symmetry between helping and not harming, just demonstrated, is that there is no rationally defensible middle ground. There is no way of defending, to purely rational egoists, why the initial baseline should be set anywhere in between zero and one. There is no reason, from their point of view, why that baseline should protect any of people's initial holdings and any of the things that they might do to help or harm others, without protecting all of them.

Some of us would settle quite comfortably onto the one horn of that dilemma. We would be happy to see that everything be put onto the bargaining table; we would be happy to make all initial endowments subject to social redistribution. Those, like Gauthier, who want to resist that conclusion seem to be forced to rely for justification of that stance upon a highly moralized distinction between acts and omissions, between helping and not harming. But if Gauthier insists upon persevering with this conclusion, with only that to justify it, then he is once again guilty of the sin of 'morality in, morality out' that he had hoped all along to avoid.

Now, 'not worsening' might just have been an unfortunate choice of phrase in fleshing out the 'no interaction' baseline. What Gauthier really had in mind might have been simply that bargaining should proceed from the baseline that each would have had, if none of the others had existed at all. Anything that you have, over and above that baseline, is something that is in some sense a 'joint product' – attributable, if not exactly to the efforts of others, anyway to the existence of others. It is, therefore, appropriately on the bargaining table for division among them all. Anything you have, independently of their existence, is yours alone.

Morally, there is much to be said for that proposition. But there is not much to be said for it, purely rationally, except in one very special case. What each would have if others did not exist would indeed be rationally relevant, if the issue were one of whether to bring those others into existence. Imagine a hyper-democratic family, in which procreation occurred only with the unanimous consent of all of its existing members. Bargaining over who gets what, come a new baby, would in that case rightly proceed from consideration of what each would enjoy if the new baby were not to be born at all.

Such a baseline is rationally relevant, there, precisely because the issue at stake in the bargaining is whether or not that other person, presently not in existence, is to be brought into existence. Once in existence, however, counterfactual questions of how much you would have, if others did not exist, is rationally irrelevant (unless of course the question is whether to snuff them out of existence). There is no pragmatic purpose to be served in discussing what else would be true if the moon were made of green cheese, given that it is not. Neither is there any pragmatic purpose to be served in discussing what else would be true if others did not exist, given that they do.

That is not necessarily to deny the merit in a 'no interaction' baseline, counterfactually construed. That the starving of the world would be starving, even if we were not ourselves here feasting, might provide good grounds for resisting the hyper-utilitarian proposal that the rich redistribute most of their wealth to the poor worldwide. My point here is just that the sort of grounds provided by such counterfactual facts – facts about how others would fare if we did not exist – are *moral* grounds.

That we are here is certainly not immaterial – not pragmatically irrelevant – to how others fare, for obviously the more of our wealth we share with them the better off they will be. That we are here at all is only irrelevant, if at all, morally. What is established by appeal to the notion of a baseline of how well off others would be, were we ourselves absent, is (at most) that others have no claims upon us, morally.

The moral merits of that case are debatable, but it is a debate which need not be joined here. For if the 'no interaction' baseline, counterfactually construed, is defensible only by appeal to considerations of morality, then it cannot provide independent grounding for a derivation of morality. Here again, we find a classic case of 'morality in, morality out'. Gauthier, like many before him, has failed in his greatest ambition.

Notes

1. Gauthier compares his approach with those of Rawls and Harsanyi in *Morals by Agreement*, pp. 4–6. I say 'perhaps', because actual uncertainties confronting people might sometimes be almost that dramatic. I have developed these themes in other work (Goodin and Le Grand, 1987; Goodin, 1990; Goodin, 1992, Chapter 3).
2. Strictly speaking, it is a weaker form of egoist – a 'non-tuist' – to whom such demonstrations are addressed. All that matters for purposes of the formal logic is that none internalize the preferences of any of the others with whom he interacts. See Buchanan and Tullock (1962, Chapters 3–4).
3. I elaborate on these issues in Goodin (1975).
4. The classic piece of social anthropology on that score concerns the reluctance of impoverished Southeast Asian peasants to plant new 'wonder rice', which has higher average yield but also more variation from year to year in its yield than traditional strands. This is a perfectly rational response for those who

are so poor that a single year's bad crop would drive them off the land altogether. Scott (1976, p. vii) effectively evokes, in this connection, Tawney's image of the peasant as a man up to his neck in water, who would be drowned by a single swell.

5. See Taylor (1976, pp. 281–99) and Rawls (1982, pp. 159–86). One can concede that needs differ from mere wants in ways that impact upon the fairness of bargaining based upon them, without jumping to some grander conclusion such as that satisfying needs deserves absolute priority over satisfying mere wants. I argue against that in Goodin (1988, Chapter 2).
6. The difference to which I refer is, of course, that between choosing institutions and choosing outcomes. Here there is the large literature on 'indirect consequentialism' to be taken on board. See, e.g., Hardin (1988).
7. See Barry (1989b, pp. 111–69).
8. See Braithwaite (1955) and Zimmerman (1981). Nozick (1972) presents an opposing view.

8

Bargaining and morality[1]

Ken Binmore

The purpose of this chapter is to offer a game-theoretician's perspective on Gauthier's *Morals by Agreement*. My own philosophical views on social contract questions differ sharply from Gauthier's. I think he goes astray, for example, in his second sentence, when he argues that David Hume (1777, Section 9, Part 2) was mistaken in asking: 'what theory of morals can ever serve any useful purpose, unless it can show ... that all the duties which it recommends, are also the true interest of each individual?' However, this chapter is not about the differences I have with Gauthier on his *conclusions*; it focuses instead on his *methodology*. I agree very much with Gauthier that the notion of a rational bargain belongs at the heart of any social contract theory, and hence that game theory has an important place in the tool-kit of a moral philosopher. But Gauthier is not orthodox in his use of game-theoretic tools. And such deviations from the straight and narrow path are especially dangerous in game theory because the path marks a route through a veritable minefield of paradoxes and fallacies.

In discussing where I believe Gauthier has wandered into the minefield, I plan to concentrate on bargaining theory. Gauthier (p. 146) is dismissive of 'infighting among bargaining theorists', and it is true that the views I offer do not command unanimous support. But what I shall be describing is undoubtedly the mainstream position from which deviations need to be justified. Aside from bargaining questions, something will also be said about Gauthier's notion of 'constrained maximization' which, along with all game theorists, I find unacceptable as a rationality principle.

The next section summarizes the five major 'conceptions' that Gauthier lists as fundamental to his theory. Section 2 comments on his notion of 'constrained maximizaton' in the context of the Prisoner's Dilemma. Later sections provide a user's guide to bargaining theory together with a commentary on Gauthier's heterodoxy.

1 Gauthier's five major conceptions

Gauthier (pp. 13–17) founds his theory on the ideas listed below. They are repeated here with some brief commentary in order to set the scene for the rest of the chapter.

(i) *The Archimedean point*

The first notion is that of an Archimedean point from which moral issues can be viewed impartially (Rawls, 1971, p. 584). In Rawls, this is provided by his device of the original position, in which people imagine themselves bargaining about which social contract should be adopted behind a veil of ignorance that conceals the role that the bargainer will occupy in the society being negotiated. Gauthier uses no such device. His bargaining over a social contract is hypothetical, just like Rawls's, but everybody knows exactly what role they will occupy during the hypothetical negotiations.

(ii) *The state of nature*

The second notion concerns the *status quo* from which the hypothetical bargaining commences in Gauthier's story. Wolff (1966) has been forceful in criticizing Rawls on this issue, and a similar criticism can be directed at Harsanyi (1977).

I agree with Wolff about the importance of properly identifying a *status quo* in a bargaining situation. However, I am not at all comfortable with the 'initial bargaining position' that Gauthier selects (pp. 190–232). To my mind, indeed, the state of nature should not be selected at all, but should be rendered inevitable by the manner in which the Archimedean point is specified. However, Gauthier takes a Lockean view of how the state of nature should be determined that he adapts from Nozick (1974). The criteria he employs seem to me to have an *ad hoc* flavour, but the point I want to make is rather different. Since Gauthier sees the set of feasible contracts over which negotiation takes place as being determined only by *rationality* considerations, and since he and I agree that the manner in which he resolves the bargaining problem is without moral content, then all the moral content in the hypothetically agreed social contract

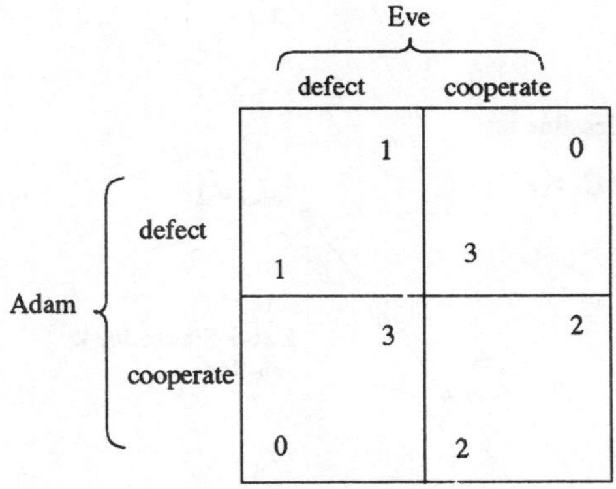

Figure 8.1 The Prisoner's Dilemma.

necessarily falls on his choice of the state of nature. Whether the argument he offers in defence of his state of nature can bear such a burden is something I leave others to discuss.

(iii) *Constrained maximization*

To quote Gauthier: 'We distinguish the person who is disposed straightforwardly to maximize her satisfaction ... from the person who is disposed to comply with mutually advantageous moral constraints, provided he expects similar compliance from others. The latter is a constrained maximizer' (p. 15). The notion that constrained maximization is *rational* is anathema to game theorists. Constrained maximizers will, for example, cooperate in the Prisoner's Dilemma of Figure 8.1, whereas game theorists regard it as almost tautological that defection is rational in the Prisoner's Dilemma.[2]

Gauthier's idiosyncratic view of the nature of rationality in games allows him to take a very optimistic view of the possible agreements available to his hypothetical bargainers. An orthodox view of rationality in games would restrict his bargainers to choosing some kind of *equilibrium* in the game of life as their social contract.

(iv) *Bargaining*

The fourth notion is Gauthier's (p. 145) concept of 'minimax relative concession' from which he deduces a bargaining solution equivalent to

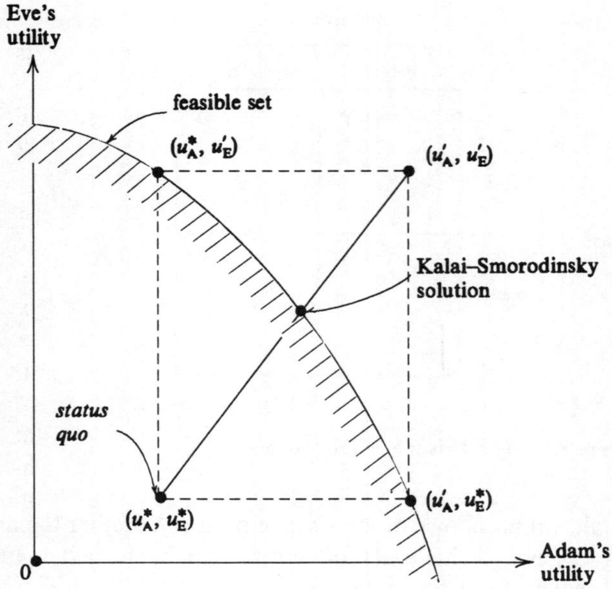

Figure 8.2 Minimax relative concession.

that of Kalai and Smorodinsky (1975) for the two-person case. The bulk of this chapter is devoted to expounding the orthodoxy he thereby violates. In so far as it ever was the case that the 'Nash–Harsanyi–Zeuthen theory' was the touchstone against which alternatives like Gauthier's needed to be measured (p. 133), this is no longer true. It is correct that it remains orthodox to defend the Nash bargaining solution, but the basis for its defence is now very much more securely grounded in non-cooperative game theory. In particular, it is no longer considered adequate to appeal to *ad hoc* criteria like 'Zeuthen's Principle'.

Gauthier (p. 133) envisages rational bargaining as a two-stage process in which each bargainer makes a claim followed by a concession. Suppose, with his notation, that there are just two bargainers, Adam and Eve, who begin by making claims, u_A' and u_E'. The *status quo* is (u_A^*, u_E^*).

The rational claims, so Gauthier asserts, are those that maximize u_A' and u_E' subject to the requirement that (u_A^*, u_E'), (u_A', u_E^*) correspond to feasible agreements (see Figure 8.2). The bargainers then make concessions according to an unspecified process. This leads to agreement on a utility pair (u_A, u_E). Gauthier defines the 'relative magnitude of a player's concession' as $c_i = (u_i' - u_i)/(u_i' - u_i^*)$. He emphasizes the scale-invariance of this quantity. (That is, replacing each u by $Au + B$ leaves c_i unchanged.)

He next insists that rational bargainers will select (u_A, u_E) so as to ensure that the larger of c_A and c_E is minimized. This is the 'principle of minimax relative concession'.

His defence of the last requirement is very brief. He asserts that the condition

> expresses the equal rationality of the bargainers. Since each person, as a utility-maximizer, seeks to minimize his concession, then no one can expect any other rational person to be willing to make a concession if he would not be willing to make a similar concession. (p. 143)

In this quote, the word 'concession' is used in two different senses. At its first appearance, no more than Gauthier's algebraic definition seems to be intended. It is, of course, tautologous that a maximizer of u_i is a minimizer of c_i. At its later appearances, it has acquired a more complex meaning that needs careful examination.

It is certainly attractive to entertain the proposition that no rational person would expect another rational person to take an action that he himself would not take under *identical* circumstances. Having granted this, it is tempting to extend the proposition by requiring that no rational person would expect another rational person to take an action that he would not take himself under *equivalent* circumstances. The question then arises: When are the circumstances under which rational players operate equivalent? Gauthier's answer seems to be: When the sets of concessions from which they choose are the same – other structure being irrelevant. It may be that such a proposition could be defended if the definition of the word 'concession' were tailored to the situation. But Gauthier offers no defence at all for the use of his simple algebraic definition in this context. It is, indeed, difficult to see what form such a defence would take without specific reference being made to the concession *strategies* available to the players.

One modelling approach might be to assume that, after making their claims, each player simultaneously announces a take-it-or-leave-it concession. But, with any such model, it is hard to see why the final outcome should depend on the initial claims in the manner Gauthier suggests. Indeed, unless some reason is given why backing down from an initial claim should be costly, it is hard to say why *rational* bargainers should regard the initial claims as having any relevance at all to what follows.

(v) *Morally free zone*

Gauthier (p. 13) tells us that a morally free zone is to be identified with a perfectly competitive market. Moreover, 'Were the world such a market, morals would be unnecessary'. To me it seems that if all human activity were organized using the market mechanism then morals would be needed to relieve some of the suffering that would result. However, I plan to say nothing more on this topic since, in spite of the emphasis accorded to it by Gauthier, it seems to me to be only peripheral in the development of his theory.

2 Game theory and commitment

Gauthier's notion of 'constrained maximization' requires departing from the most fundamental principle of non-cooperative game theory – namely, that players will not use a strongly dominated strategy. I plan to explain why game theorists regard this principle as almost a tautology, and then to say something about why I believe Gauthier's reasoning has gone awry.

Figure 8.1 shows a version of a toy game called the Prisoner's Dilemma.[3] The strategy *defect* strongly dominates the strategy *cooperate* because a player gets more by defecting whatever the other player may do. Unfortunately, such statements invite a certain type of fallacy. This is the fallacy that a person chooses action A rather than action B *because* the utility $u(\mathrm{A})$ of action A exceeds the utility $u(\mathrm{B})$ of action B. However, modern utility theory has long outgrown its Benthamite origins and is now based, in principle, on the choice behaviour of the decision-maker. In modern utility theory, a decision-maker does not choose A over B because $u(\mathrm{A}) > u(\mathrm{B})$. On the contrary, the utility function u is chosen so that $u(\mathrm{A}) > u(\mathrm{B})$ because the decision-maker chooses A over B. Thus modern utility theory has abandoned the attempt to *explain* coherent choice behaviour, and contents itself with seeking to *describe* it.

So what do Adam's payoffs in the matrix of Figure 8.1 mean? If Adam *knows* that Eve will choose *defect*, then he gets a payoff of 1 from defecting himself, and a payoff of 0 from cooperating. The payoff 1 was chosen to be larger than the payoff 0 because Adam will choose *defect* over *cooperate* when he knows that Eve will use *defect*. Similarly the payoff 3 was chosen to be larger than the payoff 2 because Adam will choose *defect* over *cooperate* when he knows that Eve will choose *cooperate*. (One may ask: Why 1 and 0 in the first case but 3 and 2 in the second? The answer is irrelevant to the point in hand but, for the record, the payoffs are von Neumann and Morgenstern utilities that provide information about how the player will choose when he faces an uncertain future.)

To conclude an analysis of the Prisoner's Dilemma, we now need a rationality principle. The idea is a watered-down version of Savage's (1954) *Sure-Thing Principle*. It says that, if a decision-maker will choose A over

B when he knows T is true, and he will also choose A over B when he knows that T is false, then he will choose A over B whatever he may know about T. This principle is applied in the Prisoner's Dilemma with A taken to be *defect*, B taken to be *cooperate*, and T taken to be the proposition that Eve will choose *defect*.

One may complain that this argument makes defection in the Prisoner's Dilemma almost into a tautology, and therefore that game theory is not telling us very much. Game theorists will gladly agree that this is correct. In fact, they will be pleased at being thought to be promulgating tautologies since they are mostly closet mathematicians.

I do not want to itemize the various fallacies that are commonly offered in seeking to justify cooperation in the Prisoner's Dilemma (on which, see Binmore (1991)). In brief, they mostly proceed by arguing that the Prisoner's Dilemma is really some other game in which cooperation is not irrational. Game theorists do not object to some other game being analyzed: only to the analysis of some other game being offered as an analysis of the Prisoner's Dilemma.

An exception to this method of escaping from the supposed paradox represented by the Prisoner's Dilemma is the *fallacy of the twins* (see Binmore (1989)). This fallacy argues that, since it is common knowledge that both players are rational, therefore both will make the same choice. The final outcome will therefore be either D = (*defect*, *defect*) or C = (*cooperate*, *cooperate*). Since both players prefer C to D, so the story goes, it follows that rationality requires C to be chosen. The fallacy lies in the final sentence. Rationality may perhaps restrict the final outcome to the set S = {C, D}. But it does not therefore follow that C is a feasible choice for rational players, because it is possible that rationality may restrict the final outcomes to a smaller set than S. In fact, game theorists argue that rationality restricts the set of final outcomes to {D}.

Gauthier offers a version of the fallacy of the twins in which the difficulties are finessed as follows:

> Since our argument is to be applied to ideally rational persons, we may simply add another idealizing assumption, and take persons to be *transparent*. Each is directly aware of the disposition of his fellows, and so is aware whether he is interacting with straightforward or constrained maximizers. Deception is impossible. (pp. 173–4).

A little later he observes that transparency can be replaced by translucency. By this he means that it does not matter if mistakes are sometimes made in identifying the disposition of one's opponent.

Making people's skulls transparent or translucent certainly pulls the rug out from under the feet of critics of the twins fallacy. But is it a legitimate manoeuvre? I can think of two reasons why not. The first is the obvious objection that one cannot simply add 'idealizing assumptions' willy-nilly. People cannot see inside each other's heads and it is idle to examine models in which they can.

The second reason is more subtle but is of overwhelming importance. Since the work of Schelling (1960), game theorists have learned to deal with the problem of commitment very carefully. When commitments can be made, they are modelled formally as moves *within* the game and then the game is analyzed without further commitment opportunities being attributed to the players. Gauthier rides roughshod over these eggshells. He assumes that people can *choose* a disposition to be a constrained maximizer. That is, they can make a commitment not to make certain choices in the future. In the Prisoner's Dilemma, for example, they make a commitment not to defect when they see a corresponding commitment inside the transparent skull of their opponent.

In attributing players with the power to make commitments in a game, Gauthier runs afoul of another game-theoretic tautology. To illustrate this point, the Kidnapping Game of Figure 8.3(a) will be used. The discussion will also serve to introduce some game theory ideas that will be needed in studying bargaining theory later in the chapter.

The Prisoner's Dilemma of Figure 8.1 is a game in *strategic form.* (Von Neumann and Morgenstern used the term *normal form.*) Each player chooses a strategy simultaneously. The kidnapping game is given in *extensive form.* Adam moves *first* and Eve may then get an opportunity to move *later*. The story is that Adam has kidnapped Eve and the ransom has been paid. Eve has promised not to reveal Adam's identity and he would like to release her, but he knows that she will have the opportunity to fink on her promise once out of his power.

Game theorists use backwards induction in such a game to compute a *subgame–perfect equilibrium.* First consider what Eve would do if she were released. She gets 2 from finking and 1 from remaining silent. This means that she finks. This choice is indicated in Figure 8.3(a) by doubling the line that represents the choice *fink*. Adam can predict this behaviour. He therefore knows that, if he releases Eve she will fink and he will get a payoff of 0. But, by murdering Eve, he gets a payoff of 1. Thus Adam murders Eve, as indicated in Figure 8.3(a) by doubling the line representing the choice *murder*.

Why do game theorists call the strategy pair (*murder*, *fink*) a subgame–perfect equilibrium? First it is necessary to know what a *Nash equilibrium* is. The pair (*murder*, *fink*) is a Nash equilibrium because *murder* is a best reply for Adam to Eve's choice of *fink* and *fink* is simultaneously a best reply for Eve to Adam's choice of *murder*. (If Adam is going to murder Eve, it makes no difference what she plans to do if released.) The pair

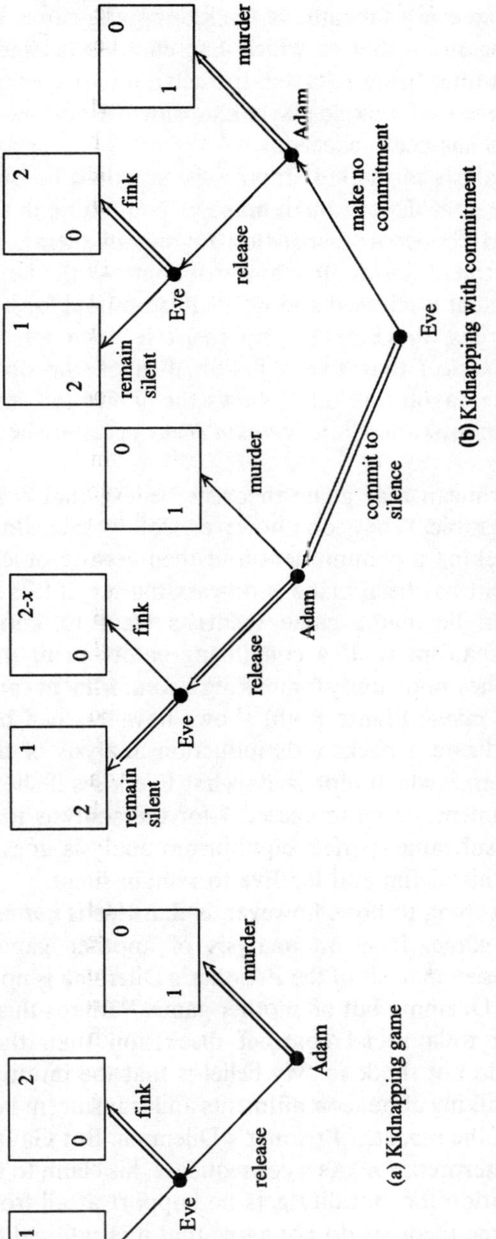

Figure 8.3 Subgame-perfect equilibrium

(*murder, fink*) is a subgame–perfect equilibrium because it induces Nash equilibrium play in every subgame of the kidnapping game. There is only one (proper) subgame – that in which Eve chooses between remaining silent and finking after being released. In such a one-player game, a Nash equilibrium reduces to the single player choosing the optimal action given that the subgame has been reached.

Gauthier's analysis of the kidnapping game would be quite different. He would argue that Eve should make a commitment to remaining silent: she should choose a 'disposition to remain silent'. When Adam sees this commitment inside Eve's transparent skull, he knows that she will remain silent if released and hence it is optimal for him to release her. Game theorists, however, see no merit in such an analysis. For them, it is *tautological* that Eve will fink if given the opportunity. A 2 is written in the payoff box that follows the choice *fink* and a 1 in the payoff box that follows the choice *remain silent* because she *would* fink if released.

This does not mean that game theorists believe that commitment is necessarily impossible. They do, however, follow Schelling (1960) in believing that making a commitment and then getting others to believe that a commitment has been made is no easy matter. If it is claimed that commitments can be made, game theorists want to know what the enforcement mechanism is. If a convincing enforcement mechanism is described,[4] then the opportunity for making a commitment can be included *as a move in the game*. Figure 8.3(b) shows how this can be done. The doubled lines indicate a backwards induction analysis of this modified game. The number x, which represents what Eve loses if she backs down from her commitment, needs to exceed 1 for the analysis to be correct.[5] Notice that this subgame–perfect equilibrium analysis does indeed lead Adam to release his victim and for Eve to remain silent.

The important thing to note, however, is that this is *not* an analysis of the kidnapping game. It is an analysis of another game. Similarly, Gauthier's supposed analysis of the Prisoner's Dilemma is not an analysis of the Prisoner's Dilemma but of another game. Perhaps this other game is more relevant to a social contract discussion than the Prisoner's Dilemma, but I do not think so. My belief is that the intuition Gauthier is tapping when talking about commitments and translucent heads belongs in a discussion of the *repeated* Prisoner's Dilemma. But Gauthier (p. 169) refuses such an interpretation. As a consequence, his claim to be supplying a *rational* foundation for morality gets no support at all from orthodox game theory. Game theorists do not agree that it is rational to cooperate in the Prisoner's Dilemma. The mainstream view is that rationality calls for the use of an *equilibrium* of some kind – and the only available equilibrium in the Prisoner's dilemma is (*defect*, *defect*).

3 Nash bargaining theory

As explained in the opening paragraphs, the focus of this chapter is on Gauthier's views on bargaining theory. These views conflict with what I am representing here as the mainstream view among game theorists. This knows nothing of 'minimax relative concessions' and defends instead the *Nash bargaining solution* (which is not at all the same thing as a Nash equilibrium). Since it is many years since Nash (1950) wrote, the philosophy of his approach has had a long time to percolate, but, at the risk of boring many readers, the ideas will be repeated here. Nash's axiomatic defence of the Nash bargaining solution is what is best known. His second defence depends on the analysis of a specific model of a negotiation process in which both bargainers are restricted to making simultaneous take-it-or-leave-it *demands*. With some vestigial uncertainty about precisely what is available, Nash shows that optimal non-cooperative play in this demand game leads to an outcome which approximates his bargaining solution. I believe that Nash's axiomatic defence cannot properly be understood without an appreciation of at least some of the non-cooperative bargaining games of which Nash's demand game is one example. The two lines of attack are simply different aspects of a single conceptual approach nowadays referred to as the *Nash programme* (Nash, 1951, 1953).

The idea is very reductionist. Where opportunities for negotiation exist, the proposal is that the various ploys open to the negotiators be modelled as formal moves in a non-cooperative game. The term 'non-cooperative' refers to the manner in which the negotiation game is to be analysed. The players are assumed to be motivated only by rational self-interest, and attention therefore centres on locating *equilibria* of the negotiation game. If one *can* formalize the relevant negotiation procedure adequately and then locate an appropriate equilibrium, whether Nash or some more refined variant, that is unequivocally the 'right' equilibrium, then the bargaining problem is solved. The solution of the bargaining problem is the 'right' equilibrium outcome – i.e. the payoffs the players receive if they both use their equilibrium strategies during the play of the negotiation game.

Of course, major difficulties exist. (See the introduction to Binmore and Dasgupta (1987) for a fuller account.) Nash's axiomatic approach is designed to short-circuit these. He asks what properties one might anticipate the equilibrium outcome to have. He then codifies these properties as 'axioms' and demonstrates that only one pair of payoffs satisfies the axioms: namely, the Nash bargaining solution. Having arrived at this conclusion, it is tempting to discard the conceptual framework of non-cooperative negotiation games as redundant scaffolding. But this would be a serious mistake. One *must* have a view on what the relevant negotiation game is before one can make a judgement on what properties its equilibrium outcome ought to have. If the negotiation game does not belong to the class of those Nash had in mind when formulating his axioms, then the Nash bargaining solution will be wrong. Even when the Nash bargaining solution is right, it is easy to go astray by applying it wrongly.

This section continues with a list of possible interpretations of the Nash bargaining solution that are *not* compatible with the ideas laid down in the Nash programme.

(i) *Collective rationality interpretations*

Gauthier asks '[w]hether there are principles of rational bargaining with the same context-free universality of application as the principle of expected utility maximization' (p. 129). I think that the answer to his question is 'No'. Without the context of a negotiation *procedure*, the bargaining problem is *indeterminate*. The Nash programme calls for a relevant context to be established and then asks that the appropriate principles of rational bargaining *for that context* be *deduced* from the principle of expected utility maximization. Nash's axioms, notably the 'independence of irrelevant alternatives', are *not* to be seen as context-free, collective rationality principles.

(ii) *Behavioural interpretations*

Von Neumann and Morgenstern (1947) say that the bargaining problem is outside the scope of game theory because its resolution depends on the *psychology* of the bargainers. Nash (1951) refers to equal bargaining *skill* on the part of the players – although he explicitly corrects himself later (Nash, 1953). Harsanyi (1977) quantifies such a notion, in the context of an informal dynamic bargaining model, by reviving an idea of Zeuthen (1930) and elevating this to the status of a principle: *Zeuthen's principle.* More recent advances in game theory mean that it is possible to dispense with such *ad hoc* behavioural assumptions provided that what the players actually can or cannot do is adequately tied down. It is true that a price is paid for this. The game-theoretic analysis for a chimpanzee playing chess, for example, becomes the same as for Alekhine.[6] If both *optimize*, both will do the same. But this is the price that is always paid for using *homo economicus* as a model for *homo sapiens*. In any case, interpretations of the Nash axioms in terms of the psychology of the players, or in terms of variants of Zeuthen's obsolete principle, are *not* to be admitted.

(iii) *Ethical interpretations*

These are the most invidious. Raiffa (1953) compared a number of axiom systems, of which Nash's was one, as candidates for a 'fair' arbitration scheme. Since then, the idea that the Nash bargaining solution is properly to be interpreted in this manner has taken on a life of its own and the Nash bargaining solution is routinely rejected on the grounds that it has no merit as an ethical concept. My own view, which simply echoes what is orthodox in social choice theory, is that ethical decisions require inter-personal comparison of utility units. Such comparisons are expressly ruled out of court by Nash's axioms. That is to say, *it is agreed* that the Nash bargaining solution has no merit as an ethical concept. When used, it is to predict what the result would be, under certain ideal circumstances, if agents were to act as individual optimizers. The issue is therefore never whether or not one *likes* the result. As with $2 + 2 = 4$, the only issue is whether the result is accurate. This is at least one area in which Gauthier and I are in agreement, since he says exactly the same of the result of using his 'minimax relative concession' principle as I am now saying of the Nash bargaining solution.

4 Nash's axioms

If Adam and Eve are rational in their attitudes to risk, in the sense axiomatized by von Neumann and Morgenstern, their personal preferences can be represented by utility functions $\phi_A: S \to \mathbf{R}$ and $\phi_E: S \to \mathbf{R}$ in such a way that Adam and Eve always behave as though maximizing *expected* utility. The set S_0 of feasible deals on which Adam and Eve might agree is a subset of the set S on which their preferences are defined. A particular member s_0 of S_0 represents the current *status quo*. In terms of von Neumann and Morgenstern utilities the *feasible set* is

$$X = \{(\phi_A(s), \phi_E(s)) : s \in S_0\}$$

The point $d = (\phi_A(s_0), \phi_E(s_0))$ will be called the *disagreement point*. The pair (X, d) is said to be a 'Nash bargaining problem'. Figure 8.4(a) illustrates a pair (X, d). The diagram incorporates the assumptions about X that will routinely be made: namely, that X is closed, bounded above, convex and comprehensive.[7] It will also be assumed that d is an interior point of X.

Figure 8.4(a) also illustrates the *weighted Nash bargaining solution* n for (X, d) corresponding to the *bargaining powers* $\beta_A > 0$ and $\beta_E > 0$. This is the value of $x = (x_A, x_E)$ at which the weighted 'Nash product'

$$\pi = (x_A - d_A)^{\beta_A}(x_E - d_E)^{\beta_E}$$

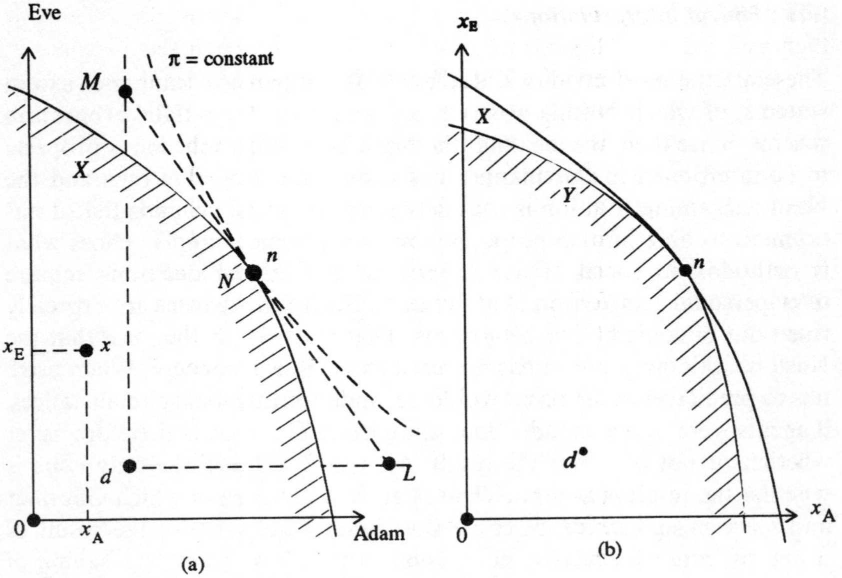

Figure 8.4 Nash bargaining solution.

is maximized subject to the requirements that $x \in X$ and $x > d$. Notice that only the ratio β_A/β_E is significant. The alternative geometric characterization, that $LN/MN = \beta_A/\beta_E$ as illustrated in Figure 8.4(a), is often less cumbersome to use.

Two properties of the weighted Nash bargaining solution require emphasis. The first is that the deal that results from its use – i.e. the deal t which satisfies $n = (\phi_A(t), \phi_E(t))$ is *independent of the calibration of the utility scales* built into ϕ_A and ϕ_E. (Nothing changes if, for example, x_A and d_A are replaced, in the definition of the Nash product, by $Bx_A + C$ and $Bd_A + C$, where $B > 0$ and C are constants.) A bargaining solution which failed to satisfy this requirement would be incoherent from the viewpoint of the Nash programme. Recall that the primitive notion in modern utility theory is the choice behaviour of the agents. Preferences are deduced from coherent choice behaviour and then utility functions are deduced from the preferences. It bears repeating that an individual does *not* prefer s to t because $\phi(s) > \phi(t)$: on the contrary, $\phi(s) > \phi(t)$ *because* s is preferred to t. In particular, $B\phi + C$ represents an individual's preferences just as well as ϕ.

In the von Neumann and Morgenstern theory, $B\phi + C$ and ϕ are *indistinguishable*. But an ethical theory needs to distinguish them as a preliminary to a discussion of the inter-personal comparison of utilities. Such a theory therefore needs to add *further primitive assumptions* to those of von Neumann and Morgenstern. There is, of course, a tradition in which utility functions themselves are taken as primitives. Significance is then assigned to utility scales by *fiat*. Such an approach seems to me to beg the question. Bertrand Russell said that Mathematics is the subject where we do not know what we are talking about and do not care whether what we are saying is true. But this surely ought not to be true of Ethics.

The *independence of irrelevant alternatives* is illustrated in Figure 8.4(b). The feasible set X has been replaced by a smaller feasible set Y that still contains the bargaining solution n for the problem (X, d). The condition requires that the bargaining solution for (Y, d) *remains* at n under such circumstances. The following result of Roth (1979)[8] concerns functions f that map each pair (X, d) onto a point $n = f(X, d)$ in the set X. *Strong individual rationality* is an unfortunate way of expressing the very mild requirement than $n > d$.

> *Proposition.* A function f satisfies the properties
>
> 1. Strong individual rationality
> 2. Independence of utility calibration
> 3. Independence of irrelevant alternatives
>
> if and only if $\beta_A > 0$ and $\beta_E > 0$ exist such that $n = f(X, d)$ is the weighted Nash bargaining solution corresponding to β_A and β_E.

Nash (1951) also required *Pareto efficiency* and *symmetry*. The first of these is a *conclusion* in the above formulation. The role of an additional assumption of *symmetry* is simply to ensure that $\beta_A = \beta_E$. This is the case normally understood when the Nash bargaining solution is mentioned.

The first requirement of the proposition is very mild. It has been argued that the second is no constraint at all in the current context. All therefore rests on the much maligned third property. It may be that 'collective rationality' is genuinely meaningful in some situations in spite of Arrow's theorem and other impossibility results. If so, then the *independence of irrelevant alternatives* is certainly one of the candidates for a property that collective rationality should satisfy. But I do not think it should be defended on such grounds in a bargaining context, although its name clearly invites such an interpretation (the alternatives in X but not in Y being 'irrelevant', since they are not chosen when n is available).

In game theory jargon, the *independence of irrelevant alternatives* should be seen as an *implementability* requirement.[9] Roughly speaking, a payoff pair is *implementable* if there exists a game (of some specific type) for which the payoff pair is an equilibrium outcome. The water is somewhat muddied by the existence of theorems that are not strictly relevant. These concern the impossibility of *precise* implementation in certain circumstances. But one ought only to care about being able to implement within as small a margin of error as one chooses. However, this is a technical point. What needs to be emphasized is that, if it is indeed true that the *independence of irrelevant alternatives* can sensibly be seen as an implementability requirement, then it is *necessary* that it be insisted upon, given the aims of the Nash programme. But is it sensible to see it this way? This is not a question that is easy to answer in the abstract. It seems necessary to look at some specific bargaining games.

5 Nash's demand game

Adam demands x. Simultaneously, Eve demands y. Each gets his or her demand unless these are incompatible, in which case each gets nothing. The probability that a pair (x, y) of demands is compatible is $p(x, y)$. If the demands are von Neumann and Morgenstern utilities,[10] and (a, b) is a Nash equilibrium, then $x = a$ must maximize $xp(x, b)$ and $y = b$ must maximize $yp(a, y)$. The reason is that $xp(x, b)$ is the *expected* payoff to Adam given that Eve has chosen b. Similarly, $yp(a, y)$ is the *expected* payoff to Eve given that Adam has chosen a.

When differentiation is legitimate, it follows that

$$ap_x(a, b) + p(a, b) = 0$$

and

$$bp_y(a, b) + p(a, b) = 0$$

If the contour $p(x, y) = p(a, b)$ admits a tangent line at the point (a, b), this is given by

$$p_x(a, b)(x - a) + p_y(a, b)(y - b) = 0.$$

From the first two equations, it follows that the tangent line is

$$(x/2a) + (y/2b) = 1$$

as illustrated in Figure 8.5(a). That is to say, (a, b) is the Nash bargaining solution for the problem $(Y, 0)$, where Y is the set shaded in Figure 8.5(a).[11]

Of course, when there is no uncertainty about what demands are compatible, then differentiation is *not* legitimate because p is discontinuous (since then $p(x, y) = 1$ when $(x, y) \in X$, and $p(x, y) = 0$ when $(x, y) \notin X$). In this case, *any* Pareto-efficient (x, y) of X with $x > 0$ and $y > 0$ is a Nash equilibrium. Without a criterion for selecting one of these as a solution of the demand game, one is left therefore with an *indeterminate* situation. To obtain a determinate result in Nash's formulation, some *vestigial*

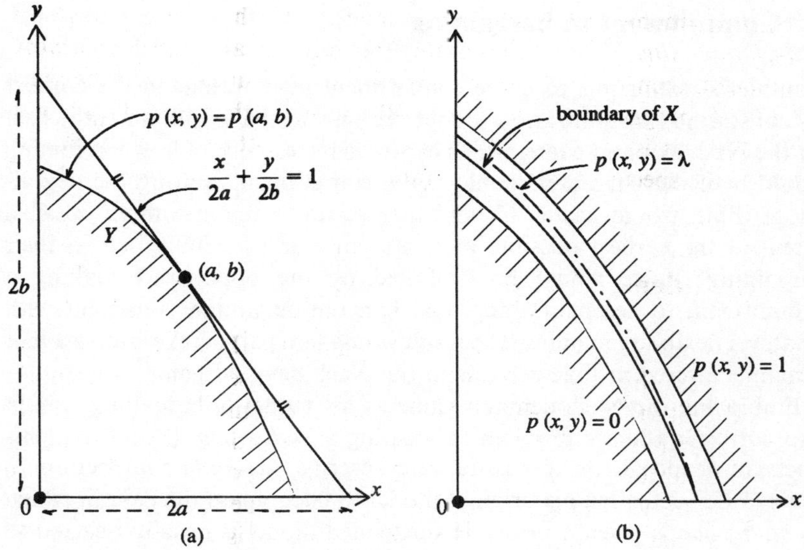

Figure 8.5 Nash demand game.

uncertainty is required. It is natural to model this by supposing that each contour $p(x, y) = \lambda$, with $0 < \lambda < 1$, approximates the boundary of X as indicated in Figure 8.5(b). Any Nash equilibrium of the demand game with such a dash of uncertainty will then approximate the *Nash bargaining solution* for the problem $(X, 0)$.

Is it genuinely appropriate to attach such significance to the possible existence of vestigial uncertainties? An easy answer is that nothing is ever certain in life, not even death and taxes. However, we shall soon encounter alternative non-cooperative bargaining models whose equilibria also implement the Nash bargaining solution, and hence the question becomes less crucial than at the time Nash was writing.

Returning now to the *independence of irrelevant alternatives* and consider the following abstract bargaining game based on Nash's demand game. Two players choose negotiation strategies s_1 and s_2 from strategy sets S_1 and S_2, which are fixed independently of X and d. A fixed function g: $S_1 \times S_2 \rightarrow \mathbf{R}$ determines the payoffs. The payoff pair is $g(s_1, s_2)$, unless $g(s_1, s_2) \notin X$, in which case the payoff pair is d. Suppose the game always has a *unique*, non-trivial Nash equilibrium[12] generating the outcome n. What now happens if X is replaced by Y as in the *independence of irrelevant alternatives*? Observe that the *same* negotiation strategies *remain* in equilibrium and so generate the *same* outcome n. In this situation the equilibrium outcome *must* therefore satisfy the *independence of irrelevant alternatives*.

6 Commitment in bargaining

Gauthier's willingness to make commitment assumptions in the context of 'constrained maximization' ought perhaps to make him an enthusiast for the Nash demand game, which captures the essence of how bargaining would be if the bargainers could make commitments during the negotiations. Both would hasten to bind themselves to the maximum possible extent at the earliest possible moment, since any flexibility left in their bargaining stance would be exploited by the opponent's making a commitment to accept nothing less than the maximum consistent with whatever flexibility remains. The result would be a pair of take-it-or-leave-it demands uttered at time zero, as in the Nash demand game.

Embracing the Nash demand game as his model of bargaining would also solve Gauthier's problem in locating a *status quo*. (Recall that his Lockean proposals on this issue were described as *ad hoc* in Section 1.) Nash (1953) extended his original model to encompass the case in which no *status quo* is given a priori. His extended model is usually referred to as his *variable threats model* (as opposed to the fixed threats model, in which the only available threat is forcing adherence to the *status quo*).

In the variable threats model, each bargainer begins by announcing what action he or she will take if there should fail to be agreement in the subsequent bargaining. These threats are interpreted as commitments from which no backing down is possible. They serve to determine a *status quo* for the Nash demand game which is played after the threats have been uttered. Gauthier rejects such a model for his purposes, saying:

> fortunately we need not face the problem of determining maximally effective threat strategies ... They play a purely hypothetical role in the Nash–Harsanyi analysis, since [Adam] and [Eve] do not actually choose them ... But if [Adam] and [Eve] would not choose these strategies, then they cannot credibly threaten with them. Maximally effective threat strategies prove to be idle. (p. 200)

I do not think this is meant as a condemnation of hypothetical reasoning in game theory. If it were such a condemnation, Gauthier would be attacking the very foundations of the subject. After all, the reason that players use their equilibrium strategies is because of what *would* happen *if* they didn't. I think the passage is condemning the commitment assumption built into Nash's notion of a threat. He is saying that threats need to be credible to be effective. That is, the opponent has to believe that you actually would carry out your threat *if* the occasion to implement it did in fact arise. This is exactly what game theorists say when defending subgame–perfect equilibria.

If I interpret Gauthier correctly, his reasons for rejecting both Nash's fixed and variable threat models are therefore entirely orthodox – albeit not perhaps consistent with his views on 'constrained maximization', or the model of bargaining that he proposes (in which some level of commitment to the initial 'claims' must be present for them to be relevant to what follows).

However, more on this last point will need to wait until Ariel Rubinstein's model of bargaining has been discussed. This dispenses with Nash's commitment assumptions, but still leads to the Nash bargaining solution.

7 Rubinstein's bargaining game

(Woe to Ariel – Isaiah 29:1.) As an introduction, imagine the Nash demand game without uncertainty, modified so that Adam makes his demand *first*. Eve is then left with a take-it-or-leave-it ultimatum. If Adam's ultimatum leaves her with more than her *status quo* payoff, rationality says that she must accept.[13] To express this more grandiosely, the only Nash equilibrium in the one-player *subgame* which follows such an ultimatum from Adam requires Eve to make the maximum demand compatible with that already made by Adam. Adam, knowing that Eve will behave rationally in these subgames, therefore optimizes by minimizing the amount that his demand leaves for Eve. Thus Adam scoops the pot.[14]

Of course, with the Nash bargaining solution demands n_A and n_E, Adam does *not* scoop the pot. Nevertheless, the pair (n_A, n_E) is a *Nash equilibrium* for the ultimatum game (along with many others). If Eve is *always* going to use the strategy of demanding n_E whatever Adam does, then Adam cannot gain by demanding more than n_A. The point here is that the definition of a Nash equilibrium is too crude to capture the fact that a threat by Eve to play this way is just not credible. When *time* is relevant, the Nash equilibrium idea needs to be *refined*. This is why game theorists introduce the notion of a *subgame-perfect equilibrium*. Its power, as compared with the idea of a Nash equilibrium, will become evident in the following analysis of Rubinstein's model.

Why would Eve not make a counter-bid in the ultimatum game after rejecting Adam's original bid? Only because the rules forbid it. Rubinstein (1982) formulated a game without such an artificial constraint. (See also Stahl (1972).) Adam and Eve alternate in making proposals until a proposal is accepted. Hitherto it has been the players' attitudes to *risk* which has been crucial, but now their attitudes to *time* must also be considered. As Cross (1969) remarks, 'If it did not matter *when* the parties agreed, it would not matter *whether* they agreed at all.'

In the discussion that follows, the assumption will be that a deal s reached at time t is worth $\delta_A^t \phi_A(s)$ to Adam and $\delta_E^t \phi_E(s)$. to Eve. The numbers δ_A and δ_E are therefore *discount factors.* They are assumed to lie between 0 and 1. The corresponding discount *rates,* ρ_A and ρ_E, are defined by $\delta_A = e^{-\rho_A}$ and $\delta_E = e^{-\rho_A}$. A time interval of $\tau > 0$ is assumed to separate consecutive proposals, the first of which is made by Adam at time 0. A utility of zero is assigned by both players to the event that agreement is *never* reached.

Rubinstein's result is that such games have a *unique* subgame–perfect equilibrium.[15] Rubinstein's model is certainly a natural one, but it still incorporates unexplained constraints. Why does Adam go first? Why do the players politely wait their turn? Who chose the time interval of τ between successive proposals?

Such difficulties evaporate when the limiting case $\tau \to 0^+$ is considered. This is the interesting case because a player will want his or her next bid on the table as soon as possible after a rejection has been registered. But, in the limiting case, the problem of who goes first disappears since the first-mover advantage becomes vanishingly small.

The limiting case of Rubinstein's game *minimizes* on the fictions that need to be promulgated to explain the behaviour of those playing the bargaining game. In particular, the rules of the game leave players with no obvious motive for cheating on the rules. One does not therefore need to hypothesize exogenously determined penalties for infringements of the rules. Nor is it necessary to hypothesize an exogenous mechanism for sustaining commitments. It is therefore a striking vindication of Nash's insight that the unique equilibrium outcome in the limiting case as $\tau \to 0^+$ is a weighted *Nash bargaining solution.* To see this is not hard, given that there is a unique subgame–perfect equilibrium.

With $\tau > 0$, let $P = (a, b)$ be the equilibrium outcome in the Rubinstein game with Adam as first mover. If Adam's opening proposal is refused, then a subgame is entered in which Eve is the first mover. Let $Q = (c, d)$ be the equilibrium outcome in the Rubinstein game if Eve were first mover. Since the subgame after Adam's opening proposal is refused begins at time $t = \tau$, the equilibrium outcome of the subgame is necessarily ($\delta_A^\tau c$, $\delta_E^\tau d$). It follows that, in equilibrium, Eve must accept any proposal $(x, y) \in X$ made by Adam for which $y > \delta_E^\tau d$, because the latter is what she will get from refusing. Similarly she will refuse if $y < \delta_E^\tau d$. The equilibrium proposal by Adam must therefore be $y = \delta_E^\tau d$. Similar considerations apply when it is Eve who proposes. Thus,

$$b = \delta_E^\tau d \qquad \text{and} \qquad c = \delta_E^\tau a$$

Raise both sides of the first of these equations to the power $\beta_E = 1/\rho_E$. Do the same for the second equation using the power $\beta_A = 1/\rho_A$.

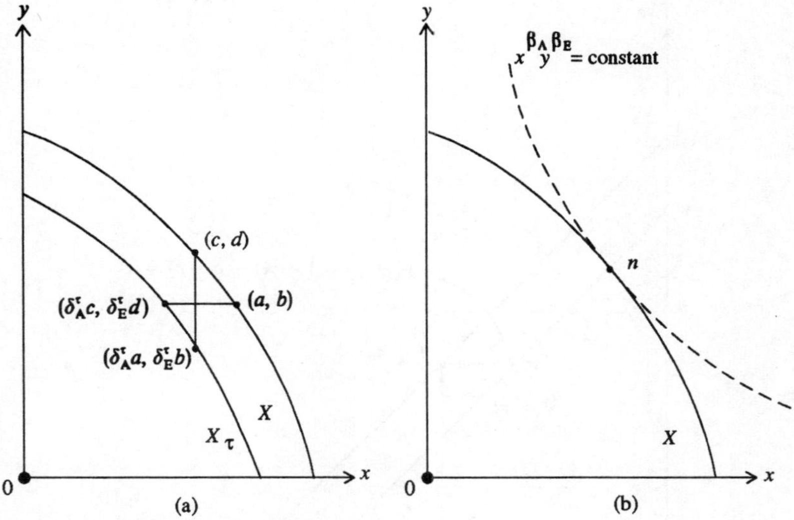

Figure 8.6 Rubinstein's model.

Multiplying the equations then yields the result that

$$a^{\beta_A} b^{\beta_E} = c^{\beta_A} d^{\beta_E}$$

and hence the points $P = (a, b)$ and $Q = (c, d)$ both lie on the same contour $x^{\beta_A} y^{\beta_E} = k$, where k is a constant. The situation is illustrated in Figure 8.6(a) (in which $X_\tau = \{(\delta_A^\tau x, \delta_E^\tau y): (x, y) \in X\}$).

Figure 8.6(b) shows the limiting case as $\tau \to 0^+$. The points P and Q converge to a common limit n at which a contour $x^{\beta_A} y^{\beta_E} = k$ touches the frontier of X. It follows that n is the weighted Nash bargaining solution for $(X, 0)$ with bargaining powers $\beta_A = 1/\rho_A$ and $\beta_E = 1/\rho_E$.

Aside from providing a minimalist defence of the Nash bargaining solution, the model also yields some input on the interpretation of the 'bargaining powers' in the asymmetric case. These do *not* quantity differing bargaining 'skills'. One cannot do better than be a rational optimizer, and this is assumed of both players. The asymmetries, in the Rubinstein game, arise from their differing attitudes to the unproductive passage of time. The more impatient player has less bargaining power. For simplicity, in the examples that follow, only the symmetric case $\rho_A = \rho_E$ is considered.

8 Gauthier's bargaining model

Gauthier's bargaining model is described in Section 1. I want now to offer an orthodox analysis of his model adapted from a recent paper of Muthoo

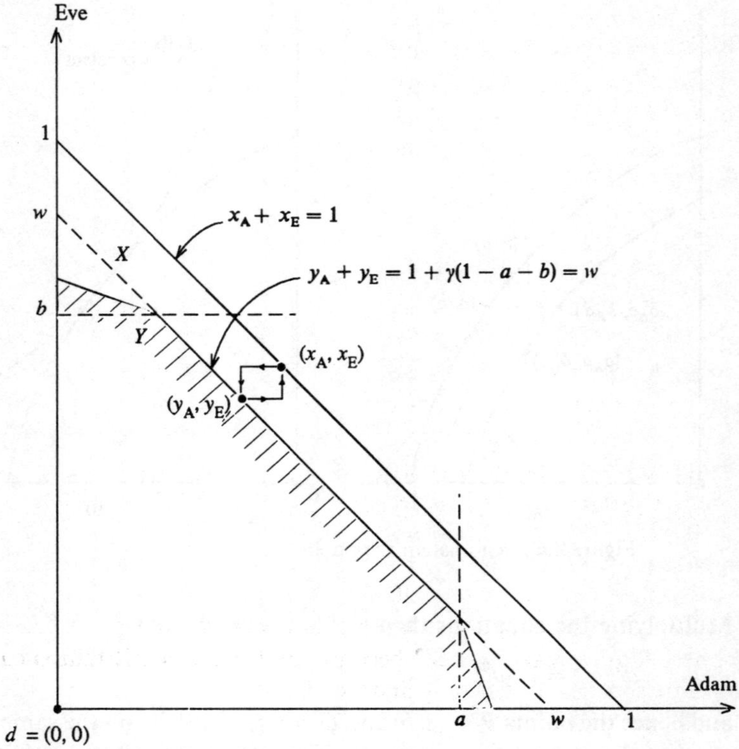

Figure 8.7 Claims and concessions.

(1991). However, before this is possible, it is necessary to fill in some of the gaps that Gauthier leaves to the imagination of the reader. Recall that, in his models, the players begin by simultaneously announcing claims. In this section the claims will be denoted by a and b. Gauthier does not explain why these claims should be relevant to the bargaining that then follows. Rational players would simply ignore the first stage of Gauthier's process unless there were some cost of backing down from an initial claim. Muthoo (1991) introduces such a cost. He assumes that Adam loses $\gamma(a - x)$ utils if he finally agrees to accept $x < a$ and Eve loses $\gamma(b - y)$ utils if she finally agrees to accept $y < b$ utils.

The second gap that needs to be filled is the question of what happens during the bargaining that follows the initial claims. We shall assume that the bargaining follows Rubinstein's procedure and so use the Nash bargaining solution to predict its outcome.

Only the simple case illustrated in Figure 8.7 will be considered. The feasible set X is then the triangle with vertices (0, 0), (0, 1), and (1, 0). The disagreement point is $d = (0, 0)$. The effect of making the claims a and b is to change the shape of the feasible set from X to Y for the bargaining that follows. Figure 8.7 shows the set Y in the case when $a + b > 1$. If there is agreement on (x_A, x_E) in the bargaining with $x_A < a$ and $x_E < b$, then Adam pays $\gamma(a - x_A)$ and Eve pays $\gamma(b - x_E)$. The result is the pair (y_A, y_E) with $y_A = x_A - \gamma(a - x_A)$ and $y_E = x_E - \gamma(b - x_E)$. The locus of such pairs is given by

$$y_A + y_E = (1 + \gamma)(x_A + x_E) - \gamma(a + b) = 1 - \gamma(1 - a - b)$$

When $a > w/2$ and $b > w/2$, the Nash bargaining solution for the problem $(Y, 0)$ is $(w/2, w/2)$, where $w = 1 + \gamma(1 - a - b)$. It follows that Adam's final payoff is a *decreasing* function of a when both a and b are sufficiently large. Adam will therefore certainly *not* want to make a as large as he can in the manner proposed by Gauthier. On the contrary, for each large enough b, he will want to decrease a at least until $a = w/2$. Similarly, Eve will wish to decrease b at least until $b = w/2$.

If $a = b = w/2$, then $a = b = 1/2$. This pair of claims is a Nash equilibrium because the best thing to do when the opponent claims 1/2 is also to claim 1/2 for oneself. We check this only for Adam. We already know that, when $b = 1/2$, Adam will not want to make $a > 1/2$. Nor does it help him to make $a < 1/2$ because the feasible set Z that such a claim creates satisfies $Y \subseteq Z \subseteq X$ and hence the Nash bargaining solution for $(Z, 0)$ remains $(1/2, 1/2)$.

Gauthier may object to such an analysis in various ways. He may argue that he did not intend making concessions to be costly. However, the analysis remains valid for all $\gamma > 0$. We may therefore take the limit as $\gamma \to 0$. He may argue that he did not intend a Rubinstein model to be used for the bargaining. If so, he should suggest an equally plausible alternative. He may argue that alternative Nash equilibria may exist, but Muthoo (1991) shows otherwise. He may argue that the solution (1/2, 1/2) is identical with the Kalai–Smorodinsky solution that he advocates and hence that the analysis actually supports his conclusion. However, the solution remains (1/2, 1/2) even if everything in X to the right of the line $x_A = 3/4$ is discarded, but the Kalai–Smorodinsky solution is then quite different.

9 The Kalai–Smorodinsky solution

(And Ehud said, I have a message – Judges 3:20.) Gauthier would presumably reject the analysis of his model given in Section 8. Instead he argues that a rational analysis leads to the solution illustrated in Figure 8.2, and first proposed by Ehud Kalai and Meir Smorodinsky. Notice that he makes no ethical claims for the Kalai–Smorodinsky solution. This shares with the Nash bargaining solution the property of being independent of utility calibration. It therefore incorporates no inter-personal comparison of utilities and hence has no virtue as an ethical concept.

Gauthier's (p. 133) defence of the Kalai–Smorodinsky solution depends on an idiosyncratic version of the outmoded Zeuthen principle that I do not propose to discuss. But what of Kalai and Smorodinsky's (1975) own defence? They have no bargaining model, only axioms. Nash's *independence of irrelevant alternatives* is replaced by a *monotonicity* axiom (usually now called 'individual monotonicity').

Suppose that the disagreement point u^* and the ideal point u' are left fixed in Figure 8.2, but the feasible set changes so that, for each of Eve's possible utility demands, there will be more left in the new situation for Adam if he concedes the demand than there would have been in the old situation. The monotonicity axiom says that Adam should get more in the new situation than in the old. The grounds are that his bargaining position has improved. But what basis is there for this claim? It is certainly *false* as a general proposition. The Nash and Rubinstein bargaining models provide *counter-examples*.

I know of only one model that implements the Kalai–Smorodinsky solution. This is due to Moulin (1984). Moulin's game requires Adam and Eve to begin by simultaneously naming a probability. The player who wins this auction, by bidding the higher probability p, then gets to propose an outcome s. If the other player assents to this proposal, a referee then organizes a lottery that generates the final result. The lottery yields s with probability p, and the *status quo* d with probability $1 - p$. If the other player refuses, she gets to make a counter-proposal which, if accepted, leads to the same rigmarole as before (with the *same* probability p). If the counter-proposal is refused, d occurs for certain.

Moulin's game has been given in detail to make clear how 'unnatural' its rules are as a bargaining model. Who organized this game and why? Where did the referee come from? And, most importantly, *what constrains the players to obey the rules*?

I am sure Gauthier is right to make the notion of hypothetical bargaining fundamental to a social contract theory. I am also sure that he is right not to confuse the issue by allowing ethical considerations to enter into an analysis of how the bargaining proceeds. After all, the purpose of the bargaining is to *decide* ethical questions. But I see no good reason for not using the orthodox theory in predicting the result of the bargaining process. As I have tried to argue, the orthodox theory is soundly based on models that seek to minimize on the fictions that need to be promulgated, whereas nothing similar can be said for the Kalai–Smorodinsky solution, or for Gauthier's multi-person analogue.

10 Conclusion

This chapter has been a remorseless attack on Gauthier's use of game theory. The reason for writing at length is that I am sure that game theory has much to offer moral philosophy, but there is a risk of its becoming discredited if not used with the utmost care. Fortunately, Gauthier has broad shoulders, and my criticism will leave him undaunted. In any case, I look forward to his criticizing the unconventional philosophy in my planned book *Playing Fair* with the same vigour that I have criticized his game theory. As Samuel Johnson said: 'I dogmatize and am contradicted, and in this conflict of opinions and sentiments I find delight.'

Notes

1. This is a rewrite of 'Social Contract II: Gauthier and Nash', which was to be the second of a seven-paper series on the social contract, of which four papers were written (Binmore 1988, 1989, 1990, 1992) before I realized that a book was necessary to do justice to the subject. The rewrite suppresses references to other papers in the series where possible. The proposed book is to be called *Playing Fair: Game theory and the social contract*. The first chapter, which overviews the theory is available.
2. Gauthier (p. 169) makes it clear that he is not talking about reciprocity in a repeated game. The idea is to be applied in the one-shot case.
3. Adam's payoffs appear in the bottom left of each cell and Eve's payoffs in the top right. I assume that the story that goes with the Prisoner's Dilemma is well known.
4. Perhaps Eve can put Adam in possession of some disgraceful fact about her past that he will reveal if she finks.
5. If her commitments are literally unbreakable, remove the finking choice altogether on the left of Figure 8.3(b).
6. Alekhine is reported as saying, 'Position, what does position matter? It is my will that counts.' To model him as *homo economicus* would therefore be as fruitless as to do the same for the chimpanzee.
7. The formal definitions are: (1) *Closed*: X contains its boundary points; (2) *Bounded above*: there is a vector b such that $x \in X$ implies $x \leqslant b$; (3) *Convex*: if X contains x and y then it contains the line segment joining them; (4) *Comprehensive*: if X contains x and y, then $x \leqslant z \leqslant y$ implies $z \in X$.
8. See also the first paper of Binmore and Dasgupta (1987).
9. For those familiar with Maskin's (1985) *monotonicity*, a preference relation can be defined on $\{x: x > d\}$ as follows. Make Adam indifferent between d and any $x \notin X$ (i.e. any non-feasible payoff pair). If x and y are both in X, make Adam strictly prefer x to y if and only if $x_A > y_A$. Proceed similarly for Eve. With these preferences, the independence of irrelevant alternatives follows from monotonicity.
10. Section 2 does not say that utility scales should not be used: only that they should not be abused.
11. If the choice of incompatible demands led to the payoff pair d, the result would be the same except that $(Y, 0)$ becomes (Y, d). Technical matters are discussed in Binmore and Dasgupta (1987, Chapters 4 and 8).

12. This is a lot of supposing. A more careful discussion is really necessary here.
13. One is not entitled to argue that she would not *want* to accept a 'derisory' offer. She is a maximizer of expected utility by definition. In real life, she might easily turn down a derisory monetary offer in favour of nothing without being irrational. But this would imply that her utility for the latter option was greater in the circumstances of the decision.
14. If Adam is able to make arbitrarily low offers, Eve will actually get nothing at all in *equilibrium.* It cannot be optimal to offer Eve even a tiny amount if she is going to accept half as much. Of course, in real life, goods come in discrete units.
15. See Chapters 3, 5 and 6 of Binmore and Dasgupta (1987), particularly p. 109 for a quick proof for the current special case.

9

Rationality and impartiality: Is the contractarian enterprise possible?[1]

Robert Sugden

'Nature hath made men so equal', Hobbes wrote in a famous passage,

> in the faculties of the body, and mind; as that though there be found one man sometimes manifestly stronger in body, or of quicker mind than another; yet when all is reckoned together, the difference between man, and man, is not so considerable, as that one man can thereupon claim to himself any benefit, to which another may not pretend, as well as he. (1651, Chapter 13)

Hobbes's state of nature, in which every man has a right to every thing, even another's body, is thus a state of rough equality. From this premiss of initial equality, Hobbes deduces his second law of nature:

> that a man be willing, when others are so too, as far-forth, as for peace, and defence of himself he shall think it necessary, to lay down this right to all things; and to be contented with so much liberty against other men, as he would allow other men against himself. (1651, Chapter 14)

Rational men, starting from a position of equality in a state of nature, would agree to a set of principles of mutual and equal restraint. Or so Hobbes claims.

This claim is echoed by many modern contractarians. Contractarians seek to derive principles of morality by analyzing the problem that would be faced by rational individuals in a state of nature. Such individuals, it is argued, would recognize that they could best further their separate interests by agreeing to abide by certain rules, prescribing cooperation and mutual restraint. But what makes these rules moral?

A common answer is to appeal to certain properties that rules of conduct must have in order to qualify for the adjective 'moral'. Foremost among these properties is some form of universality or impartiality: moral rules must require like cases to be treated alike. If it can be shown that rational individuals in a state of nature would agree to follow impartial rules, then contractarianism has generated a system of morality. Some contractarians would add that there should be some correspondence (or 'reflective equilibrium') between the rules generated by the contractarian thought experiment and our pre-theoretical moral convictions.

On one view, which I shall call weak contractarianism, deriving such moral rules is the whole purpose of the exercise. To ensure that the principles agreed are impartial, it is permissible to inject impartiality into the specification of the initial bargaining position. This means that the theory has a moral input as well as a moral output. Locke's (1690) conception of a state of nature governed by natural law is the classic example of this approach. The 'veils of ignorance' that Harsanyi (1955) and Rawls (1971) build into their initial bargaining positions provide other examples.

A more ambitious approach is taken by strong contractarians such as Gauthier who work in the Hobbesian tradition. For such contractarians, the fundamental question is: 'What is it rational to do?' It is essential for the enterprise that it should not start from any moral premisses: the only premisses allowed are those of rational choice. We must then be fearless in following through the implications of these premisses.

The result will be theorems about rational choice. If it turns out that it is rational to abide by self-imposed constraints that are impartial, then we have succeeded in showing that it is rational to be moral. This, of course, is what Gauthier claims to be able to show. But if instead we find that partiality or non-cooperation is rational, we must bite the bullet.

Common to both traditions is the idea that rational bargaining from a fair initial position will generate impartial rules. Weak contractarians deliberately construct the initial position so that it is fair; strong contractarians (like Hobbes in the passage I quoted, arguing that there will be rough equality in the state of nature) provide non-moral reasons why the initial position will be fair in the relevant sense.

I wish to dissent from this conclusion. I shall argue that rational bargaining, even from an initial position of equality, does not guarantee the kind of impartial outcomes that contractarians typically suppose it does. Rational bargaining is necessarily dependent on mutual expectations. There are many possible sets of mutual expectations, any one of which could be held by rational bargainers in a position of initial equality. Some of these lead to equal bargains, some to unequal ones. Contractarianism, therefore, cannot generate a uniquely impartial code of morality. If contractarian reasoning can generate any moral conclusion at all, it must be that morality is, in important respects, a matter of convention. Or to put this another way: contractarian reasoning leads not to morality, but to norms.

1 Bargaining games

Gauthier's *Morals by Agreement* represents modern contractarianism in its most fully developed and uncompromising form. I shall use this book as my principal exhibit of contractarian argument, although later in the chapter I shall discuss the rather different approach of Rawls's *A Theory of Justice* (1971).

Gauthier tries to show that it is rational to abide by certain self-imposed constraints of impartiality. His argument for this conclusion involves two stages. First he presents a theory of rational bargaining for any set of individuals who start out with a given baseline of entitlements but who are in a position to generate a cooperative surplus (that is, a surplus that comes into existence only if they all agree to cooperate). The theory prescribes how this surplus will be divided between the bargainers. At this stage it is assumed that any agreement made will be enforced. Then Gauthier relaxes the assumption of enforcement, and argues that it will be rational for individuals to comply with their agreements if and only if bargaining begins from an essentially Lockean system of natural rights. Since there is no point in making agreements unless people can be expected to comply with them, this implies that rational individuals will recognize these natural rights as the baseline for bargaining.

My concern is with the first stage of this argument. Gauthier's theory of bargaining implies that the cooperative surplus will be divided according to a principle of 'minimax relative concession'. Although this principle is justified in terms of rationality, it corresponds fairly closely with some common intuitions about fairness or impartiality. This correspondence is crucial for Gauthier's claim to be able to show that it is rational to be moral. I wish to challenge Gauthier's argument at this point. My objection is not just to Gauthier's own theory of bargaining, but to any theory that claims to derive a unique and impartial division of a cooperative surplus from the assumption that the bargainers are equally rational.

Gauthier uses a model of bargaining that derives from Nash (1951): I shall call it the Nash bargaining game. To keep things simple, I shall consider the case of just two bargainers. The bargaining game is described in terms of the utilities of the two players. There is an 'initial bargaining position', representing the utilities the players would achieve if they failed to reach agreement. Then there is a set of possible outcomes, any one of which could be achieved were the players so to agree. This set is assumed to be closed, bounded and convex in utility space.

Gauthier does not specify the rules of his bargaining game beyond this, although he insists that 'bargaining is cost free, in terms of both utility and time' (p. 156) – which leaves it unclear why the players ever reach agreement at all. In not specifying the rules of the game in any detail,

Gauthier is following a precedent set by Nash and by other contributors to the theory of cooperative games. But as Nash (1953) himself recognized, any bargaining game must in principle be capable of being fully described in terms of strategies and outcomes, with each player independently choosing a strategy (that is, a complete plan specifying how he will play in every possible contingency) and the chosen strategies jointly determining the outcome for each player. In appraising Gauthier's bargaining theory, it is useful to have in mind some particular specification of the rules of the game.

I suggest the following formulation, which seems to be in the spirit of Gauthier's analysis. The two players are allowed a fixed time in which to negotiate. Negotiating during this period is costless. At the end of this period, each player must simultaneously make a final claim. This is the level of utility that each demands. If these claims are compatible – that is, if taken together they represent one of the possible outcomes of the game – then each gets what he has claimed. If the claims are incompatible, each remains in the initial bargaining position. In the theoretical sense, this game is non-cooperative. Each player independently chooses a strategy – the level of his final claim – and the strategies chosen by the two players jointly determine the outcome of the game for each of them. Although the players can discuss the game with one another before choosing their strategies (this is the significance of the period of negotiation), they cannot bind themselves to choose particular strategies. Nor is there any external mechanism to enforce any agreement they might make about the strategies they will play.

Although very simple, this game captures something of the flavour of real bargaining. If in the process of discussion the players reach agreement about their final claims, it is in each player's interest to keep to the agreement provided he expects the other to do so. Thus it is possible for the players to reach a meaningful agreement during the negotiation period. But the game also allows for the possibility of deadlock: the two players might hold out for incompatible claims. This allows us to pose the question of whether fully rational players could fail to agree. Pe!rhaps, as Gauthier claims, they could never fail to agree, but in order to show this we need a model in which players who were not fully rational could be deadlocked.

I shall often find it convenient to consider a special case of this game, which I shall call the Division Game. In the division game, two players A and B with identical utility functions have to agree on how to divide one unit of some good between themselves. The marginal utility of the good is constant for each player. This allows us to measure utility in the same unit as the good. Then the initial bargaining position is (0, 0): if the players fail to agree, each gets a utility of zero. The set of possible outcomes contains all combinations of utility (u_A, u_B) for which $u_A, u_B \geq 0$ and

$u_A + u_B \leq 1$. The usefulness of this game is that it allows us to sidestep what Gauthier calls the 'infighting among bargaining theorists' (p. 146) over the merits of their various criteria for identifying rational solutions for bargaining games: for reasons that will emerge later, these criteria all point to the same solution for the division game.

2 Rationality in games

Gauthier's argument depends on his showing that the bargaining problems he analyzes have what I shall call uniquely rational solutions. By this I mean the following. Suppose a game is described in a purely formal way, in terms of the logical structure of its rules and the utility functions of its players. Any other information which might be used to label the players or their strategies, or to put the game in a social or historical context, is suppressed. We suppose the players to be perfectly rational, with rationality being defined according to the axioms of expected utility theory. (For the purposes of this chapter I shall leave to one side the question of whether these axioms really are necessary properties of rational preferences.) Further, we suppose the rules of the game and the rationality of the players to be matters of common belief. That is, each player believes the other players to be rational, believes that each of them believes that every other player is rational, and so on. We treat the game as a one-off interaction between people who have no previous experience of playing it. Then if these assumptions imply a particular choice for each player, the game has a uniquely rational solution.

Gauthier starts from the following three 'conditions for strategically rational choice':

A: Each person's choice must be a rational response to the choices she expects the others to make.

B: Each person must expect every other person's choice to satisfy condition A.

C: Each person must believe her choice and expectations to be reflected in the expectations of every other person. (p. 61)

Conditions A and B are unexceptionable, given the assumption of perfect rationality on the part of the players. A rational player must form some expectation about what her opponents will do, and then do the best she can in the light of those expectations. And if she knows that her opponents are rational, she must expect them to do the same. Condition C, however, is less obviously compelling. What this condition is saying is that if a player is going to choose some strategy, it must be a matter of common belief that this is what she will choose, and that if she forms some expectation about another player, it must be a matter of common belief that this is what she expects.

Explaining Condition C, Gauthier says that in the ideal case he is considering, the structure of the game and the utilities the players derive from the various outcomes are common knowledge. 'But then', he goes on, 'each person's reasoning from these data to his own expectations and choices must be accessible to every other person. In effect individual choice must emerge from common reasoning' (p. 60). And again: each player 'believes that her reasoning about interaction replicates, and is replicated by, everyone else's reasoning' (p. 61). The idea, then, is that ideally rational players can replicate one another's reasoning and hence that each must be able to work out what the others will expect and choose.

It is clear that if a rational player's analysis of the structure of the game leads her to the conclusion that a particular choice is uniquely rational, then she must know that other rational players can replicate her reasoning. The same must apply to any expectation that she can reach by rational analysis. So if we could assume that rational analysis was always determinate in this way – that is, if we could assume that every game had a uniquely rational solution – we should be entitled to impose Condition C. I shall call this assumption the principle of *rational determinacy*. Lying behind Condition C, I suggest, is Gauthier's belief in rational determinacy. But is this belief well founded?

The principle of rational determinacy is very powerful. To see why, just suppose we could prove it was valid. We might be able to prove this without being able to identify the uniquely rational solution for every game. (Take an analogy: we know that in chess, one of the following must be true: either White can force a win, or Black can force a win, or either player can force a draw. So we know that chess would have no interest for perfectly rational players: the result of every game would be a foregone conclusion. Fortunately for those of us who enjoy chess, however, we do not know how perfectly rational players would play.) Merely knowing that every game had a uniquely rational solution might allow us to identify such solutions for some particular games. Suppose we draw up a list of necessary conditions for uniquely rational solutions. This list need not be exhaustive: it simply gives a number of conditions that we can be sure are necessary. Then, for any given game, we can eliminate all those solutions that fail to satisfy one or more of these conditions. If only one solution remains, we know that this is uniquely rational – if, that is, we know that every game has a uniquely rational solution.

This type of argument was used by von Neumann and Morgenstern (1947, pp. 146–8) in support of the maximin solution for zero-sum games. The same argument can be used in relation to Nash equilibrium. A Nash equilibrium is a combination of strategies, one for each player, such that each player's strategy is optimal for him, given the strategies of the others. Now suppose we can prove that every game has a uniquely rational solution. If we can prove this, so too can perfectly rational players. This implies that perfectly rational players will be able to predict one another's strategies. But a rational player must choose a strategy that is optimal for him, given his beliefs about his opponents. Thus perfectly rational players must choose strategies that are in Nash equilibrium with one another. So Nash equilibrium is a necessary condition for a uniquely rational solution. Looking for Nash equilibria can thus be thought of as a way of drawing up a shortlist of candidates for the position of 'uniquely rational solution'. Gauthier presents almost precisely this argument, showing that it is an implication of Conditions A, B and C that rational players must choose strategies that are in Nash equilibrium with one another (p. 65).

Here Gauthier is being quite conventional: game theorists generally assume that perfectly rational players in one-off games will choose Nash equilibrium strategies. Thus if a game has a unique Nash equilibrium, it is treated as uncontroversial that this equilibrium would be reached by rational play. But it is hard to see how this practice can be justified, other than by assuming that every game has a uniquely rational solution. In this sense, then, the principle of rational determinacy is implicitly used throughout the theory of games. But this is not to say that it is valid.

Another necessary property of uniquely rational solutions is the following: the uniquely rational solution of a symmetrical game must itself be symmetrical. Consider any game in which the positions of the players are completely symmetrical. Then if rational analysis can show one player that he must choose a particular strategy, it must show the same thing to the other players. So in the case of a symmetrical game, the only candidates for the position of 'uniquely rational solution' are symmetrical Nash equilibria.

In the Nash tradition of bargaining theory, it is conventional to impose an axiom that requires symmetrical games to have symmetrical solutions. Nash (1950) explicitly states a symmetry axiom of this kind. So too do Kalai and Smorodinsky (1975), whose solution to the two-person Nash bargaining game is identical with Gauthier's. Gauthier regards symmetry as an implication of his assumption that the bargainers are equally rational: 'Since each person, as a utility-maximizer, seeks to minimize his concession, then no one can expect any other rational person to be willing to make a concession if he would not be willing to make a similar concession' (pp. 143–4). In a symmetrical game, therefore, the concessions made in reaching agreement must be symmetrical; and this guarantees a symmetrical solution. Given what I take to be his acceptance of the principle of rational determinacy, Gauthier is entirely consistent in insisting on symmetry as well as Nash equilibrium.

The force of these two conditions for uniquely rational solutions can be seen by applying them to the division game. The only pure-strategy Nash equilibria in this game are those in which the players claim u_A and u_B where $0 \leq u_A, u_B \leq 1$ and $u_A + u_B = 1$, that is, in which the players' claims exactly exhaust the good. To see why, notice that if one player claims some proportion s of the good, the best reply for his opponent is to claim $1 - s$, and vice versa. But the mathematical structure of the division game is completely symmetrical between the players. So if we invoke the symmetry condition, we can restrict ourselves to symmetrical solutions. The only pure-strategy solution that is both symmetrical and a Nash equilibrium is the one in which $u_A = u_B = 0.5$, that is, in which the bargainers agree to divide the good equally.

Aficionados of game theory will have noticed the qualification about pure-strategy equilibrium. The division game has many symmetrical mixed-strategy equilibria. For example, it is an equilibrium if each player claims one-quarter of the good with probability one-third and three-quarters with probability two-thirds. But all of these equilibria are strictly Pareto-inferior to the equal-division solution. In general, of course, we have no reason to expect uniquely rational solutions to be Pareto-efficient (think of the Prisoner's Dilemma). However, the present case has two significant features. First, the players are allowed to discuss their strategies before playing them. (Recall that this is one of the rules of the division game.) Second, the equal-division solution is a strict Nash equilibrium: if one player expects the other to claim a half-share, it is uniquely rational for the first player to claim a half-share too. Thus an agreement to go for an equal division – unlike an agreement to cooperate in the Prisoner's Dilemma – would be self-enforcing. Given this, we may conclude that none of the mixed-strategy equilibria is the uniquely rational solution to the division game.

Notice what is proved by this line of argument. It does not show that an equal division is the uniquely rational solution to the division game: it shows only that if there is a uniquely rational solution, this is what it must be. This is the result that lies at the core of Gauthier's (and Nash's) bargaining theory. It encapsulates the sense in which the outcome of rational bargaining is impartial. But it is an empty theorem unless we can prove that bargaining games have uniquely rational solutions.

3 Do all games have uniquely rational solutions?

It is tempting to think that every game must have a uniquely rational solution – that if every detail of a game is common knowledge between perfectly rational players, rational analysis must be capable of prescribing what each should do. But, I wish to argue, this is not the case.

Consider the Battle of the Sexes Game shown in Table 9.1. This is a simple game of coordination. Each player benefits from choosing the same strategy (i.e. 'left' or 'right') as his opponent does, but the players have opposing preferences between the two alternative ways in which they could coordinate: A prefers that they both choose 'left' while B prefers that they both choose 'right'. This game is of particular interest in relation to contractarian arguments because it can be interpreted as a simple model of bargaining. (We may think of the two players trying to reach agreement. There are two sets of terms on which they might settle: 'left', which favours A, or 'right', which favours B. If they fail to agree – that is, if one chooses 'left' and the other 'right' – both are worse off than under the terms of either possible agreement.)

Table 9.1 The battle of the sexes.

		player B's strategy	
		left	right
player A's	right	0, 0	2, 3
strategy	left	3, 2	0, 0

This game has three Nash equilibria. In one equilibrium, both play 'left'; in the second, both play 'right'; in the third, A plays 'left' with probability 0.6 and 'right' with probability 0.4 while B plays 'left' with probability 0.4 and 'right' with probability 0.6. If the game has a uniquely rational solution, it must be one of these equilibria.

Notice that the game is entirely symmetrical apart from the labelling of the players and strategies. Thus if there is a uniquely rational solution, it must be a symmetrical one. We must therefore conclude that neither the Nash equilibrium in which both players play 'left', nor the equilibrium in which they both play 'right', can be uniquely rational. (Whatever reason could be given for the rationality of one could also be given for the rationality of the other.) This leaves us with the mixed-strategy equilibrium, which is symmetrical. But how could this solution be uniquely rational? What reason can we give to show player A that he must choose 'left' with probability 0.6 and 'right' with probability 0.4? As an expected-utility maximizer, A must choose whichever of 'left' or 'right' leads to the higher expected utility, given his beliefs about what B will do. The only case in which it could be rational for A to choose a mixed strategy is that in which 'left' and 'right' lead to exactly the same expected utility; and then any probability-mix of 'left' and 'right' is as good as any other. There simply are no beliefs that A could hold that would make a 0.6:0.4 mixed strategy uniquely optimal.

This is a well-known problem in game theory, and Gauthier recognizes its significance. He rejects the possibility of concluding that such games do not have uniquely rational solutions. Revealing his attachment to the principle of rational determinacy, he says he is 'unwilling to leave rational choice undefined' for situations like these (p. 70). His principal response to the problem is the following argument:

> A person may be genuinely indifferent among several strategies given his expectations. But these expectations may themselves reflect the choice of one and only one of the strategies among which he is indifferent. He must then choose that strategy in order to sustain his expectations. (p. 70)

Applying this argument to the battle of the sexes game, suppose A believes that B will play 'left' with probability 0.4. Then A is 'genuinely indifferent' between 'left' and 'right'. But (Gauthier seems to be saying) A cannot rationally hold this belief unless it is 'reflected' in his own choice. That is, A cannot believe that B will play 'left' with probability 0.4 without also believing that this is an optimal response by B, not just to what B believes A will choose, but also to what A actually will choose. So A must play 'left' with probability 0.6 because this is the only choice that will confirm the expectations that A believes B holds: this must be what Gauthier means by sustaining one's expectations.

This argument has some similarities with the argument for opening just one box in Newcomb's problem – and, I think, to involve the same error. B's choice is causally independent of A's. So A cannot use the supposition that his choice will be 'reflected' in B's as a reason for choosing in a particular way. If, after careful reflection, A comes to the conclusion that B will play 'left' with probability 0.4, then it really does not matter to A which strategy he chooses: by choosing to play 'left' with probability 0.6 he cannot make his belief about B any more likely to be true. The correct conclusion to draw, I suggest, is this: the supposition that the battle of the sexes game has a uniquely rational solution generates a contradiction. It must therefore be false. More generally, the principle of rational determinacy – the principle that every game has a uniquely rational solution – is false.

This is not to deny that some games have uniquely rational solutions. In the Prisoner's Dilemma, for example, it is uniquely rational for each player to defect. This follows from the fact that for each player, defection is a strictly dominant strategy: whatever one player's expectations about the other may be, it pays him to defect. This must be a sufficient reason for a utility-maximizing player to defect in a one-off game. My point is this: to show that a particular solution is uniquely rational, we must show why it is rational for each player to play in the relevant way. We may not simply assume that a uniquely rational solution exists, and then use this assumption to help us identify a particular solution as uniquely rational.

What does it mean to say that some games lack uniquely rational solutions? The implication is that there can be circumstances in which a person has to act, but cannot find rational grounds for choosing one action rather than another. Equally, a person may (in order to choose rationally according to the principles of expected utility theory) have to attach probabilities to various contingencies, but be unable to find rational grounds for using one probability rather than another.

Gauthier seems to think that ideally rational people would never find themselves in this position. Looking for a principle for determining rational expectations, he says: 'One may not form expectations about others' choices simply at will.' There must, he implies, be some way in which rational persons can ground their expectations (p. 71). I agree that we cannot will our expectations. But this does not mean that we can always arrive at our expectations by rational analysis. Perhaps some expectations are necessarily subjective, in much the same way that tastes are. Tastes are typically not the product of rational analysis, but neither are they things we can will. You and I may be rational, and our rationality may be common knowledge, but I may be unable to discover your tastes by replicating your reasoning processes. (If we were identical, of course, I would be able to discover your tastes by introspection about my own: it would not matter whether or not your tastes were in some way rationally grounded. But the ideally rational persons of game theory are not meant to be identical – except in respect of their rationality.) For much the same reasons, I suggest, there can be circumstances in which we are unable to discover one another's expectations by rational analysis.

4 Experience

Does this mean that reason cannot guide us in problems of strategic interaction? No, because I have been discussing only a very special type of problem – that of one-off games. These problems have the property that we cannot be guided by experience in choosing what to do. I want to suggest that it is experience that allows rational players to ground their expectations and to escape from the infinite regressions of reasoning that bedevil one-off games.

Consider the concept of Nash equilibrium. This can be interpreted as a system of self-confirming beliefs: in Nash equilibrium, each player's beliefs about his opponent make it optimal for him to act in a way that confirms his opponent's beliefs about him. In a one-off game, I have argued, the fact that a particular set of beliefs is self-confirming is no reason for anyone to hold them. (Why should I care whether my action confirms your beliefs about me?) But if a game is played repeatedly, only self-confirming beliefs will survive. Imagine a large population from which pairs of individuals are repeatedly drawn by some random process and made to play some game. Then each individual can use his experience of the game when forming his beliefs about the actions of future opponents.

The argument that follows depends on the assumption that games are anonymous, so that each person remembers only his experience of playing the game against opponents in general, but not how he has fared against particular individuals. Or, equivalently, it has to be assumed that the population is so large that the probability of meeting the same opponent twice is vanishingly small. This is very different from the kind of repetition that occurs when the same two individuals play a sequence of games against one another. In particular, anonymous play implies that no one can hope to build any kind of individual reputation for playing the game in a particular way. I realize that the assumption of anonymous play is a strong one. My hunch is that we could relax it quite a lot and still derive much the same conclusions; but I cannot prove this.

As a first example, consider a pure coordination game – say, Rule of the Road. This is the simple game faced by two drivers who are approaching each other on a narrow road which is just wide enough for their vehicles to pass. Each must either steer to the left or steer to the right. If both steer left, or if both steer right, they pass each other. If one steers left and the other steers right, they don't. Suppose someone has played rule of the road many times and in every case his opponent has chosen 'left'. Then surely it must be rational for him to believe there is a high probability that any future opponent will play 'left' too. Given this belief, it will pay him to play 'left', thus providing his opponent with further evidence of the prevalence of left-playing behaviour in the population. So the 'steer left' rule is self-sustaining. The underlying idea here is that of an evolutionarily stable equilibrium. This concept of equilibrium was developed by theoretical biologists to explain the genetic evolution of animal behaviour (see Maynard Smith, 1982), but it can be adapted so as to explain the evolution of social conventions among rational human beings (Axelrod, 1981; Sugden, 1986).

Among a population of players with a shared experience of playing a game, stable patterns of expectations – or conventions – can evolve, such that it becomes rational for each person to hold these expectations and to act in a way that sustains these expectations in others. (This latter effect, of course, is not intended: it is just a by-product of rational choice.) Such a pattern of expectations will be a Nash equilibrium. If it is to persist, it must also have certain properties of evolutionary stability. But must the expectations associated with a symmetrical game be symmetrical? In the case of rule of the road, which is a symmetrical game, the 'steer left' and 'steer right' equilibria each treat the two players symmetrically (although they do not treat the two strategies symmetrically). But now consider the division game.

If the division game is played repeatedly within a population, a stable pattern of expectations can evolve. But provided there is some asymmetry between the players – however trivial, and however unrelated to the mathematical structure of the game – there can be stable expectations that do not involve equal claims. Suppose, for example, that the structure of the division game is exactly the same whatever the gender of the players. Thus the logical structure of the game is symmetrical even if one player is a man and the other a woman. But suppose that everyone expects that in a male–female encounter, the man will claim two-thirds of the good and the woman one-third. (In a same-gender encounter, let us say, each player is expected to claim a half.) These expectations are self-confirming. In a male–female encounter, the man expects the woman to claim one-third; given this expectation, it is rational for him to claim two-thirds. The woman expects the man to claim two-thirds; given this expectation, it is rational for her to claim one-third. So each acts in a way that confirms the other's expectation.

Is such a convention consistent with the assumption that the players are equally (and perfectly) rational? Gauthier would say 'No', because only an equal division satisfies his principle of minimax relative concession. Recall how he justifies this principle: 'Since each person, as a utility-maximizer, seeks to minimize his concession, then no one can expect any other rational person to be willing to make a concession if he would not be willing to make a similar concession.' And: 'No rational person can be willing to make unnecessary, or unnecessarily large, concessions' (pp. 144–5). In my example, the woman makes a concession that is twice as large as the man's. Nevertheless, the man can quite rationally expect the woman to concede so much. It is common knowledge that they both have experience of playing the game, and that this experience has shown both of them that in male–female encounters, men invariably claim two-thirds and woman one-third. This provides the man with a reason to expect the women to claim one-third. Had their common experience been the opposite – had it been their experience that women invariably claimed two-thirds and men one-third – the man would have responded in the way he expects the woman to do. So there is no conflict with the assumption of equal rationality: the man is not expecting the woman to make a concession that he, in similar circumstances, would not make. Nor is the woman making an unnecessarily large concession. Given her well-grounded expectation that the man will claim two-thirds, she is conceding no more than rationality requires. Gauthier is simply presupposing that an 'irrelevant' asymmetry like gender cannot have significance for rational bargainers.

Many readers, I am sure, will feel uncomfortable with this analysis, even if they find the corresponding analysis of rule of the road unexceptionable. In the case of rule of the road, there are two possible conventions – 'steer left' and 'steer right'. These are equally good from everyone's point of view. It is an arbitrary accident of history that British drivers steer left rather than right, but no unfairness is involved. In contrast, it is unfair for men consistently to get more than women, merely because they are men.

But remember that what we are considering is what it is rational for bargainers to do, not what is fair. The purpose of this paper is to ask whether rational bargaining from an initial position of equality must necessarily produce impartial results. If the example is correct, the answer to the question must be that rationality does not guarantee impartiality: it is possible for rational bargainers to agree on unfair outcomes. This is not to say that unfair bargains are good.

Many people have suggested to me that if a convention systematically favours one group of people at the expense of another, some individuals in the disfavoured group will refuse to go along with the convention in an effort to change it. But notice that what is at issue here is whether it would be rational to behave in this way, when 'rationality' is defined in terms of the efficient pursuit of individual interests. The whole point of contractarian theory is to derive moral principles from such an instrumental conception of rationality. From a Kantian point of view, for example, it would indeed be irrational to acquiesce in unfair conventions; but if we can accept a Kantian conception of rationality we have no need for contractarianism (cf. Gauthier's remarks on Kantian reasoning (pp. 6–7)).

Given an instrumental view of rationality, it will rarely be rational for an individual to challenge a well-established convention. Consider any convention that is a strict Nash equilibrium (for example, the rule 'Men claim two-thirds, women claim one-third' in the division game). Considering any game in isolation, rationality clearly requires each player to behave exactly as she believes her opponent expects her to behave: unilateral deviations from conventions are irrational. (In the case of the division game, suppose B believes that A expects her to claim only one-third. Then B must expect A to claim two-thirds. So rationality requires B to claim one-third, thus confirming what she believes to be A's expectations.) We should, of course, also consider the long-run benefits that would accrue to any member of the disfavoured group if the unfair convention were to collapse and be replaced by a fair one. But there is a free-rider problem here: when an individual challenges a convention, the benefits of this action (the weakening of the convention) are spread among all members of the disfavoured group while the costs fall only on the individual who makes the challenge.

Does it make a difference if, as in my formulation of the division game, the players are allowed to discuss the game with one another before choosing their strategies? To answer this question, we must ask what rational players could usefully say to one another. We know that when it comes to making final claims, each player must make whatever claim she believes her opponent expects her to make. Being rational, the players must know this too. So if discussion is to serve any purpose, each player must try to change her opponent's expectations about her.

Suppose I am playing you. There is an unfair but well-established convention that favours you. You come to the game expecting me to follow this convention, and so you are planning to follow it too. How am I to dislodge your expectation about me? Your expectation is grounded in your experience of opponents who have invariably followed the convention. If you tell me that this has been your experience, I cannot credibly claim not to believe you. Nor can I credibly deny that my experience has also been of opponents who follow the convention. If I am to make any progress, I must convince you that our common experience is irrelevant, that somehow the game we are playing now is different from all those other games we have played in the past. I may say that the difference is that in this case you are hearing my arguments for coordinating on the fair solution. But this is empty unless I can produce some new argument that you have not heard before.

In trying to persuade you to ignore your experience, I am trying to persuade you to treat your game with me as a one-off interaction. The problem is that this one-off game has no uniquely rational solution, and that any attempt to construct a deductively rational argument for one solution rather than another will collapse in an infinite regress of reasoning. In a one-off version of the division game, the best that each of us can do is to identify some solution that is especially 'prominent' or 'salient'. A salient solution somehow sticks out or suggests itself as a focal point for coordination by virtue of some property that both players can recognize, can expect each other to recognize, and so on (Schelling (1960), Sugden (1986, Chapters 3 and 5)). There must be something common to the two players with which the salient solution can connect. Usually what is common is experience: when a rational player is guided by experience in predicting the behaviour of a rational opponent, he is making use of a particular form of salience. Playing the division game, neither of us has any option but to search around for a solution that is salient, and a particularly 'natural' (that is, particularly salient) place to start is with our common experience of how analogous problems have been resolved before. So in trying to persuade you to ignore your experience, I start out at a disadvantage: our common experience just is a source of ideas of salience. Whatever I may say, you know that I know this. The best I can do is to try to persuade you to look for some other form of salience.

Could a common standard of fairness provide an alternative focal point? Clearly, it could. If it is a matter of common belief between us that a fifty-fifty division is the fair solution – or even that most people believe a fifty-fifty division to be fair – then that solution does have a special prominence. (This is not, of course, to say that it will always be perceived to be the most prominent solution: common experience is relevant too.) But a contractarian cannot use such an argument. The whole point of the contractarian enterprise is to derive principles of fairness from an analysis of rational bargaining. We cannot presuppose a particular, non-contractarian principle of fairness and then feed that in to the bargainers' rational calculations.

5 Is the contractarian enterprise possible?

I have argued that bargaining problems typically do not have uniquely rational solutions. Rational bargainers, starting out from an initial position of equality, may agree to unequal divisions of their cooperative surplus. Rationality does not guarantee impartiality. Where does this leave the contractarian enterprise?

Recall the distinction I made at the beginning of this chapter, between weak and strong contractarianism. Weak contractarians try to derive impartial moral principles from an analysis of rational bargaining, starting from a fair initial position or state of nature. If the argument of this chapter is correct, this enterprise cannot succeed. When individuals interact strategically with one another, each person's rational choices must be based on expectations about other people's choices. There can be many patterns of expectations, each of which is self-confirming: once one of these patterns becomes established, it becomes rational for everyone to act in a way that sustains the pattern. Among the patterns of expectations that can be self-sustaining are some that lack the impartiality that would qualify them to be called moral; but these expectations are no less rational than the impartial ones.

It might be objected that unequal agreements cannot result unless there are some asymmetries in the expectations of the bargainers, and that in this case, some people must be unfairly disadvantaged in the initial position. If, for example, there is a common expectation that women will settle on less favourable terms than men, mustn't this be the product of a common experience of inequality between the sexes? If the initial position were truly fair, it may be said, it would not be contaminated with the residue of past unfairness.

But how, then, are we to construct a fair initial position? If we make it part of the definition of the original position that the bargainers already have a common experience of abiding by moral principles, contractarian reasoning becomes circular. The only alternative seems to be to require that the past casts no shadow at all, that it is as if the bargainers' experience had been totally erased. But this takes us back to classical game theory, and to the attempt to ground expectations in rational analysis alone. I have argued that this attempt cannot succeed. If experience is erased, rationality has nothing on which to grip.

There is a way out of this problem for the weak contractarian, but it has heavy costs. This is the route taken by Rawls.

In Rawls's 'original position', the contracting parties are not allowed to know their gender, race, class or natural talents, or any other facts about themselves as individuals: the only facts they know are about people in general (Rawls, 1971, p. 137). At first sight, this veil of ignorance may seem no more than a way of dramatizing a particular view about the fairness of initial endowments. For example, Rawls holds that because no one deserves his natural talents, the distribution of talents should be regarded as a common asset (pp. 101–2). On this view, a fair starting point for bargaining must have the property that everyone has an equal claim on the product of everyone's talents. The veil of ignorance, which prevents the contracting parties from knowing their own talents, seems to be a way of imposing this property on the original position.

However, as Rawls points out, the veil of ignorance has a much more drastic effect:

> since the differences among the parties are unknown to them, and everyone is equally rational and similarly situated, each is convinced by the same arguments. Therefore, we can view the choice in the original position from the standpoint of one person selected at random. If anyone after due reflection prefers a conception of justice to another, then they all do, and a unanimous agreement can be reached. . .
>
> Thus there follows the very important consequence that the parties have no basis for bargaining in the usual sense. No one knows his situation in society nor his natural assets, and therefore no one is in a position to tailor principles to his advantage. We might imagine that one of the contractees threatens to hold out unless the others agree to principles favourable to him. But how does he know which principles are especially in his interests? (pp. 139–40)

Notice the difference between this and Gauthier's argument that the outcomes of symmetrical bargaining games must be symmetrical. Gauthier's bargainers know who they are, and so we can make sense of the idea that one of them might demand more favourable terms than he is prepared to concede to the others. Gauthier then tries to show that if the bargainers' preferences and endowments are the same, and if they are equally rational, such a demand cannot rationally be made (since a rational opponent would not concede to it). This is the argument that I have questioned. Rawls, in contrast, sets up his original position so that the idea of demanding differentially favourable terms has no meaning. Such a demand would have to be made on behalf of some person or class of persons in the society beyond the veil of ignorance, and the contracting party making the demand must know that this is the person he will be, or that this is a class to which he will belong. And this is precisely the kind of knowledge that the veil of ignorance is designed to hide.

Thus, I suggest, Rawls is entitled to claim that his form of contractarianism generates unique and impartial principles. But he has to pay a high price for this.

It is a recurring theme in *A Theory of Justice* that society should be viewed as a 'voluntary scheme' (p. 13), as a form of 'social cooperation among equals for mutual advantage' (p. 14), as a 'system of cooperation designed to advance the good of its members' (p. 178). This contractarian vision is contrasted with that offered by utilitarianism, in which there can be no assurance that social arrangements work to everyone's benefit. In a utilitarian society, some people may have to 'forgo advantages for the sake of the greater good of the whole' (p. 177); 'the violation of the liberty of a few might be made right by the greater good shared by many' (p. 26). It is Rawls's rejection of this feature of utilitarianism that lies behind his famous remark that utilitarianism does not take seriously the distinction between persons (p. 27).

In a contractarian theory such as Gauthier's, in which the bargainers know their identities, it is quite clear that what will be agreed will be a system of cooperation for mutual advantage. If (as Gauthier and other contractarians assume) the bargainers are motivated by their own interests, then no one will agree to sacrifice his own interests for the greater good of others. Perhaps the benefits of cooperation will not be shared equally, but at least everyone must get some share. But as soon as we lower Rawls's veil of ignorance, we have to recognize the possibility that the contracting parties will agree to sacrifice the interests of some people for the greater good of others. Since the contracting parties do not know their identities, each may gamble on finding himself one of the people who share in the greater good and not one of those whose interests have been sacrificed. To put this another way, Rawls's argument that choice in the original position can be viewed from the standpoint of any one person comes uncomfortably close to the utilitarian concept of the impartial spectator. And the impartial spectator, for Rawls, is the personification of the error of not taking seriously the distinction between persons (pp. 26–7).

Rawls, of course, argues that his contracting parties will choose according to the maximin criterion. This leads to principles of justice that do take seriously the distinction between persons, and that are in this sense recognizably contractarian. Nevertheless, this feature of Rawls's theory must be regarded as the result of the particular and controversial position he takes on rational choice under uncertainty. The deep structure of the theory – the idea of choice in the original position – is not contractarian in the same sense that this can be said of the theories of Hobbes or Locke or Gauthier.

So far I have considered the implications of my argument for the weak form of contractarianism in which the initial bargaining position is characterized in moral terms. Strong contractarians, in contrast, want to find out what rules would be agreed by rational people who consulted only their own interests. We might hope that this enquiry will show the rationality of impartial rules, but showing this is not its purpose. Having committed ourselves to the enquiry, we must accept the way the chips fall. On this view, we cannot make it a matter of decree that the bargainers do not know the facts about themselves that would allow them to try to hold out for principles that work to their individual advantage. Nor can we decree that all experience of previous interaction is erased from their memories. The object is to show what is rational for real people in the real world.

My conclusion is that we cannot show that impartial rules are uniquely rational. Rational bargainers will choose their strategies using expectations about one another that are grounded in their common experience. This common experience may be of conventions that divide the fruits of cooperation unequally, and in ways that seem morally arbitrary. Nevertheless, it can be rational for each person to expect every other person to continue to follow such a convention; and hence it can be rational for each to follow the convention herself. This may be unfair, but it is not irrational.

Note

1. This chapter was previously published as 'Contractarianism and norms' in *Ethics*, vol. 100 (July 1990), pp. 768–86; 0014-1704/90/004-0010$01.00. I thank the editors of *Ethics* for permission to reprint it.

   I presented earlier versions of this paper to: a conference on 'Rationality and Moral Choice' in Munich in December 1988; to an *Ethics* symposium on norms at the University of Chicago in May 1989; and to a seminar at Nuffield College, Oxford in July 1989. I am grateful to the participants at these meetings for their comments, and in particular to Richard Arneson, Bruce Coram, Alan Hamlin and Susan Hurley.

10

Uniting separate persons

David Gauthier

In the first chapter of *Morals by Agreement* I identify the conceptions at the heart of my theory. Three of these – minimax relative concession, constrained maximization, and the proviso – are structurally central, and I shall organize these reflections around them. But I have found a unifying leitmotif in Weale's chapter: 'any adequate theory of justice will have to strike a justifiable balance between the principle of the separateness of persons on the one hand and the ideal of a social union on the other' (see page 78 above).[1] Until I read his instructive account, I should not have thought to formulate my project in these terms, but it now seems to me quite illuminating.

Before proceeding, let me note that whether or not I have an adequate theory *of* justice, I am under no illusion that I can actually *do* justice to the chapters in this volume in the few pages at my disposal. I make no attempt to reply adequately, or in many cases even inadequately, to the many concerns they raise. What I do hope to do is to suggest what now seems to me viable in the main conceptions of *Morals by Agreement* and in the theory that they structure.

1 Minimax relative concession

Treating society as 'a cooperative venture for mutual advantage' (Rawls, 1971, p. 4),[2] we think of social interaction as yielding a cooperative surplus, a gain over what persons could expect interacting in a state of nature. Both the overall size of this surplus, and its distribution among individuals, will depend on the particular institutions and practices that define the society. Think of each person as having an *expectation* about the share of the cooperative surplus she may be able to gain for herself: this expectation will of course vary with different social institutions and practices. Mutual advantage sets both a lower bound to her expectation in requiring that she must benefit as a participant in society, and an upper bound in requiring that others must benefit from her participation. (Thus one's upper bound must be compatible with all others expecting at least their lower bound.) Without loss of generality we may set the lower bound at zero. Then we may define the *relative benefit* to an individual of any particular set of social arrangements as the proportion her expectation under those arrangements bears to the upper bound on her expectations.

I claim that social institutions and practices are just if and only if they afford no member of society a relative benefit less than some person must receive, i.e. than some person would receive given any feasible alternative to the institutions and practices. This claim formulates a requirement of *maximin relative benefit*,[3] and I seek to establish it by deriving its dual, *minimax relative concession* (MRC), as the outcome of the social contract, conceived as a rational *ex ante* bargain over the terms of social interaction. In this way I seek to establish a principle of justice on purely rational grounds, without introducing any moral premisses into the derivation.

Here are four objections to my claims:

1. Rational bargaining does not yield MRC, but rather the Nash bargaining solution.
2. Rational bargaining does not yield a unique outcome.
3. Rational bargaining, as I characterize it, includes moral premisses.
4. MRC misses an important element of justice.

These are simplified formulations of arguments that may be found in the chapters in this volume; I associate them respectively with Binmore, Sugden, Goodin and Lehning.

Several months ago I attended the International Conference on Game Theory in Fiesole, and heard Ariel Rubinstein lecture on non-cooperative bargaining and the Nash solution. And it was clear to me that what I say about bargaining in *Morals by Agreement* is simply undercut by the non-cooperative approach. And so, although I see good reason to be suspicious of Nash's independence of irrelevant alternatives axiom taken in itself, and to reject Harsanyi's use of 'the outmoded Zeuthen principle' (as Binmore (page 154 above) calls it), I have to agree that in the light of Rubinstein's argument, 'the orthodox theory is soundly based on models that seek to minimize on the fictions that need to be promulgated' and thus provide 'a minimalist defence of the Nash bargaining solution' (Binmore, page 154 and page 151 above). Were I Binmore, I should have chosen a different verse from Isaiah: 'And the multitude of all ... that fight against Ariel, ... shall be as a dream of a night vision' (Isaiah 29:7).

Must I then abandon MRC? My present view is this. The argument in Chapter V of *Morals by Agreement* cannot stand in its present form. At most it may have heuristic value in presenting the idea of minimax relative concession as uniting rationality and morality. But the real work of defending MRC as a bargaining outcome, if as I still believe it is defensible, requires a different argument. It requires arguing that in the circumstances of the social contract, MRC coincides with the Nash bargaining solution.

A sufficient condition of coincidence is that the *ex ante* bargain on the terms of social interaction may be represented as symmetric in its individually rational outcomes. (An outcome is individually rational if and only if each person's expectation is at least as great as her lower bound.) Let the measure of each person's expectations be determined by setting the lower bound at zero and the upper bound at one. Let each feasible social arrangement among which the bargainers must choose be represented by an ordered set of expectations, one for each bargainer. Then the bargain is symmetric in its individually rational outcomes if for each feasible arrangement with only non-negative members in its ordered set of expectations, every permutation of this ordered set of expectations is also a feasible arrangement.

What would this symmetry imply for the social contract? In effect, if the bargaining situation is symmetric, then in bargaining over social arrangements, we may choose among feasible sets of expectations independently of assigning the expectations to the actual members of society. Of course, both the Nash solution and MRC would require choosing the set of greatest equal expectations. And indeed, MRC requires this as long as the set of greatest equal expectations is optimal, whether or not the bargain is itself symmetric.

To avoid misunderstanding, note that symmetry is defined relative to each person's measure of expectation. Thus there need be no *absolute* symmetry among social alternatives, and no substantive similarity among expectations of equal magnitude held by different persons. In so far as we may compare the expectations of different persons, we may find that both the lower and upper bounds on expectation may vary significantly from person to person without this affecting the possibility of symmetry in the structure of the bargaining situation.

A real bargain may fail to be symmetric if the rate at which one party's benefits can be exchanged for another's while preserving optimality varies independently of the relation between the parties. If my relative benefit is high and yours is low, I may need to lose little for you to gain considerably, whereas if your relative benefit is high and mine is low, you may need to lose considerably for me to gain a little. But the social contract is the outcome of a *hypothetical* bargain. Once we establish each participant's upper and lower bounds of expectation and use them to fix a measure for his expectation from each feasible social arrangement, there seems no reason not to represent the bargain as symmetric at least in those arrangements that are individually rational.

But these comments do not constitute an argument. And so I conclude this discussion of the viability of MRC simply by noting the state of play. MRC requires that the social contract distribute the cooperative surplus optimally and with equal expectations of relative benefit, given that these are compatible. The Nash solution makes a similar requirement provided the social contract results from a bargain that is symmetric in individually rational outcomes. Assuming this symmetry, I can defend the requirement of MRC without straying from the path of orthodoxy represented by Binmore and Rubinstein.

But does this defence meet Sugden's objections to any attempt to provide a determinate solution to the bargaining problem? He argues that 'the result that lies at the core of Gauthier's (and Nash's) bargaining theory ... is an empty theorem unless we can prove that bargaining games have uniquely rational solutions' (see page 164 above). I am tempted to say, 'Sugden, meet Rubinstein'. For as Binmore notes, 'Rubinstein's result is that such games have a *unique* subgame–perfect equilibrium' (see page 150 above). To be sure, 'such games' does not refer to all bargaining games, but only to those treated in Rubinstein's model. And one might deny that the bargaining solution need be a subgame–perfect equilibrium. But if one allows, as Sugden does, that the solution must be in equilibrium, then the further requirement of subgame–perfection is, I think, compelling, and gives the uniqueness proof that Sugden claims is lacking.[4]

Nevertheless, there is an important dimension of Sugden's argument that an appeal to Rubinstein does not even begin to capture. Sugden rightly insists that 'strong contractarians' such as I must 'show what is rational for real people in the real-world'. And real-world bargaining reflects expectations that agents have about each other 'that are grounded in their common experience', which 'may be of conventions that divide the fruits of cooperation unequally, and in ways that seem morally arbitrary' (see page 175 above). Therefore real-world bargaining need not result in a division of the cooperative surplus that is impartial, or fair, or could plausibly be represented as meeting the demands of justice. But such bargaining may be rational.

Sugden, it seems to me, addresses two quite different issues. First, there is the question whether, if one represents the social contract as a hypothetical *ex ante* rational bargain among all members of society to determine the terms of their interaction, a bargain that is conceived to be prior to any actual experience of interaction or any actual conventions governing their interaction, then one can derive a determinate solution.

To this question, Rubinstein's uniqueness proof is surely relevant. Second, there is the equally important question whether actual persons have adequate reason to interact on the basis of such a contract. And of course, if their actual conventions, social institutions and practices are not those that such a contract would endorse, then the simple answer is negative. For as Sugden says, 'it will rarely be rational for an individual to challenge a well-established convention' (see page 170 above). And to this extent, there is a clear gap between what is rational and what would be just.

But as I have argued previously, as persons come to awareness of the idea of a social contract, they will come to consider social conventions, institutions and practices as justifiable only in so far as they can be represented as plausible outcomes of such a contract, conceived as a rational *ex ante* bargain about the terms of social interaction (Gauthier, 1988a, pp. 177–90 and 1991, pp. 25–9). They may rationally acquiesce in conventions that they consider unjustifiable, given that adherence to them is generally expected and, in some cases, enforced. But over time expectations change, and the enforcement of unjustifiable conventions is increasingly recognized as arbitrary. Thus only those conventions and institutions that can be represented as plausible outcomes of a social contract will prove sustainable, for only they will keep (if they are already in place) or gain (if they are not initially in place) the willing support of the members of society. What it is rational to adhere to in real-world interaction will come to conform to what it would be rational to agree to in determining *ex ante* the terms of interaction. The gap between what is rational and what is just will close.

Let me now turn to Goodin's concern, that the assumption of the equal rationality of the parties to the social contract introduces a moral element into the premisses from which the principle of justice is derived. The objection seems to be not to equal rationality as such, but to my use of it, in which what may initially seem innocuously formal takes on a significant, substantive role. For I argue that equal rationality constrains the concessions that rational bargainers will make to one another, where concessions are measured in terms of relative benefit. Doesn't this measure, which is hardly implicit in instrumental rationality, smuggle a particular moral perspective into my argument?

But the appeal to equal rationality is part of the flawed argument that I am now persuaded I must abandon. Rather than answer Goodin, I can bypass him by appealing to Rubinstein, whose bargaining model contains no such measure of concessions in terms of relative benefit, and no suspect premiss of equal rationality. To be sure, Binmore notes that the bargaining outcome defended in Rubinstein's account is sensitive to the bargaining powers of different individuals as reflected in their 'attitudes to the unproductive passage of time' (see page 151 above). And Goodin may see this as an objection to investing the outcome with moral significance. But this leads me to the more general point raised by Lehning, that I have 'missed an important element of what justice is really about' (see page 114 above). If this is true, then my success at avoiding ethical premisses would be coupled with failure at reaching morally sound conclusions.

Here I must emphasize the revisionist character of my project. There are different views of justice, and the attempt to ground justice in rational choice is not neutral among these views. Lehning rightly contrasts my view with that of Rawls. 'In Rawls's view, the well-ordered society corrects the arbitrariness of natural, social and accidental contingencies. In Gauthier's view, the social order should mirror the partiality of the natural order. The inequalities in basic endowment should be transmitted to the social order when talking about just benefits. Differences in talents *should* make a difference' (see page 113 above). This contrast precedes Lehning's claim that I have missed an important element of justice. But for me, this contrast reveals what is central to a view of justice grounded in rational choice – that it does transmit natural inequalities into society. Social institutions and practices that failed to do this would not be rationally acceptable in failing to recognize the separateness of persons.

At the outset of these reflections I referred to Weale's thesis that 'any adequate theory of justice will have to strike a justifiable balance between the principle of the separateness of persons on the one hand and the ideal of a social union on the other'. The *principle* of separateness is not the simple *fact* of separateness. How should we understand it? I suggest that the principle rests on the capacity each person has for normative motivation, determining herself to act on what she takes to be reasons. Allan Gibbard (1990, pp. 56–7) suggests that 'peculiar to human beings' is a 'psychological faculty' that we might call 'the *normative control system*'. Gibbard suggests this system makes possible 'both complex coordination among individuals and complex individual plans'; think of these as the roles of *intrapersonal integration* and *interpersonal coordination.* I interpret the former as leading to the idea of the individual as a normative unit, and the latter then as concerning the relations among these units. If this is indeed a correct interpretation of normative motivation, then it supports my emphasis on the normative separateness or independence of persons.[5] This account affords no rationale for the *interpersonal integration* of persons into a single normative unit, and no basis for treating the natural differences of persons as arbitrary contingencies to be 'corrected' in a 'well-ordered society'. I shall expand on my idea of a social union presently, but I want to insist that its primary role is to enable each individual to improve on her natural condition by effectively coordinating the exercise of her basic endowment with those of her fellows. To pursue these matters further, I turn to another of the ideas structurally central to *Morals by Agreement*.

2 The proviso

Don't better by worsening. Do not make yourself better off than you would have been in someone else's absence, by making that person worse off than he would have been in your absence.[6] That is what the proviso says, according to my refinement of Nozick's (1974, pp. 175–9) refinement of Locke's (1690, Second Treatise, Section 27) 'enough and as good' original.

There is a corollary. You need not better someone else by worsening yourself. He would violate the proviso if he bettered himself by worsening you, and you are not required to do for him what he is not permitted to do for himself. Travelling across the desert you encounter someone whose water supply has given out and who is dying of thirst. You could give him some of your water; you came well supplied. But the corollary tells you that you are under no obligation to do so, at least if giving him water would worsen your situation in any way, even by simply diminishing your assurance that you have enough water for (almost) any emergency that might befall you. He may not take, since that would be bettering himself by worsening you, and you need not give, since that would be bettering him by worsening yourself.

And there is another corollary. You may, without violating the proviso, worsen another, if the alternative would be to worsen your own situation from what it would be in that other's absence. If you find yourself cast up on a barren and remote island with another person and meagre supplies,[7] you worsen his situation by using any of the supplies. But you would worsen your own (from what it would be in his absence) if you didn't use them. In unfortunate situations like this, the very presence of each person is a cost to the other, and the proviso is silent. Or largely silent – you may use the supplies but you may *not* seize the fish that the other person manages to catch.

The proviso is not intended to be the last word on morality, but only the first. Starting from the proviso, rational persons will agree to principles that require them to accept and even to bring about small worsenings of themselves, when these lead to significant betterings of others. They will agree because their expectations are greater if everyone acts on these principles than if everyone observes the proviso and its corollaries. But although the proviso may be rejected as a ground of action, it remains as a baseline. Departures from the proviso must be expected to be Pareto-improvements.

What is the proviso doing in a contractarian moral theory? I treat it as constraining the lower bound on expectations in bargaining to the social contract. That is, each person considers his share of the cooperative surplus to be his gain over what he would expect in interaction constrained only by the proviso. I argue in *Morals by Agreement* that the effect of this constraint is to equip each bargainer with a set of rights, to the exclusive use of his body and its powers, mental and physical, and also to the exclusive use of particular resources, in so far as – and only in so far as – this benefits the user without *net* cost to those no longer entitled to treat these resources as in common use.

The rights determined by the proviso express the normative separateness or independence of persons. But the proviso also removes one of the obstacles to linking this separateness with the ideal of a social union. Indeed, it is the *strongest* constraint on natural interaction (i.e. interaction outside the framework of a social contract) that is compatible with separateness, and the *weakest* constraint on the initial bargaining situation for the social contract that is compatible with social union. A stronger constraint would either restrict some betterings that do not involve worsenings, or would require some worsenings of the agent's situation to prevent worsenings of others. In either case, the agent would be required to give others' concerns normative priority over his own. He would not enjoy the exclusive use of his capacities and his independence would be violated.

A weaker constraint would allow some betterings at the price of worsenings. But an interaction that worsens a person's situation disadvantages him in relation to what he would have expected in its absence. If such interactions affect the lower bound from which agents measure shares of the cooperative surplus, then some agents will begin from a position of disadvantage. And this limits the extent to which the resulting social contract establishes a cooperative venture for mutual advantage. It undermines the ideal of social union.

Let me now turn to two objections to my use of the proviso:

1. The proviso introduces a moral, and not a rational, premiss into the derivation of the social contract.
2. The initial bargaining position for the social contract should be established by agreement rather than by natural interaction constrained by the proviso.

Again these are simplified formulations of arguments that may be found in the chapters in this volume. I associate the first with Goodin and the second with Lehning.

I agree that the proviso is a moral premiss. The question then is whether it is rational to accept it as a constraint on bargaining to the social contract.

In *Morals by Agreement* I appeal to considerations of both equal rationality in agreeing to the social contract and stability in complying with it to support the claim that the proviso is a rational requirement on bargaining to the terms of social interaction. I cannot develop this argument in detail here, but it seems to me that Goodin raises the legitimate worry that it 'ends up assuming what it is meant to prove'. I appeal to stability to support the rationality of the proviso. But Goodin objects that my claim that an agreement that did not incorporate the proviso would be unstable, presupposes that without the proviso persons would 'take moral offence, which may give rise to resistance and enforcement costs', and assumes that 'it would be rational for people increasingly to resent and resist [this] increasing coercion' (see pages 125–6 above). And why would 'rational egoists' take moral offence, or what 'rational reason' would they have for resentment and resistance?[8] Note that Goodin's objection not only threatens my defence of the proviso, but also my reconciliation of rationality and justice as sketched in the preceding section. What basis do I have for appealing to such notions as 'moral offence'?

Let me first insist that I do not characterize persons as rational egoists. I have referred to the role of individual plans in achieving intrapersonal integration; I suppose that full or ideal integration would involve the adoption of an overarching life-plan, subject of course to reflective revision, which a person endeavours to realize. But such a life-plan need be neither substantively nor formally egoistic. A rational life-plan need not and at least normally does not include only self-directed objectives, and it must not require only straightforwardly maximizing behaviour.

Think then of a person as seeking on the one hand to choose a life-plan and on the other hand to agree with her fellows on the terms of their interaction. Now in the real world a person is born into the terms of interaction – the ongoing social institutions and practices – and chooses her life-plan from the possibilities that these terms allow. But the social institutions and practices are themselves choiceworthy only in so far as they make possible the more effective realization of life-plans.[9] I propose therefore to incorporate both of these features into my account; think of persons agreeing on those terms of interaction that they expect to be maximally responsive to whatever life-plans they then choose.[10]

In *Morals by Agreement* I offer an account of Archimedean choice in which I claim that the proviso would be selected as defining 'the initial position from which ... the forms of social interaction proceed, as the intersection between individual liberty and mutual benefit' (p. 259). An adaptation of that argument would, I think, show the place of the proviso among the terms of interaction that make possible the most effective realization of life-plans.

Lehning suggests that my project 'would have gained in strength if it had been built on . . . an agreement on the initial bargaining position' (see page 99 above). At first I found this suggestion puzzling, wanting to ask from what bargaining position *this* contract would proceed. If the initial bargaining position is to be the output, what position is to be the input? But perhaps I have actually provided an answer to my question. If we think of persons as bargaining over the terms of interaction *prior* to choosing their life-plans, then nothing is incorporated into their bargaining position save their desire to reach agreement in a way that will be most responsive to that subsequent choice. And if the proviso is accepted among the terms of interaction, then the rights derived from the proviso may be incorporated into the basis from which that choice, of one's particular life-plan, is made.

These remarks may help to make clear at least what I think the proviso is doing in a contractarian moral theory. But I need to say more to support my denial that I characterize persons as rational egoists. And I need to show that I characterize them in a way that permits me to speak of them taking moral offence. To do this, I turn to my third central conception.

3 Constrained maximization

I remain convinced that this is the most fruitful idea in *Morals by Agreement*, despite Binmore's offhand dismissal of it (see pages 131, 133 above). I have referred to each person determining herself to act on what she takes to be reasons. In so far as we may understand the orthodox theory of rational choice as giving an account of reasons for acting, we may find it in the idea of an agent's utility function, where utility is a measure of her preferences over possible outcomes, and so derivatively over her possible actions. We interpret an agent's behaviour as rational in so far as we represent it as maximizing expected utility as determined by this function. Utilities (or the preferences they measure), and only utilities, provide reasons for acting, and they do so directly; an agent has sufficient reason to choose one action rather than another if and only if the former affords her an expected utility greater than the latter.

I suggested above that a fully integrated person would endeavour to realize an overarching life-plan as fully as possible. What underlies constrained maximization is the recognition that such a person would be less successful if she were to take her reasons for acting exclusively and directly from her utilities, than if she were to include among her reasons other considerations only indirectly related to her utilities. Among these considerations would be the execution of a plan or the honouring of a commitment even if in so doing, she would not, and would know that she would not, be maximizing her expected utility at that time, *given* (i) that the plan or commitment had been rationally undertaken (in terms of her expected utilities) and (ii) that in executing or honouring it she would expect to be doing better (in those terms) than she would be doing had she not undertaken it. A *constrained maximizer*, as I shall use the term in a way that generalizes somewhat from my use in *Morals by Agreement*, is someone who takes her reasons for acting, not only directly from the utilities of possible outcomes she may bring about, but also from her plans and commitments in the manner that I have just sketched.

Suppose for example that I promise to assist you next week in some way, provided you assist me now. I reasonably expect to benefit more from so promising than from any alternative open to me, since I have no alternative way of gaining your assistance, and its benefit to me is much greater than the cost of reciprocating. Suppose you accept my promise and in consequence assist me. Next week I may have no directly utility-based reason to assist you; neither reputation effects nor prospects of future interaction between us need outweigh the costs of actually giving you the promised assistance. Nevertheless I may expect to be doing better honouring my promise than I should be doing had I made no promise – and in consequence, not received your assistance. And given this expectation, my promise affords me sufficient reason to carry it out – not of course according to the received theory of rational choice, but according to the alternative theory that embraces constrained maximization.

Binmore says that 'In attributing players with the power to make commitments in a game, Gauthier runs afoul of another game-theoretic tautology' (see page 138 above). This can be true only if a player's choices are interpreted as directly revealing his utilities. But this view leaves no conceptual space between preferences and choices, and a view that leaves no such space is simply too impoverished, in the distinctions that it admits, to provide a model of rational action. And indeed, this is my real objection to Binmore and 'all game theorists' who find constrained maximization unacceptable (see page 131 above). For them, the view that utilities and only utilities provide reasons for acting, and do so directly, is true *by definition*. In this way they pretend to convert a substantive and mistaken thesis into a tautology. Taken in by this pretence, they think about issues of rationality in a conceptually inadequate way. There are reasons for acting that remain undreamt of in their philosophy.

In my sketch of constrained maximization, I have defended constraints on maximizing behaviour entirely from the standpoint of what might be considered the maximizing agent – at any rate, the agent who seeks to realize an overarching life-plan as fully as possible. I have made no reference to mutual benefit, or to fair optimality, or to anything that would establish the constraints as moral or as collectively rational. And indeed, I should want to deny that ideas of collective rationality or morality have any independent weight in establishing the role of constrained maximization, so that, for example, I should reject Nida-Rümelin's 'negative criterion for practical reason: one should never act in such a way that there is no system of rules of behaviour in accord with collective rationality allowing that act' (see page 58 above). My account of rationality is strongly individualistic.

Thus I may seem to fall victim to the 'two serious problems' that Nida-Rümelin raises for those who wish to erect a 'bridge between maximization and morality'. For first 'it does not seem very probable' that the reasons for carrying out plans and honouring commitments that override reasons taken directly from one's preferences or utilities 'will meet moral criteria such as justice or the Lockean proviso'. And furthermore if these reasons have to be internalized as dispositions 'understood as some kind of sanctions *in foro interno*', then reason would be 'no more than the handmaiden of interest'[11] and *Morals by Agreement* 'contains an inadequate theory of moral agency' (see page 73 above).

Whether Nida-Rümelin's second concern is a problem for my account of constrained maximization turns at least in part on the interpretation of constraint. On the one hand, we may link constraint directly and solely to maximization, so that we think of plans and commitments as constraining the framework within which the agent makes maximizing choices. Having adopted a plan, an agent takes herself to have sufficient reason to disregard those of her possible actions that would be incompatible with it in deciding what to do (unless of course she finds herself with reason to reconsider her plan). I want to endorse this sense of constraint. But on the other hand, we may link constraint to the agent's psychological state, thinking of plans and commitments as introducing 'some kind of sanctions *in foro interno*'. Now an agent may experience this when she sticks to a plan or commitment, but it is certainly no part of rational agency, and indeed, its presence is a sign of weakness, and in some cases of moral weakness. In the past I have not distinguished these two senses of constraint, and I have at times thought of constrained maximization as involving internal sanctions, but Nida-Rümelin's illuminating comments have, I hope, enabled me to clarify and amend my position.

Underlying both of Nida-Rümelin's concerns, underlying also Hollis's concluding insistence that I must answer 'urgent questions about moral psychology' that are causing ferment in 'the Church of Reflective Reason' (see page 52 above), and central to Weale's concern with balancing the principle of the separateness of persons with the ideal of social union, is the place of constrained maximization in *moral* agency. So far I have focused exclusively on its role in rational agency; I must now conclude these reflections by defending its moral significance.

First, let me emphasize that taken simply in itself, constrained maximization is *not* a moral conception. A person may find it advantageous to be a credible threatener, and may find this possible only if he is actually disposed to carry out his threats, even when doing so is not supported by a direct appeal to his utility. Reasons for executing threats, just as reasons for keeping promises, in the face of direct advantage, are constraining reasons. But they are hardly *moral* reasons.

What constrained maximization does is to provide for the possibility of morality. The agent who takes her reasons for acting exclusively and directly from her utilities is an amoral agent. She pursues her concerns, whatever they may be, without constraint. In her behaviour she may indeed conform perfectly to the demands of some moral code. But her conformity can only be a matter of preference; were she to suppose that she had some reason, either for preferring to conform to the code or for conforming whether or not she preferred, then she would not be taking her reasons exclusively and directly from her utilities.

Constrained maximization creates a space for moral reasons. Whether moral reasons actually fill that space, or some part of it, depends on an agent's circumstances and concerns. The key idea is that the interaction with her fellows made possible by social institutions and practices that express a double mutuality – of agreement and of advantage – is a constitutive and core element in the agent's overarching life-plan. For then the constraints that those institutions and practices impose, and that I have identified with justice, will fall among those considerations that the agent takes from her life-plan as reasons for acting. Nida-Rümelin's first serious problem will be met.

But a life-plan that requires just interaction can be implemented only if society embodies justice. That such a society would be chosen by persons agreeing *ex ante* on their terms of interaction does not give us grounds to think that we live in such a society. In so far as our reasons for acting must reflect our actual circumstances, they may fall far short of the moral ideal. I do not see this as deeply problematic for my argument,[12] although no doubt much should be said (but not by me here) about the relation of rationality and morality in non-ideal settings.

What I do need to defend is the limitation on life-plans imposed by taking interpersonal interactions based on mutual agreement and advantage as a constitutive ideal. My aim in *Morals by Agreement* was to defend the rationality of morality, and so the incorporation of moral considerations among an agent's reasons for acting, whatever her concerns might happen to be. In effect I sought to impose no material restrictions on the contents of her life-plan. But this is unsound. Consider an agent whose life-plan is focused on the destruction of his fellows, who lives to kill. He has no interest in interactions that reflect mutual agreement and advantage, though he might find his victims more easily were he to simulate such interest. But of course others have no interest in interacting with him at all; knowing his life-plan, they would want to exclude him from their midst. And the impossibility of reaching genuine agreement with him on mutually advantageous terms of interaction, and so of making him party to a social contract, gives them a principled basis for such exclusion.

I must therefore amend my aim. My defence of the rationality of morality must be limited to those persons whose overarching life-plans make them welcome participants in society. Such persons are potential parties to an agreement that would determine mutually advantageous terms of interaction. And then I claim that for such persons, a life-plan (LP) that constitutively incorporates a concern with interactions that reflect such terms, and so makes social participation itself an aim or objective, is superior to any alternative (LP′) that although otherwise similar, does not incorporate, or incorporates only instrumentally, a concern with social participation. For LP fits the person better for obtaining the objectives of LP′ and so is superior to LP′ in its own terms.[13] Furthermore, since by hypothesis LP′ establishes objectives that are congruent with being welcomed as a participant in society, LP enriches LP′ by adding, as an objective, that very participation.

Hollis recognizes very clearly the problem that my argument must face. 'The snag is that the disposition to be a [constrained maximizer] is both constitutive and regulative, with the value of morality consisting both in the constitutive fact that moral agents do not have a further goal thus served and in the regulative claim that the further goal of maximising utility will be best served thereby. This seems to me an untenable position' (see page 51 above). In the preceeding paragraph, the counterpart of the constituent claim appears in the last sentence, and the counterpart of the regulative claim in the second last. And it seems to me that they give rise to a coherent moral psychology that is neither Humean nor Kantian.

To develop that moral psychology would be to trace out an affective structure that would relate the moral dispositions and emotions to life-plans that constitutively incorporate interpersonal relationships expressive of mutual agreement and advantage. Within this structure attitudes such as moral offence would play an important place. Without carrying out this task I cannot claim to have answered Hollis, but I should hope to avoid having simply 'to *declare* some relationships, like love and friendship, essential to persons' (see page 52 above, emphasis added). I agree with him in doubting that *Kantian* autonomy will emerge at the end, but I do not share his concern that what will result is 'a situated ethics ... inimical to the universal, impersonal demands of the moral point of view' (see page 52 above). For as I insist in *Morals by Agreement*, the terms of interaction of the 'essentially just society, with respect to the aims of its members' must adapt to 'bringing their fulfilment into optimal relative equality' (p. 341). The 'personal ties and special duties' that arise from particular aims and objectives must then fit into the universal framework set by justice.

Whether these remarks, delivered with suitable embellishment from its pulpit, would still the ferment in the Church of Reflective Reason, I must leave to the judgement of the parishioners. But perhaps one point deserves further emphasis. A constrained maximizer, as I have characterized him here, does not see the reasons for acting that he finds in the plans he adopts, the commitments he undertakes, the social institutions and practices to which he subscribes, as an overlay on a more basic set of reasons that relate directly to the attainment of his objectives. It is not as if a straightforward maximizer lurks deep within every constrained maximizer. To achieve the full integration of the self, a life-plan must both express and ensure the integrity of reason.

I began with Weale's insistence that 'any adequate theory of justice will have to strike a justifiable balance between the principle of the separateness of persons on the one hand and the ideal of a social union on the other'. I see this balance struck in the life-plans of the separate persons. For the constitutive role of interaction on mutually agreed and mutually advantageous terms embraces the 'shared final ends and common activities valued for themselves' that characterize social union (Rawls, 1971, pp. 520–9; quotation from p. 525). But in a world in which, as Weale says, 'individuals are redundant', may they not find themselves alienated from their terms of interaction?

My account has emphasized the significance of social participation, viewed from the standpoint both of the participating agent and of her prospectively welcoming fellows. But if individuals are socially redundant, then no value is attached to participation. Weale suggests that 'the only conception of rationality capable of moving individuals to conformity [with social institutions and practices] in this context is not one that rests upon the practical advantages to individuals of conformity, but is one which instead appeals to the rationality of being able to will only that which could be rationally willed by all' (see pages 93–4 above).[14] Although I have not appealed merely to the instrumental value of conformity in realizing one's life-plan, it may seem that Weale could accommodate this and argue that although in ideal circumstances individuals would recognize a constituent place for conformity in their life-plans, in circumstances of redundancy they would not recognize such a place and in consequence would not be rationally motivated to conformity. But Weale's positive, essentially Kantian proposal seems to me far less promising than my own approach. The effect of redundancy is to weaken ties among individuals, but appeal to a Kantian conception of rationality would seem to demand even stronger ties than are present in or required for social union.

Perhaps the real problem lies with the idea of society as a cooperative venture for mutual advantage. That it has been plausible to view society in this way throughout much of our recent history is implicit in the view that it is desirable for population to increase in a society, either through natural growth or through immigration. For the obvious explanation and justification of this view is found in increasing returns to scale – the more people, the greater the cooperative surplus *per capita.* But in today's world, overall population growth seems a cost rather than a benefit. And in those countries where 'the cooperative surplus ... is large, people are on the outside struggling to get in' (Weale, see page 93 above) although increasingly they are not wanted by those on the inside. If our social world no longer affords increasing returns to scale, then the idea of it as an overall cooperative venture for mutual advantage may be supplanted by the idea of society as a marginal zero-sum competition for relative advantage. Even in these social circumstances mutually agreed constraints would be a shield against the Hobbesian war of all against all, but sufficient rationale for internalizing them may be lacking. Only if we maintain the social circumstances in which the normative separateness of persons is congruent with the ideal of social union can we ensure that morals by agreement will not become an idea whose time has passed.

Notes

1. At the end of his chapter, Weale speaks of 'respect for persons' (see page 94 above) rather than 'the separateness of persons'. This seems to me an unfortunate shift; what needs to be put in the balance with social union is not the moral idea of respect, which depends on the normative status of its objects, but *that normative status itself.*
2. Viewing society in this way enables me to accept Weale's proffered third line of defence for 'the legitimacy of redistribution from market exchanges' (see page 92 above) – the claim that social interaction affords significant increasing returns to scale. Weale's chapter has been especially helpful to me in articulating the economic underpinning needed by my account of justice.
3. And indeed, of *maximum equal relative benefit*, where this is compatible with optimality.
4. Note that Rubinstein's proof is restricted to bargaining games; there is no implication that 'every game must have a uniquely rational solution', which Sugden (page 164 above) rightly disputes.
5. Whether Gibbard would agree with my interpretation and the support it gives to the normative separateness of persons is outside the scope of the present discussion.
6. Henceforth when I speak of bettering and worsening without any qualification, they should be interpreted as here.
7. Assume that neither you nor the other person is responsible for the supplies being on the island.

8. The quoted phrases are Goodin's (pages 125 and 126 above).
9. As Lehning says, 'the state has a duty to ensure for all persons a reasonable opportunity to pursue the good of their own choosing' (see page 106 above) and I should add that this is society's *only* (primary) duty.
10. In *Morals by Agreement* I characterize the 'essentially just society' as adapting 'to whatever their [its members'] aims may be, bringing their fulfilment into optimal relative equality' (p. 341).
11. Nida-Rümelin here quotes *Morals by Agreement*, p. 1.
12. But Weale's discussion of the redundancy of individuals, that 'no one can trade his or her compliance for a share of the cooperative surplus' (see page 93 above) might give me pause. Perhaps what I call the moral ideal has no relevance to our world. I return to this concern in my conclusion.
13. In effect LP proceeds from the recognition that, as Weale says, 'social union is the condition for individual advantage rather than a derivative from it' (see page 92 above).
14. Thus Weale's account ends in agreement with Nida-Rümelin's 'negative criterion for practical reason'.

References

Alexander, L. and Schwarzschild, M. (1987), 'Liberalism, neutrality, and equality of welfare vs. equality of resources', *Philosophy and Public Affairs*, vol. 16, pp. 85–110.

Arrow, K. J. (1984), *Social Choice and Justice*, Oxford: Basil Blackwell.

Atiyah, P. S. (1979), *The Rise and Fall of Freedom of Contract*, Oxford: Clarendon Press.

Axelrod, R. (1981), 'The emergence of cooperation among egoists', *American Political Science Review*, vol. 75, pp. 306–18.

Axelrod, R. (1984), *The Evolution of Cooperation*, New York: Basic Books.

Baier, A. C. (1988), 'Pilgrim's progress', *Canadian Journal of Philosophy*, vol. 18, pp. 315–30.

Barry, B. (1989a), *Theories of Justice*, Hemel Hempstead: Harvester Wheatsheaf.

Barry, B. (1989b), 'Power: an economic analysis', in B. Barry, *Democracy, Power and Freedom*, Oxford: Clarendon Press.

Becker, G. (1976), *The Economic Approach to Human Behavior*, Chicago: Chicago University Press.

Bergson, A. (1967), 'Market socialism revisited', *Journal of Political Economy*, vol. 75, pp. 655–73.

Binmore, K. (1988), *Social Contract II: Gauthier and Nash*, Technical Report CREST 89-04, University of Michigan.

Binmore, K. (1989), 'Social contract I: Harsanyi and Rawls', *Economic Journal*, vol. 99, pp. 84–102.

Binmore, K. (1990), 'Social contract III: evolution and utilitarianism', *Constitutional Political Economy*, vol. 1, pp. 1–26.

Binmore, K. (1991), *Fun and Games*, Lexington, Mass.: D. C. Heath.

Binmore, K. (1992), 'Social contract IV: evolution and convention', in R. Selten (ed.), *Rational Interaction: Essays in honor of John C. Harsanyi*. Berlin: Springer-Verlag.

Binmore, K and Dasgupta, P. (1987), *The Economics of Bargaining*, Oxford: Basil Blackwell.

Braithwaite, R. B. (1955), *The Theory of Games as a Tool for the Moral Philosopher*, Cambridge: Cambridge University Press.

Buchanan, J. M. (1975), *The Limits of Liberty*, Chicago: University of Chicago Press.
Buchanan, J. M. and Tullock, G. (1962), *The Calculus of Consent*, Ann Arbor: University of Michigan Press.
Cohen, G. A. (1986a), 'Self-ownership, world-ownership, and equality', in F. S. Lucash (ed.), *Justice and Equality Here and Now*, Ithaca, N.Y.: Cornell University Press.
Cohen, G. A. (1986b) 'Self-ownership, world-ownership, and equality: part II'. *Philosophy and Public Affairs*, vol. 3, pp. 77–96.
Cohen, G. A. (1989), 'On the currency of egalitarian justice', *Ethics*, vol. 99, pp. 906–44.
Coleman, J. L. (1985), 'Market contractarianism and the unanimity rule', *Social Philosophy and Policy*, vol. 2, pp. 69–114.
Coleman, J. L. (1988) 'Morality and the theory of rational choice', in J. L. Coleman, *Markets, Morals and the Law*, Cambridge: Cambridge University Press.
Cross, J. (1969), *The Economics of Bargaining*, New York: Basic Books.
Diekmann, A. and Mitter, P. (eds), (1986), *Paradoxical Effects of Human Behaviour: Essays in honour of Anatol Rapoport*, Heidelberg: Physica Heidelberg.
Elster, J. (1979), *Ulysses and the Sirens: Studies in rationality and irrationality*, Cambridge: Cambridge University Press.
Elster, J. (1983), *Sour Grapes: Studies in the subversion of rationality*, Cambridge; Cambridge University Press.
Foot, P. (1978), *Virtues and Vices and Other Essays in Moral Philosophy*, Oxford: Oxford University Press.
Frankfurt, H. G. (1971), 'Freedom of the will and the concept of a person', *Journal of Philosophy*, vol. 68, pp. 5–20.
Gauthier, D. (1974a), 'Rational cooperation', *Noûs*, vol. 8, pp. 53–65.
Gauthier, D. (1974b), 'Justice and natural endowment: toward a critique of Rawls' ideological framework', *Social Theory and Practice*, vol. 3, pp. 3–26.
Gauthier, D. (1982), 'Justified inequality?' *Dialogue*, vol. 21, pp. 431–43.
Gauthier, D. (1986), *Morals by Agreement*, Oxford: Oxford University Press.
Gauthier, D. (1988a), 'Morality, rational choice, and semantic representation: a reply to my critics', in E. F. Paul, F. D. Miller, J. Paul and J. Ahrens (eds), *The New Social Contract: Essays on Gauthier*, Oxford: Basil Blackwell.
Gauthier, D. (1988b), 'Moral artifice', *Canadian Journal of Philosophy*, vol. 18, pp. 385–418.
Gauthier, D. (1991), 'Why contractarianism?', in P. Vallentyne (ed.), *Contractarianism and Rational Choice: Essays on David Gauthier's Morals by Agreement*, New York: Cambridge University Press.
George, D. (1984), 'Meta-preferences: reconsidering contemporary notions of free choice', *Journal of Social Economics*, vol. 11, pp. 92–107.
Gibbard, A. (1990), *Wise Choices, Apt Feelings: A theory of normative judgment*, Cambridge, Mass.: Harvard University Press.
Goodin, R. E. (1975), 'How to determine who should get what', *Ethics*, vol. 85, pp. 310–21.
Goodin, R. E. (1988), *Reasons for Welfare*, Princeton, N. J.: Princeton University Press.
Goodin, R. E. (1990), 'Stabilizing expectations', *Ethics*, vol. 100, pp. 530–53.
Goodin, R. E. (1992), *Motivating Political Morality*, Oxford: Blackwell.
Goodin, R. E. and Le Grand, J. (1987), *Not only the Poor*, London: Allen and Unwin.
Hampton, J. (1986), *Hobbes and the Social Contract Tradition*, Cambridge:

Cambridge University Press.
Hampton, J. (1988) 'Can we agree on morals?', *Canadian Journal of Philosophy*, vol. 18, pp. 331–56.
Hardin, R. (1988), *Morality Within the Bounds of Reason*. Chicago: University of Chicago Press.
Harsanyi, J. C. (1955), 'Cardinal welfare, individualistic ethics and interpersonal comparisons of utility', *Journal of Political Economy*, vol. 63, pp. 309–21.
Harsanyi, J. C. (1977), *Rational Behaviour and Bargaining Equilibrium in Games and Social Situations*, Cambridge: Cambridge University Press.
Hirschman, A. O. (1982), *Shifting Involvements: Private interest and public action*, Princeton: Princeton University Press.
Hobbes, T. (1651), *Leviathan*, 1962 edition, edited by M. Oakeshott, published by Collier Macmillan, London.
Hobbes, T. (1841), *The English Works of Thomas Hobbes of Malmesbury*, edited by W. Molesworth, vol. 5. London.
Hobbes, T. (1978), *De Cive* (in English translation), in B. Gert (ed.), *Man and Citizen*, New York: Doubleday.
Hollis, M. (1988), *The Cunning of Reason*, Cambridge: Cambridge University Press.
Hollis, M. (1990) 'Honour among thieves', *Proceedings of the British Academy*, vol. 75, pp. 163–80.
Hume, D. (1748), 'Of the original contract', first published in the 1748 edition of *Moral and Political Essays*, reprinted in E. Barker (ed.), *Social Contract: Essays by Locke, Hume and Rousseau*, London: Oxford University Press, 1947.
Hume, D. (1777), *An Enquiry Concerning the Principles of Morals*, edited by L. A. Selby-Bigge, Oxford: Clarendon Press, 1975.
James, W. (1962), *Psychology: Briefer course*, London: Collier.
Jasay, A. de (1989), *Social Contract, Free Ride*, Oxford: Oxford University Press.
Jeffrey, R. C. (1974), 'Preferences among preferences', *Journal of Philosophy*, vol. 71, pp. 377–91.
Jones, P. (1989), 'The ideal of the neutral state', in R. E. Goodin and A. Reeve (eds), *Liberal Neutrality*, London: Routledge.
Kalai, E. and Smorodinsky, M. (1975), 'Other solutions to Nash's bargaining problem', *Econometrica*, vol. 45, pp. 1623–30.
Kern, L. and Räder, H.-G. (1988), 'Private goods and public bads', in G. L. Eberlein and H. Berghel (eds). *Theory and Decision: In honor of W. Leinfellner*, Dordrecht: Reidel.
Kliemt, H. (1985), *Moralische Institutionen: Empiristische Theorien ihrer Evolution*, Freiburg and München: Alber.
Kliemt, H. (1986a), *Antagonistische Kooperation: Elementare spieltheoretische Modelle spontaner Ordnungsentstehung*, Freiburg and München: Alber.
Kliemt, H. (1986b), 'Individualism, libertarianism and non-cognitivism', *Analyse & Kritik*, vol. 8, pp. 211–28.
Kronman, A. T. (1981), 'Talent pooling', in J. R. Pennock and J. W. Chapman (eds), *NOMOS XXIII: Human rights*, New York: New York University Press.
Larmore, C. E. (1987), *Patterns of Moral Complexity*, Cambridge: Cambridge University Press.
Locke, J. (1690), *Two Treatises of Government*, 1960 edition, edited by P. Laslett, published by Cambridge University Press, Cambridge.
Luce, R. D. and Raiffa, H. (1957), *Games and Decisions*, New York: Wiley.
McClennen, E. F. (1988), 'Constrained maximization and resolute choice', in E. F. Paul, F. D. Miller, J. Paul and J. Ahrens (eds), *The New Social Contract:*

Essays on Gauthier. Oxford: Basil Blackwell.

McClennen, E. F. (1990), *Rationality and Dynamic Choice*, Cambridge: Cambridge University Press.

McPherson, M. S. (1982), 'Mill's moral theory and the problem of preference change', *Ethics*, vol. 92, pp. 252–37.

Maskin, E. (1985), 'The theory of implementation in Nash equilibrium: a survey', in D. Schmeidler, L. Hurwicz and H. Sonnenschein (eds), *Social Goals and Social Organization*, Cambridge: Cambridge University Press.

Maynard Smith, J. (1982), *Evolution and the Theory of Games*, Cambridge: Cambridge University Press.

Moulin, H. (1984), 'Implementing the Kalai–Smorodinsky bargaining solution', *Journal of Economic Theory*, vol. 33, pp. 32–45.

Muthoo, A. (1991), 'Revocable commitment and sequential bargaining', *Economic Journal*, vol. 102, pp. 378–87.

Narveson, J. (1989), 'The justice of the market: comments on Gray and Radin', in J. W. Chapman and J. R. Pennock (eds), *NOMOS XXXI: Markets and justice*, New York: New York University Press.

Nash, J. (1950), 'The bargaining problem', *Econometrica* 18, pp. 155–62.

Nash, J. (1951), 'Non-cooperative games', *Annals of Mathematics*, vol. 54, pp. 286–95.

Nash, J. (1953), 'Two-person cooperative games', *Econometrica* 21, pp. 128–40.

Neumann, J. von and Morgenstern, O. (1947), *Theory of Games and Economic Behavior* (2nd edition), Princeton: Princeton University Press. 1st edition 1944.

Nida-Rümelin, J. (1987), 'Der Vertragsgedanke in der politischen Philosophie', *Zeitschrift für Politik*, vol. 34, pp. 200–6.

Nida-Rümelin, J. (1988), 'Plädoyer für eine kontraktualistische Philosophie der Politik', in O. Weinberger (ed.), *Philosophie des Rechts, der Politik und der Gesellschaft*, Vienna: Hölder-Pichler-Tempsky.

Nozick, R. (1972), 'Coercion', in P. Laslett, W. G. Runciman and Q. Skinner (eds), *Philosophy, Politics and Society*, 4th series, Oxford: Basil Blackwell.

Nozick, R. (1974), *Anarchy, State and Utopia*, New York: Basic Books.

Opp, K.-D. (1983), *Die Entstehung sozialer Normen: Ein Integrationsversuch soziologischer, sozialpsychologischer und ökonomischer Erklärungen*, Tübingen: Mohr.

Raiffa, H. (1953), 'Arbitration schemes for generalized two-person games', in H. Kuhn and A. Tucker (eds), *Contributions to the Theory of Games II*, Princeton, N.J.: Princeton University Press.

Rapoport, A. and Chammah, A. M. (1965), *Prisoner's Dilemma: A study in conflict and cooperation*, Ann Arbor: University of Michigan Press.

Raub, W. and Voss, T. (1986), 'Conditions for cooperation in problematic social situations', in Diekmann and Mitter (1986).

Raub, W. and Voss, T. (1988), 'Individual interests and moral institutions: an endogenous approach to the modification of preferences', paper presented at conference on the emergence, maintenance and effects of social institutions, Werner-Reimers-Stiftung, Bad Homburg, January 1988.

Rawls, J. (1971), *A Theory of Justice*, Cambridge, Mass: Harvard University Press.

Rawls, J. (1974), 'Some reasons for the maximin criterion', *American Economic Review*, vol. 64, pp. 141–6.

Rawls, J. (1978), 'The basic structure as subject', in A. I. Goldman and J. Kim (eds), *Values and Morals*, Dordrecht: Reidel.

Rawls, J. (1980), 'Kantian constructivism in moral theory', *Journal of Philosophy*,

vol. 77, pp. 515–72.
Rawls, J. (1982), 'Social unity and primary goods', in A. Sen and B. Williams (eds), *Utilitarianism and Beyond*, Cambridge: Cambridge University Press.
Rawls, J. (1988), 'The priority of right and ideas of the good', *Philosophy and Public Affairs*, vol. 17, pp. 251–76.
Raz, J. (1986), *The Morality of Freedom*, Oxford: Clarendon Press.
Roth, A. (1979), *Axiomatic Models of Bargaining*, Berlin: Springer-Verlag.
Rousseau, J.-J. (1762), *Du Contrat Social*, translated as *On the Social Contract*, ed. R. D. Masters, translated J. R. Masters, New York: St Martin's Press, 1978.
Rubinstein, A. (1982), 'Perfect equilibrium in a bargaining model', *Econometrica*, vol. 50, pp. 97–109.
Savage, L. (1954), *The Foundations of Statistics*, New York: Wiley.
Schelling, T. C. (1960), *The Strategy of Conflict*, Cambridge, Mass: Harvard University Press.
Schelling, T. C. (1978), 'Egonomics', *American Economic Review (Papers and Proceedings)*, vol. 68, pp. 290–4.
Schelling, T. C. (1980), 'The intimate contest of self-command', *Public Interest*, vol. 60, pp. 94–100.
Schelling, T. C. (1984), 'Ethics, law, and the exercise of self-command', In *Choice and Consequence*, Cambridge, Mass: Harvard University Press.
Scott, J. C. (1976), *The Moral Economy of the Peasant*, New Haven, Conn.: Yale University Press.
Sen, A. K. (1974), 'Choice, ordering and morality', in St. Körner (ed.), *Practical Reason*, Oxford: Oxford University Press.
Sen, A. K. (1982), *Choice, Welfare and Measurement*, Oxford: Basil Blackwell.
Smart, J. J. C. (1973), 'An outline of a system of utilitarian ethics', in J. J. C. Smart and B. Williams, *Utilitarianism: For and against*, Cambridge: Cambridge University Press.
Smith, A. (1776), *The Wealth of Nations*, 1978 edition, edited by R. H. Campbell, A. S. Skinner and W. B. Todd, published by Clarendon Press, Oxford.
Stahl, I. (1972), *Bargaining Theory*, Stockholm: Economics Research Institute.
Steiner, H. (1977), 'The natural right to the means of production', *The Philosophical Quarterly*, vol. 27, pp. 41–9.
Sugden, R. (1986), *The Economics of Rights, Co-operation and Welfare*, Oxford: Basil Blackwell.
Sugden, R. (1991a), 'Rational choice: a survey of contributions from economics and philosophy', *Economic Journal*, vol. 101, pp. 751–85.
Sugden, R. (1991b), 'Rational bargaining', in M. Bacharach and S. Hurley (eds), *Foundations of Decision Theory*, Oxford: Blackwell.
Tawney, R. H. (1921), *The Acquisitive Society*, London: G. Bell and Sons.
Taylor, C. (1976), 'Responsibility for self', in A. O. Rorty (ed.), *The Identities of Persons*, Berkeley: University of California Press.
Voss, T. (1985), *Rationale Akteure und soziale Institutionen*, München: RIVM Oldenbourg.
Waldron, J. (1988), *The Right to Private Property*, Oxford: Clarendon Press.
Weale, A. (1978), *Equality and Social Policy*, Henley: Routledge and Kegan Paul.
Weintraub, E. R. (1974), *General Equilibrium Theory*, London: Macmillan.
Williams, B. (1973), 'A critique of utilitarianism', in J. J. C. Smart and B. Williams, *Utilitarianism: For and against*, Cambridge: Cambridge University Press.
Wolff, P. (1966), 'A refutation of Rawls' theorem on justice', *Journal of Philosophy*, vol. 63, pp. 170–90.

Wolff, P. (1977), *Understanding Rawls: A reconstruction and critique of* A Theory of Justice, Princeton: Princeton University Press.

Yaari, M. E. (1981), 'Rawls, Edgeworth, Shapley, Nash: theories of distributive justice re-examined', *Journal of Economic Theory*, vol. 24, pp. 1–39.

Zeuthen, F. (1930), *Problems of Monopoly and Economic Warfare*, London: Routledge and Kegan Paul.

Zimmerman, D. (1981), 'Coercive wage offers', *Philosophy and Public Affairs*, vol. 10, pp. 121–45.

Index

abilities, *see* talents
acquisition, 87, 110–11
  see also proviso
altruism, 59, 66–7
appropriation, *see* acquisition
Archimedan point, 44, 45, 46, 49, 51, 52, 100–5, 132, 184
Arrow, K. J., 13, 90, 92
Assurance Game, 61–3
Atiyah, P. S., 92
autonomy, 6, 35, 43, 49, 52, 189
Axelrod, R., 168

backwards induction, 138
bargaining power, 14, 119–23
bargaining theory, 3, 12, 14–17, 131–55, 161–4
Barry, B., 16, 17
baseline, 5, 10–14, 20–2, 87, 96–100, 123–9, 132–3, 182, 184
battle of the sexes, 165–6
Becker, G., 47
Bergson, A., 84
Bramhall, Bishop, 33, 34
Buchanan, J. M., 3, 18, 21, 96

Chammah, A. M., 72
coercion, 10–11, 20–2, 96, 124–7, 184
Cohen, G. A., 113
Coleman, J. L., 96, 109
collective rationality, 57–8, 142, 145
commitment, 25, 26–31, 35, 136–40, 148–9
  see also compliance
compensation, 98, 104–5
competitive market, 2, 10, 13, 76–7, 80, 84, 86, 89–92, 135–6
compliance, 3, 6, 17–22
constitutive rules, 50–1
constrained maximization, 19, 20, 21, 23, 43–6, 48–9, 51, 56–7, 133, 136–40, 148, 149, 185–90
convention, 168–72, 175, 179–80
cooperative surplus, 3, 14–15, 20, 102, 110, 159, 176, 183
coordination game, 168
core of economy, 90
Cross, J., 149

Dasgupta, P., 141
difference principle, 2, 11, 12, 83, 84, 86, 109
dispositions, 19, 32, 41, 43, 44–5, 48, 55, 56–7, 60, 73, 92, 117, 138, 189
distribution of income, 2, 10–14, 76–92
division game, 160–1, 164, 169–72
dominated strategy, 136

economic rent, *see* factor rent
economic justice, *see* distribution of income
Euler's Theorem, 13
evolutionary stability, 168
experience, 167–73, 175, 179
expressive rationality, 9, 48, 49
extensive form of game, 138

factor rent, 12–14, 84–92, 93
fallacy of the twins, 137
Foole, the, 19, 21, 28–34, 41
Foot, P., 72

general will, 6, 25, 33, 34
Gibbard, A., 181

Hampton, J., 36, 90
handicapped people, 5
Harsanyi, J. C., 16–17, 117, 118–19, 132, 142, 158
Hobbes, T., 3, 6, 17–19, 21, 24–39, 41, 71–3, 87, 157, 158, 191
Hume, D., 26, 43, 44, 45, 46, 48–51, 131, 189

implementability, 145–6
incentives, 83–5, 86, 89 91
increasing returns to scale, 13–14, 92, 191
independence of irrelevant alternatives, 143–6, 147, 177
initial bargaining position, *see* baseline
instrumental rationality, 9, 20, 47–8, 53
interpersonal comparisons, 4, 143

James, W., 47
Jasay, A de, 6

Kalai, E., 15, 134, 153–4, 163
Kant, I., 2, 9, 30, 31, 40, 43, 44, 48–52, 53, 59–60, 71–3, 77, 170, 189, 190
Kern, L., 72
Kidnapping Game, 138–40

law of nature, *see* natural law
limited liability, 92
Locke, J., 10, 23, 26, 87, 108, 132, 158, 182

MacIntyre, A., 41
marginal productivity, 13, 79, 80, 82, 84, 88–92
Maynard Smith, J., 168
McClennen, E. F., 19–20
metapreferences, 61–71
Mill, J. S., 52
minimax relative concession, 15–16, 22, 57, 91, 133–5, 141, 143, 159, 169, 176–82
monotonicity, 154
moral intuition, 2
moral personality, 6, 30, 31, 35–9
moral psychology, 41–52, 189–90
morally free zone, 2, 10, 76, 85–6, 89, 135–6
Morgenstern, O., 142, 162
Moulin, H., 154
Muthoo, A., 151–3

Nash, J., 15, 141–2, 148, 160, 163
Nash bargaining solution, 15–17, 134, 141–7, 150–1, 152, 154, 177–9
Nash demand game, 146–7, 148, 149
see also division game
Nash equilibrium, 138, 162–3, 167–8

natural law, 10, 27–8, 30, 34, 37–8
Neumann, J. von, 142, 162
neutrality, 105–7, 112
Newcomb's problem, 166
normal form of game, 138
Nozick, R., 77, 78–82, 87, 97, 107, 108, 110, 111, 132, 182

original position, 7, 103–4, 117, 118, 132, 173–5
other-regarding game, 61–3

patterns, 78–80, 82
practical reason, 58
Prisoner's Dilemma, 3, 9, 26, 27, 28, 29, 31, 34, 53, 58–73, 133, 136–40, 166
problematic social situation, 58
promises, 20, 76, 92
proviso, the, 87, 95, 97–100, 101, 105, 107, 110, 112–13, 182–5

Räder, H.-G., 72
Raiffa, H., 143
Rapoport, A., 72
rational determinacy, 162, 163, 166, 179–80
Raub, W., 58
Rawls, J., 1, 3–7, 11–13, 24–33, 37–9, 75, 76–8, 79, 82–5, 86, 101–5, 106, 107–9, 112, 113, 117, 118, 132, 158, 173–5, 176, 181, 190
Raz, J., 106
reflective equilibrium, 7, 158
regulative rules, 50–1
revealed preferences, 64
rights, 38, 88, 95, 96–100, 101, 108, 183
risk aversion, 121–2
Roth, A., 145
Rousseau, J.-J., 6, 25, 26, 33, 34, 52
Rubinstein, A., 16, 17, 149–51, 154, 177, 179–81
rule of the road, 168, 170
rule utilitarianism, 54

salience, 171–2
Savage, L., 136
Schelling, T. C., 138, 140, 171
self-ownership, 79–80, 86, 89, 107–9, 111
Sen, A. K., 61, 76
Slaves, Parable of the, 20–2
Smart, J. J. C., 5
Smith, A., 11
Smorodinsky, M., 15, 134, 153–4, 163
social union, 75–6, 77–8, 92–4, 181–2, 183, 190–1
sovereign, 8, 28–9, 33–8
Stahl, I., 149
Steiner, H., 111

straightforward maximization, 19, 20, 43, 45, 48–9
strategic form of game, 138
subgame-perfect equilibrium, 138–40
Sure-Thing Principle, 136
symmetry, 145, 163–4, 168–9, 173–4, 178
  see also fallacy of the twins

talents, 11–14, 79–88, 107–10, 113, 173, 181
Tawney, R. H., 91

utilitarianism, 4–5, 40, 54, 174
  see also rule utilitarianism
utility, 136, 185

veil of ignorance, *see* original position

Voss, T., 58

Waldron, J., 109
Wayne Gretzky, 12–13, 88, 90–1
Weintraub, E. R., 90
welfarism, 4, 76
Williams, B., 5
Wilt Chamberlain, 78–9
Wittgenstein, L., 50
Wolff, R. P., 24–33, 38–9, 132

Yaari, M. E., 80

Zeuthen, F., 16–17, 134, 142, 154, 177